Quilters' Travel Companion

U.S.A. Edition

Edited by: Audrey Swales
Anderson

Published By:

chalet
PUBLISHING

(719) 685-5041   32 Grand Avenue
Manitou Springs, CO 80829

With all my love,
This book is dedicated to my
husband, Marlow.
Thank you for
your support and
hours of
assistance.

Cover Design By:
Get Graphic
Indianapolis, IN
(317) 849-1437

"Definitions": Marlow Anderson
& John Roberts

Original Artwork: Pamela
Whiteman

Thanks for your encouragement:
Mom and Dad, John Roberts, Chris Lee,
John Nichols,, Janet Treichler,
Ruth O'Riley & Karen Kristofik

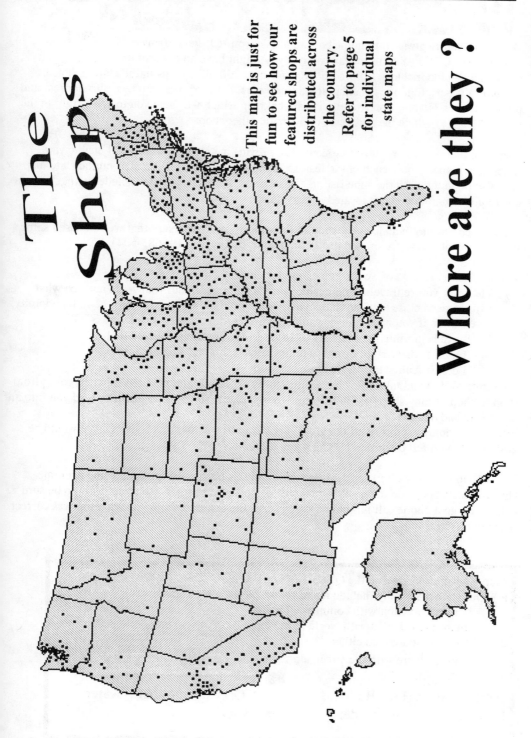

The Shops

Where are they ?

This map is just for fun to see how our featured shops are distributed across the country. Refer to page 5 for individual state maps

How to Use this Guide

Whenever you're away from home be sure to take your *Quilters' Travel Companion* (QTC). You never know when you might have an opportunity to check out a shop. This guide includes featured listings for over 750 quilt shops in the United States. There is a description of each shop, including hours, featured merchandise, plus address and phone number. In addition, we provide a local map which will help you to drive right to the door. Also we include the addresses of over 500 other shops.

The shop listings are organized by state. We provide a state map which will enable you to tell at a glance where each of the featured shops is located. The number on the state map will also be found with the shop listing. In addition, for each state we include listings of area quilt guilds and other shops located in that state.

We've tried hard to include every shop in the country, but we're sure that we've missed some. If you know of one we've missed drop us a note or call us at (719) 685-5041.

There are two basic ways we see you using our guide:
1) Whenever you're traveling on business or vacation check out your route and see what shops you may be close to. The state maps should give you an idea if you'll be in the vicinity of a store. Then if you have time or can make time give yourself a break and STOP !
> Since beginning these guides in 1992, I have certainly realized that
> I used to drive right by shops on my travels, but not stop because
> I didn't realize they were close.

2) Or go WILD and take a few days with family or friends and plan a whole trip going from shop to shop. Many shops are in historic / tourist places so your trip just may lead you into an unexpected adventure.

Either way, enjoy exploring all the great shops scattered across this country. We would be grateful if you'd tell them that QTC got you there.

We have made every effort for the information in this book to be up-to-date and accurate. Unfortunately shops do move, change hours, or go out of business; so if you want to be sure before you go a phone call might be prudent. All the featured shops' information was correct when published.

Map Conventions used in the QTC:
a) Our state maps only include major roads; please use our maps
  in conjunction with commercial maps.
b) All maps are oriented with North at the top.
c) The shops are marked either
  by a square with the street address inside (i.e. 100) or by a star ☆

* = traffic light   ■ = Business or landmark
++++++++ = Railroad   A Gray line or area = water
Dashed line = state border   ● = City

Contents

Ready, Set, GO !

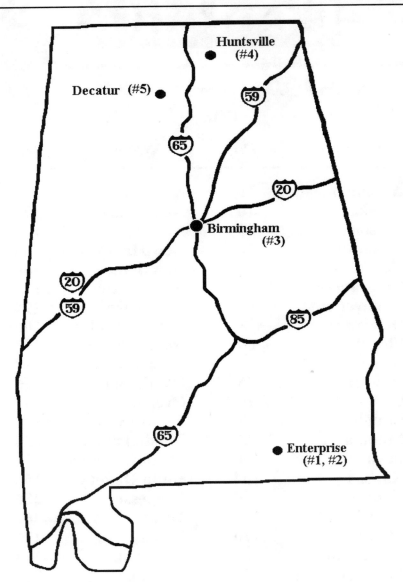

5 Featured Shops

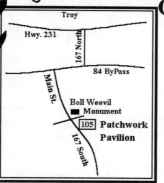

Enterprise, AL   #2

Quilters Cottage

Mon - Fri 9:30 - 5 Sat 9:30 - 2

1304 U.S. 84 Bypass   36330
(205) 393-2443
Owner: Dee Forringer
Est: 1993   1050 sq.ft.

A SPECIAL PLACE FOR QUILTERS

Classes, Books, Supplies and Fabrics.

Troy   Ozark   Dothan
Hwy. 167   Hwy. 84
1304   By Pass 84
in the Simply Southern Village Quilters Cottage
Hwy. 27
Geneva

Huntsville, AL   #4

Patches & Stitches

Mon - Thur 10 - 5 Thur til 6 Sat 10 - 4

817-A Regal Drive   35801
(205) 533-3886
Owner: Linda Worley
Est: 1978   2500 sq.ft.

Complete line of quilt supplies, classes, books, and needlework; including cross-stitch and needlepoint. Also mail order.

Bob Wallace
Patches & Stitches
Memorial Pkwy.
817   Regal
L & N Drive
Drake
Parkway City Mall

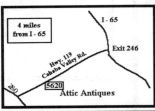

Birmingham, AL   #3

Attic Antiques

Tues - Sat 9:30 - 4:30

5620 Cahaba Valley Road
(205) 991- 6887   35242
Owners: Barbara & Howard Manning
Est: 1972   3500 sq.ft.

Year around Christmas Shop. Large selection of quilts & linens. Items made with quilts. Americana & Victorian items

4 miles from I - 65
I - 65
Exit 246
Hwy. 119 Cahaba Valley Rd.
5620   Attic Antiques

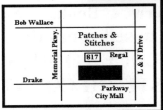

Heirloom Quilt— a hand-me-down you're glad to keep.

Decatur, AL   #5

The Crafty Bear Shop

Mon - Fri 10 - 5 Sat 10 - 4

2208 Danville Rd. S.W.   35601
(205) 351-0420   Est: 1988
Owner: Helen DeButy   1800 sq.ft.

Cotton Fabrics, books, patterns, supplies, and classes. The friendliest quilt shop for service, inspiration and sharing of ideas.

River Oaks Mall   McDonalds   to Nashville
Danville Rd.   2208 in Wes Bryan Shopping Village
The Crafty Bear Shop
Hwy. 31   I - 65
7.2 miles from I - 65   Hwy 67 N.   to Birmingham

Notes

Alabama Guilds:
Birmingham Quilters Guild, Birmingham
Enterprising Quilters, P.O. Box 30114, Enterprise, 36330
Quilter Lovers' Guild, Hartselle Library, Hartselle, 35640
Kudzu Quilter's Guild, 3933 Croydon Rd., Montgomery, 36109
West Alabama Quilters Guild, 305 Caplewood Dr., Tuscaloosa, 35401

Other Shops in Alabama :

Alexander City	Midtown Fabrics & Crafts, 209 Main Street
Anniston	Cloth Patch, 2120 Noble Street
Anniston	Quilts Plus, 1211 Noble Street
Athens	Terry's Country Craft Store, Drawbaugh Road
Birmingham	The Quilted Cat, 63 Church
Birmingham	Quilt Makers, 2403 1st. St. N.E.
Birmingham	Calico Corners, 3663 Lorna Road
Boaz	Arts & Crafts, 109 N. Main
Fairhope	A Stitch in Time, 26 S. Section
Gadsden	The Stitchin Barn, 2622 Tabor Road
Gadsden	Thornton Lake Cloth Barn, P.O. Box 247 Route #2
Hayden	Annie's Quilts, 7722 St. Hwy 160
Huntsville	Gilberg's Fabric Outlet, 2701 Patton Road S.W.
Jasper	Grandma's Treasures & Fabrics, Parkland Shopping
Mobile	Fabric by the Pound, 1508 Overlook Road
Mobile	Fabric Works, 5441 Highway 90 W.
Oxford	Quilts Plus, 1211 Noble Street
Prattville	Prattville Cloth Barn & Mill, 1351 S. Memorial Dr.
Sheffield	The Busy Needle, 931 E. Avalon Avenue
Tuscaloosa	Cloth Patch, 4331 University Boulevard E.

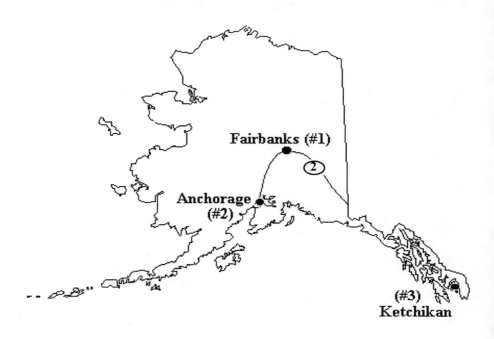

Other Shops in Alaska:

Anchorage	Calicos & Quilts Unlimited, 11900 Industry Way
Anchorage	Needlecrafters, 6311 DeBarr Road
Fairbanks	Snow Goose Fibers, 3550 Airport Way #6
Juneau	Tina's Fabrique Boutique, 8745 Glacier Hwy.
Kodiak	The Stitchery, 326 Center Avenue
North Pole	Quilts and Country Comforts, 3191 Kris Kringle Drive
Palmer	Simple Pleasures, P.O. Box 3250 Mile 1.4 Palmer-Wasilla
Wasilla	Alaska Dyeworks, 300 W. Swanson Ave. #101

Fairbanks, AK   #1

Hands All Around

927 Old Steese Hwy.   99701
(907) 452-2347
Owners: Jamie, Gayle, Janet
Est: 1991   3000 sq.ft.

Mon - Fri
9:30 - 6
Sat 9 - 5

100% Cotton
Fabrics, Books,
Notions, Classes,
Alaskan Patterns.
Commercial
Quilting Machine.
Weaving Supplies
Quilts on display

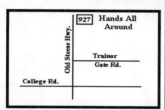

Anchorage, AK   #2

The Whiffletree

9420 Old Seward Hwy.   99515
(907) 344-5922
Owners: Rich & Diane Melms
Est: 1983   1000 sq.ft.

Mon - Wed
11 - 5
Thur - Sat
11 - 6

Full line antique
store with quality
antique Quilts, tops,
blocks, doilies,
bedcovers,
tablecloths,
hankies, buttons,
trims and laces.

Ketchikan, AK   #3

Alaska Country Workbasket

619 Mission
(907) 225-1163   Est: 1991
Owners: Karen Abuhl & Trudy
Swatch Club $20 yr.   Castle
Located 2 blocks   2500 sq.ft.
S.E. of cruise ship
docking.
Alaskan quilt patterns
and fabrics.
Gift Shop
Doll & Cross-Stitch
Patterns

Summer Hrs
Sat & Sun
8 - 5
Winter Hrs.
Mon - Fri
10 - 5
Sat 12 - 5

Bring your Quilt Guild
Pin or Charm from your
City or State and receive
a 10% discount.

Alaska Guilds:
Cabin Fever Quilters Guild, Box 83608, Fairbanks, 99708
Valley Quilter's Guild, P.O. Box 2582, Palmer, 99645

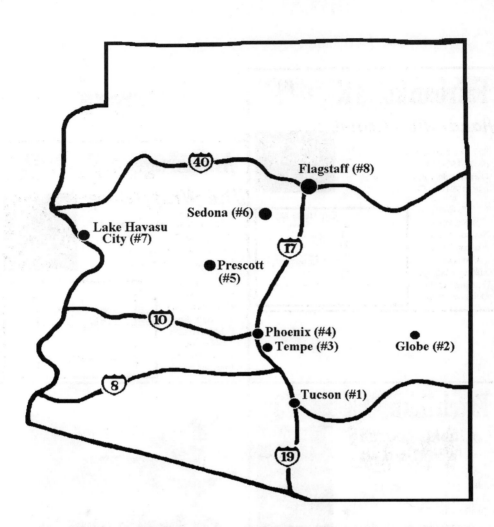

Flagstaff (#8)

Sedona (#6)

Lake Havasu
City (#7)

Prescott
(#5)

Phoenix (#4)
Tempe (#3)

Globe (#2)

Tucson (#1)

ARIZONA

8 Featured Shops

Tucson, AZ #1

Quilt Basket, Inc.

Mon - Sat 9:30 - 5

6538 C E. Tanque Verde Rd.
(602) 722-8810   85715
Owner: Peggy Peck
          Est: 1990   1500 sq.ft.

Lots & Lots of
beautiful
fabrics . . . .

Everything for
today's busy
quilter . . . .
Come see us !

Globe, AZ #2

Country Corner

Tues- Sat 9 - 5:30

383 South Hill Street   85501
(602) 425-8208
Owners: Johnny & Janice McInturff
          Est: 1986   6000 sq.ft.

Quilts, Fabric,
Notions--
Antiques
Hardware, Tack,
Boots, Vet
Supplies, Chain
saws--parts and
service.

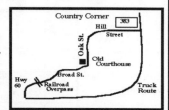

State of
The Art
Quilting
Instruction
and
Supplies

Tempe, AZ #3

Quilters' Ranch

107 East Baseline Road #6   85283
(In Mill Towne Center)
(602) 838-8350
Est: 1982   2700 sq.ft.
Owners: Anne Dutton &
Dorothy Dodds

**Mon - Sat 9:30 - 5:30
Thurs til 9**

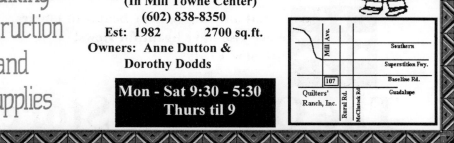

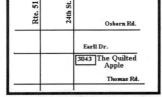

Phoenix, AZ #4

The Quilted Apple

**Mon - Sat
9:30 - 5:30
Tues till 9**

3043 North 24th St.   85016
(602) 956-0904
Owner: Laurene Sinema
Est: 1978   3600 sq.ft.   Free Catalog

100 % cotton
Fabrics, books,
patterns, notions,
classes.
Specialize in fine
hand quilting.

Rte. 51 | 24th St.
Osborn Rd.
Earll Dr.
3043 The Quilted Apple
Thomas Rd.

Prescott, AZ #5

Quilt Crossing

**Mon - Sat
10 - 5:30**

207 North Cortez   86301
(602) 776-1823
Owner: Penny Bolerjack
Est: 1990   1000 sq.ft.

Main Street
U.S.A. City,
Antique Center of
Arizona, 100%
cottons, quilting
supplies and
classes.

Old Santa Fe Depot
Quilt Crossing
207   Willis St.
Cortez
Gurley St.
Courthouse Square

Not only do we have beautiful fabrics,
we also have beautiful views!
Come Visit!

The Quilter's Store

Quilting Supplies — Classes — 100% Cotton Fabrics
Personalized Instruction Available

(602) 282-2057
Marge Elson, Proprietor

3075 West Highway 89A

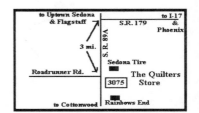

to Uptown Sedona
& Flagstaff
to I-17
&
Phoenix
S.R. 179
3 mi.
S.R. 89A
Sedona Tire
Roadrunner Rd.
The Quilters
3075   Store
to Cottonwood   Rainbows End

Sedona, AZ #6

Monday - Friday: 9 a.m. - 5 p.m.
Saturday: 9 a.m. - 4 p.m.   **Sunday**: 12 p.m. - 4 p.m.

Lake Havasu City, AZ   #7

The Cotton Patch

1685 Mesquite Ave.   86403
(602) 855-9458
Owner: Georgeann Dodge
Est: 1986   1900 sq.ft.

Mon - Fri
9:30 - 5
Sat & Sun
10 - 4

100% Cotton
Fabric,
Quilting Books,
patterns,
notions,
custom quilting
classes
Friendly Service.

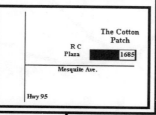

R C
Plaza

The Cotton
Patch

1685

Mesquite Ave.

Hwy 95

Flagstaff, AZ   #8

Pine Country Quilts

821 W. Riordan Rd.   86001
(602) 779-2194
Owner: Rhoda Vihel

Est: 1985   3000 sq.ft.

Glorious Historic
Building housing
internationally
acclaimed quilt
shop, fiber arts,
and antiques.
Sheer pleasure on
the way to the
Grand Canyon.

Mon - Sat
10 - 5

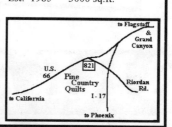

to Flagstaff
&
Grand
Canyon

821

U.S.
66   Pine
Country
Quilts

to California

Riordan
Rd.

I - 17

to Phoenix

Arizona State Guild:
Arizona Quilters Guild, P.O. Box 82416, Phoenix, 85071-2416
Arizona Guilds:
Mountain Top Quilters, P.O. Box 12961, Prescott, 86304-2961
Tucson Quilter's Guild, P.O. Box 14454, Tucson, 85732

Other Shops in Arizona:
Cottonwood	Melon Patch Quilt Shop, 529 S. Main
Lake Havasu City	Cactus Fabric Shop, 2011 Swanson Ave.
Peoria	Homestead Station, 6732 W. Sunnyside Dr.
Phoenix	By Jupiter, 6033 N. 17th Avenue
Sierra Vista	Quilter's Outpost, 2240 Golf Links Road
St. Johns	Calico Corner, 55 E. Cleveland, PO Box 1519

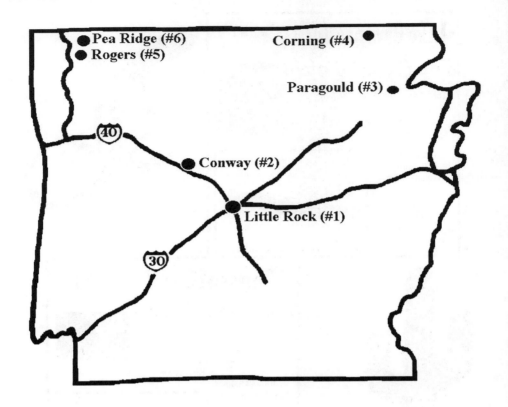

ARKANSAS

6 Featured Shops

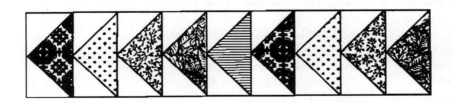

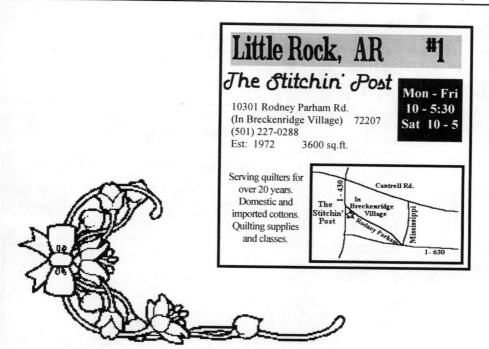

Little Rock, AR #1

The Stitchin' Post

10301 Rodney Parham Rd.
(In Breckenridge Village)   72207
(501) 227-0288
Est: 1972   3600 sq.ft.

Mon - Fri
10 - 5:30
Sat 10 - 5

Serving quilters for over 20 years. Domestic and imported cottons. Quilting supplies and classes.

Idle-Hour Quilts & Design

Tue - Sat
10 - 5

2216 Washington Ave.   72032
(501) 329-3323 Owner: Jaynette Huff   Est: 1992 1400 sq.ft.

Your Complete, Full-Service Quilt Store.

Offering superior quality supplies, fabrics (all 100% Cotton) notions, books, frames, and classes.

Free Newsletter

Conway, AR #2

Whether you are a new quilter who needs help with the basics, an intermediate quilter taking steps to stretch and develop your skills, or an accomplished quilter-extraordinaire! IDLE-HOUR QUILTS AND DESIGN can deliver the quilting service and supplies you need, promptly and professionally.

Paragould, AR   #3

Countryside Quilting Shop

**Mon - Fri 10 - 5
Sat 10 - 2
Sun by Appt.**

8425 Hwy 135 N 72450 900 sq.ft.
(501) 586-0214   Est: 1981
Owners: Connie Sidebottom & Earlene Hyde

Specializing in machine quilting, custom quilts, spreads, shams, embroidery, blocks and supplies.
Come See Us !

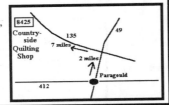

Rogers, AR   #5

Patchwork Emporium

Mon - Sat 10 - 4

224 S. 2nd. St.   72756
(501) 636-3385   Est: 1981
Owner: Nora Cope   1600 sq.ft.

Complete Quilt Shop !
1500 Bolts of Fabric—100% Cottons, Books, Patterns, Notions. Lots of Quilts! Models! Ideas!

Corning, AR   #4

Betty's Fabric & Quilts

Mon & Wed - Sat 9:30 - 5

Hwy 67 North   P.O. Box 86
(501) 857-6747   72422 - 0086
Owner: Betty Leyendecker
Est: 1981   2400 sq.ft.

Approx. 3000 Bolts of Cotton Fabric plus Quilt Blocks, 300 patterns. Around 50 quilts Hand Quilted in stock.

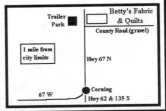

Pea Ridge, AR   #6

Country House Quilting

**Mon - Fri 8:30 - 5
Thur til 7**

16324 N. Hwy 94   72751
(501) 451-8978   Est: 1982
Owners: Charlotte & Ronald Foster   1600 sq.ft.

Quilts Machine and Hand Quilted. Supplies, Books, Patterns, Q-snap frames, Classes.

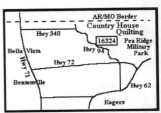

Quilt Block — this is
<u>NOT</u>
a mental condition
which prevents the
sufferer from quilting.

Arkansas State Guild:
Arkansas Quilters Guild,
4219 Sugar Maple Ln , Little Rock, 72212

Arkansas Guilds:
Belle Point Quilters' Guild, P.O. Box 3853,
Fort Smith 72913
Hill 'n Hollow Quilters Guild, Box 140,
Mountain Home, 72653
Hope Quilter's Guild, 624 Cale Rd., Prescott,
71857
Q.U.I.L.T. 823 Lakeside Dr., Fayetteville, 72701
Saline County Quilters Guild, 224 W. South St., Benton, 72015

Other Shops in Arkansas:

Batesville	Marshall Wholesale Fabrics, P.O. Box 2313
Booneville	Cheryl's General Store, 200 W. Main Street
Conway	The Quilt Patch, 273 Hwy. 36
Conway	Stitch & Sew, 2307 Washington Ave.
Eureka Springs	Sharon's Quilts, 2 Center
Eureka Springs	Calico Crafts N Things, 15 North Main
Eureka Springs	Cameo & Country Craft Shoppe, Hwy 62 East
Eureka Springs	The Cotton Patch, 1 Center
Fayetteville	Country Cupboard, 4234 N. Old Wire Rd.
Glencoe	Quilt Palace, PO Box 75
Hot Springs	Log Cabin Crafts, 450 S. Rogers Road
Little Rock	Sew Smart, 9700 N. Rodney Parham Rd.
Little Rock	Fabric Works, Inc., 5624 R Street
Lowell	Makin' Memories, R.R. #2
Mena	Quilts, Inc., 607 North
Pelsor	Country Palace Ozark Crafts, HC 30 Box 108
Pelsor	Nellie's Craft Shop, HC 30 Box 102
Pine Bluff	JM Fabrics, 2215 E. Harding #3
Russellville	Ozark Heritage Craft Village, I-40 & Hwy 7
Springdale	Creative Stitchin', 403 W. Huntsville

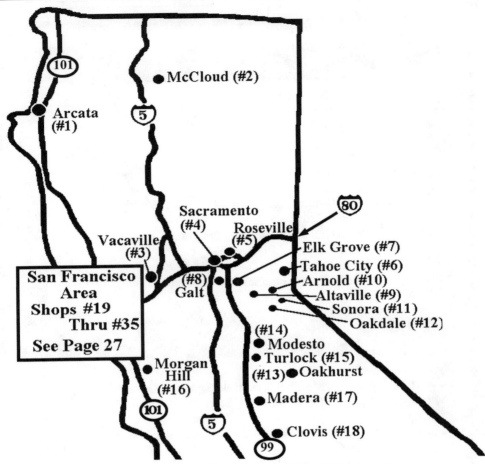

For Southern California
See Page 31
Shops #36 thru #60

Pfaff —
Pfine, Pfancy,
Pfun pfor
Pfingers.

Arcata, CA   #1

Fabric Temptations

Mon - Sat
10 - 5:30
Sun 11 - 4

942 'G' Street   95521
(707) 822-7782
Owner: Lennie   Est: 1984

Natural Fiber
Fabrics. Liberty
of London.
Battings: Cotton,
Silk, Wool &
Polyester.
Quilting &
Sewing Supplies.
Mail order.

(Map: 10th., Bank, Bus Station, Hotel Arcata, 942 Fabric Temptations 9th., Plaza, 8th., Post Office, H St., G St., 7th.)

Mail Order Welcome

Custom Quilts & Crafts

McCloud, CA   #2

207 Quincy Ave.   (916) 964-2500
Mon - Sat 10 - 5

Books
Patterns
Supplies
Friendly Service

Over 1000 Bolts of
FABULOUS FABRICS

(Map: I-5, Quincy Ave., Broadway, 207 Custom Quilts & Crafts, Minnesota, Hwy 89 to McCloud)

Vacaville, CA   #3

The Unique Spool

Hours by
Appt.

407 Corte Majorca   95688
(707) 448-1538
Owner: Roberta Whitworth
Catalog—$1.00

African Fabric
and domestic
cotton prints,
notions, quilt
frames and
quilting
patterns.

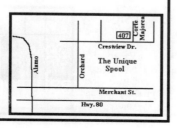

(Map: Corte Majorca, 407, Crestview Dr., Alamo, Orchard, The Unique Spool, Merchant St., Hwy. 80)

Sacramento, CA #4

Quilters' Corner

3020 'H' St. 95816
(916) 442-5768
Owner: Lindy Munday
Est: 1981

**Mon - Fri
9:30 - 5:30
Sat 9:30 - 5
Sun 12 - 4**

100% cottons, books, patterns & notions.
Classes
Seminar, retreats.
Ask about Quilt Camp

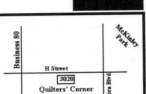

Business 80 | McKinley Park
H Street
3020 Quilters' Corner | Alhambra Blvd

Largest Selection of Patterns in Northern California

Roseville, CA #5

The Stitching Station

Est: 1989
2400 sq.ft.

**Mon - Fri
10 - 6
Sat 10 - 5:30**

1000 Sunrise Ave.
95661
(916) 773-0296
Owner: Sandra Satnowski

**Books Galore !
3000 Bolts of Fabric**

Located 14 miles from Downtown Sacramento. Take I - 80 east to Riverside exit. Right turn onto Cirby. We're on the right before Sunrise.

Tahoe City, CA #6

Windy Moon Quilts

700 N. Lake Blvd. Round House Mall
(916) 583-4011
Est: 1989   900 sq.ft.
Visit our other shop in Reno, NV See Page 179

**Daily
10 - 6**

Nestled High in the Sierra's, we make quilting easy for the mountain visitor. 1 hour classes give both the novice and experienced quilter tips & ideas.

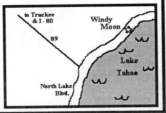

to Truckee & I - 80
Windy Moon
89
Lake Tahoe
North Lake Blvd.

Elk Grove, CA #7

The Pincushion

9639 Stockton Blvd.   95624
(916) 685-8500
Owner: Jan Gross
Est: 1988   2400 sq.ft.

**Mon - Thur
9 - 6:30
Fri 9 - 6
Sat 9 - 5**

UNIQUE FABRICS --
Q Snap frames, a variety of patterns, quality service, muslin prints and more !

to Sacramento
Elk Grove Blvd.
Hwy 99 | Stockton Blvd | 9639 | The Pincushion in Elk Park Village
to Stockton
From Hwy 99 take the Elk Grove Blvd. Exit

QUILTED TREASURES

213 S. Lincoln Way 95632
(209) 745-1605
Owner: Kim Puleo
Est: 1992   1200 sq.ft.

Galt, CA   #8

- ◆ **Fabric, Notions**
  - ◆ **Classes**
  - ◆ **Cross-Stitch**
- ◆ **Handmade Gifts & Crafts**
  Featuring:
  - ◆ **Quilt in a Day**
  - ◆ **Debbie Mumm**
  - ◆ **Patchwork Place**
AND MUCH MORE !!

Mon - Fri 9:30 - 5:30
Sat 10 - 5

Altaville, CA   #9

Country Cloth Shop

457 S. Main St. (Angels Camp)
(209) 736-4998   Est: 1980
Owners: Chuck & Ginger Duffy
1600 sq.ft.

Mon - Sat 10-5
Summer
Sundays 12 - 4

Quilting: Large
selection of
Books & Fabrics.
Cross Stitch:
Brazilian Emb.
Bernina Sales and
Service. Classes.
General Craft and
Sewing Supplies.

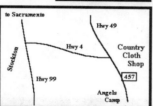

Arnold, CA   #10

Country Cloth Shop

1316 Oak Circle   95223
(209) 795-6423   Est: 1980
Owners: Chuck & Ginger Duffy
3000 sq.ft.

Mon - Sat 10-5
Summer
Sundays 12 - 4

Quilting: Large
selection of
Books & Fabrics.
Cross Stitch:
Brazilian Emb.
Bernina Sales and
Service. Classes.
General Craft and
Sewing Supplies.

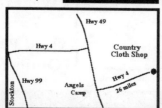

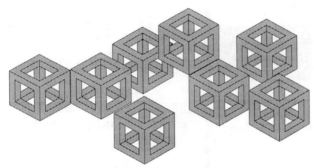

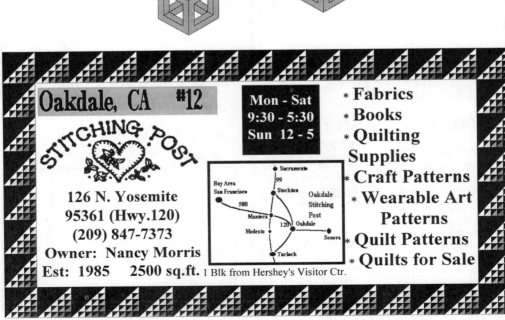

Arlene's Calico Country

A QUILTER'S HAVEN !

Enterprise Center
(209) 683-SEWS
Owner: Arlene Hartman
40092 Hwy. 49   93644
Est: 1990   2600 sq.ft.
Over 4000 Bolts of FABRIC!!!

Oakhurst, CA   #13

Happy Birthday
Come in on your birthday for a 25% discount on any fabric purchase.

Skinny Bolt Sale
Every Thursday!!
Buy the end of the bolt and get a
25% discount!

50% OFF on selected fabrics in our Treasure Trunk all year!

40% OFF
at least 1 or 2 quilt books & patterns every month!

Classes ! !
Gift Certificates !

Quilt - Pak of the Month Club!
Join Now!

Enjoy new fabric each month! You get the newest and most popular fabrics fast! 5 color coordinated fat quarters for $8.50 plus $1.95 for shipping. Q-PAK of the month offered only on an automatic credit card billing system. When you order, provide your credit card number and expiration date, authorizing us to charge your Q-PAK to it each month. Return your Q-PAK for any reason, your credit card will be credited, and you'll continue to receive future Q-PAKs. You may cancel your membership at any time.
In addition to what we have to offer on our mail order list, we will ship fabric
(1 yard minimum cuts). Send us a swatch of what you are looking for, if we have it, we'll ship it.
Quarterly Newsletter with mail order info available upon request.

Mon - Sat 9 - 5

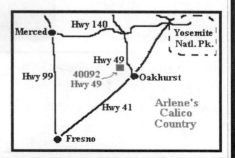

We carry Hoffman, Alexander Henry, Nancy Crow, P&B, Jinny Beyer, Kona Bay, Bali, Spiegel, Marcus Brothers, Roberta Horton, Plaids, South Seas, Concord, Debbie Mumm, VIP Color Works and many more.
All the latest Collections !

Modesto, CA #14

R. Lily Stem Quilts

815 W. Roseburg Avenue   95350
(209) 577-1919
Owner: Marilyn Nelson
Est: 1986   1400 sq.ft.

Mon - Fri
9:30 - 5:30
Sat 10 - 5
Sun 12 - 4

Fabulous fabrics, books, patterns, cross-stitch, custom comforters, classes and great service !

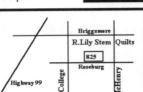

Turlock, CA #15

California QuiltMakers

134 West Main Street   95380
(209) 632-0899
Est: 1991   3000 sq.ft.
Owners: Pat Fryer & Pam Howland

Mon - Fri
10 - 5:30
Sat 10 - 5
Sun 12 - 4

Fabric, Books, Patterns, Quilts for sale, Machine Quilting. Quilting Machines. In - store quilt show.

Morgan Hill, CA #16

Quilt Blossoms

114 Cochrane Rd.   95037
(408) 779-4473

Mon, Wed -
Fri 10 - 7
Sat 10 - 6
Sun 12 - 5
Closed Tues

Quilting Classes and Supplies. Variety of 100% Cotton Fabrics, Battings, Books and Notions.

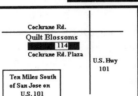

Madera, CA #17

Patchwork Pansy

121 Dwyer St. (Price's Plaza)
(209) 673-1797   93637

Owners: Lynnette & Sharon Jacobsen

Enjoy an old fashioned shopping experience at a family owned and operated store.

Clovis, CA #18

Quilter's Paradise

339 Pollasky   93612
(209) 297-7817
Est: 1978   5000 sq.ft.
Owners: Jennifer Wheeler

Tues - Sat
10 - 5
Mon & Fri
Till 8

Just What the Shop Name Says ! !

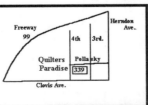

Spring Cleaning — Time to re-sort your material and oil your machine.

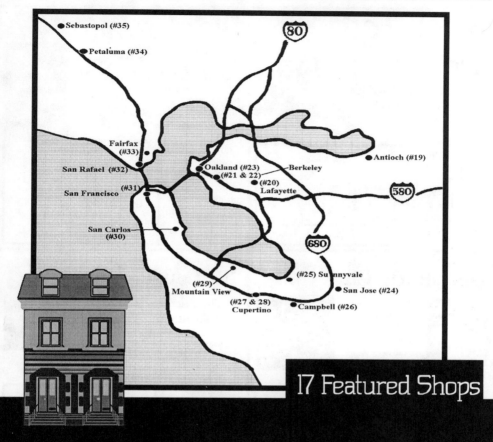

17 Featured Shops

SAN FRANCISCO AREA

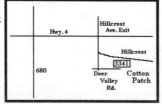

Antioch, CA #19

Cotton Patch

| Mon - Fri |
| 9:30 - 5:30 |
| Sat 10 - 5 |
| Sun 12 - 4 |

3341 Deer Valley Road   94509
(510) 757-7240
Est: 1991   1700 sq.ft.
Owner: Carolie Hensley   Mgr: Shari Vancil

Bernina Dealer.
Repair all makes &
models of
machines. Cotton
fabrics, books,
patterns, classes.
Visit our sister
shop in Lafayette.

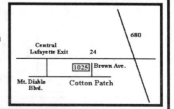

Lafayette, CA #20

Cotton Patch

| Mon - Fri |
| 9:30 - 5:30 |
| Sat 10 - 5 |
| Sun 12 - 4 |

1025 Brown Avenue   94549
(510) 284-1177
Owner: Carolie Hensley
Est: 1978   1400 sq.ft.

Bernina Dealer.
Repair all makes
& models of
machines. Cotton
prints & one
room full of solid
cottons. Patterns,
books, gifts, &
notions etc.

Berkeley, CA #21

New Pieces
Fabric & Chamber Music

Mon - Sat 10 - 6
Sun 12 - 5

1597 Solano Ave.   94707
(510) 527-6779
Owner: Carlberg Jones

Est: 1984

Stimulating, Colorful, Helpful, Knowledgeable, Convenient, Variety, Friendly, Quilt Oriented, Contemporary Fabrics, Books Exhibits

Berkeley, CA #22

The Ames Gallery of American Folk Art

Wed - Sat 2 - 6 During Exhibitions Call for Schedule

2661 Cedar Street   94708
(510) 845-4949   Est: 1970
Owner: Bonnie Grossman

An Extensive collection of antique utilitarian items as well as primitive, naive and outsider art.

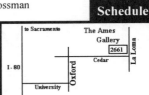

Oakland, CA #23

POPPY FABRIC

5151 Broadway
94611
(510) 655-8850
(800) 55-POPPY
Owner: Paul Eisenberg
Est: 1971

Mon - Fri 9:30 - 8
Sat 9:30-5:30
Sun 12 - 5

5000 sq.ft.

Dress and Decorator Fabrics with a large amount of imported and specialty fabrics.

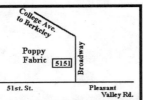

San Jose, CA #24

American Museum of Quilts and Textiles

Tues - Sat 10 - 4

766 South Second St.   95112
(408) 971-0323
Est: 1977   Non-profit Public Benefit Museum

Regularly changing exhibits of Quilts and Textiles. Museum Store has extensive assortment of books on quilting.

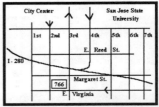

Sunnyvale, CA #25

Carolea's Knitche

Mon - Fri 10 - 6
Sat 10 - 5

586 South Murphy Ave.   94086
(408) 736-2800
Owner: Carolea Peterson
Est: 1973   1400 sq.ft.

The very latest in Hoffman, Alex Henry, Jinny Beyer, Kaufman, Tony Wentzel, Gutcheon . . . Mail orders welcome.

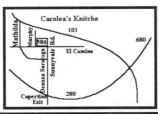

Campbell, CA #26

Needle's Eye

Mon - Sat 10 - 5:30
Sun 12 - 4

2435 South Winchester Blvd.
(408) 866-1181   95008
Owners: Steven & Cooky Schock
Opened: 1989   1600 sq.ft.

A great place for those addicted to Quilting and Cross Stitch !

Cupertino, CA #27

Whiffle Tree Quilts

Mon - Sat
10 - 6
Thurs til 8

10261 S. DeAnza Blvd.   95014
(408) 255-5270
Est: 1982   1280 sq.ft.
Owners: Marsha Burdick & Louise Horkey

A terrific store
full of fabric,
patterns, &
notions & books.
A place to share
ideas and get
inspired.

```
              I - 280
      Stevens Creek Blvd.
                                    S. DeAnza Blvd.
           Rodrigues
  10261  Whiffle Tree Quilts
         Allario
         Center
```

Cupertino, CA #28

The Granary

Mon - Thur
10 - 6:30
Fri & Sat
10 - 5

10889 North Wolfe Rd.
(408) 973-0591   95014
Owner: Karen Yancey
Est: 1973   & Michele O'Hara
1540 sq.ft.

Cotton & Calico
Fabrics, Quilting
Supplies,
Dollmaking, Tole
Painting, Patterns,
Books & Classes.
OPEN 7 DAYS

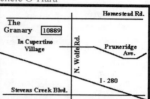

Mountain View, CA #29

The Quilting Bee

357 Castro Street   94041
(415) 969-1714
Owner: Diana Leone
Est: 1976   2,300 sq. ft.

M-F 9-8:30
Sat 9-5
Sun 11-5

4,000 Bolts
of Cotton
750 Books
Classes, Notions
Appraisals
Quilts
Bought & Sold
Special Orders
Our Specialty

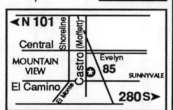

San Carlos, CA #30

The Laurel Leaf

Mon - Sat
10 - 5

648 Laurel Street   94070
(415) 591-6790
Owner: Julie Murphy
Est: 1983   2200 sq.ft.

100% Cotton
Fabric, Books,
Patterns, Quilting
Supplies, Classes.
Authorized
Bernina Dealer.

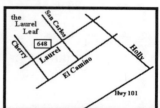

San Francisco, CA #31

Yankee Doodle Dandy

Mon - Sat
10:30 - 5:30
Sun 12 - 5

1974 Union Street
(415) 346-0346   94123-4271
Opened: 1967   2500 sq.ft
Owners: Harlan & Judith Koch

Probably the largest collection
of pre-WWII quilts in America
together with patriotic
American Folk Art. All quilts
in excellent condition supplied
by pickers from all over
America.

Located in
"Cow
Hollow" San
Francisco on
Union
between
Laguna &
Buchanan

San Rafael, CA #32

Sawtooth Quilts, Folk Art & Whimsey

Tues - Sat
10 - 5:30

1560 Fourth Street   94901   900 sq.ft.
(415) 453-1711 Owner: Susan Bradford Est: 1981

Featuring work of
local artists.
Antique Quilts &
Textiles. Quilt
Restorations.
Lessons,
appraisals, hand
& machine
Quilting.

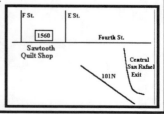

Fairfax, CA   #33

Rainbow Fabrics

**Mon - Sat
10 - 6
Sun 12 - 4**

50 Bolinas Rd.   94930
(415) 459-5100
Owner: Rose Taber

Country Store,
Cottons, Rayons,
Classes,
Latest Books &
Notions,
Beads, Crafts, &
Things
Helpful Staff

Petaluma, CA   #34

Quilted Angel

**Mon - Sat
10 - 5:30
Thur til 7:30
Sun 12 - 4**

200 G St.   94952
(707) 763-0945
Owner: Susie Ernst
Est: 1991   2200 sq.ft.

A "destination"
Quilt Store
Fabrics from all
major suppliers,
books (600 titles)
notions, patterns,
doll supplies &
classes.

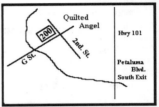

Sebastopol, CA   #35

EASTWIND ART

P.O. Box 811   95473
(707) 829-3536
Owner: Joanne Newcomb
Since 1973

Phone for Appt.

We specialize in Japanese-style
items. We carry sashiko supplies,
charms, cotton print yardage,
indigo dyed fabric. and more.
We manufacture patterns, buttons,
crafts, and other interesting stuff. Retail catalog
$2. Inquire about whole-
sale.

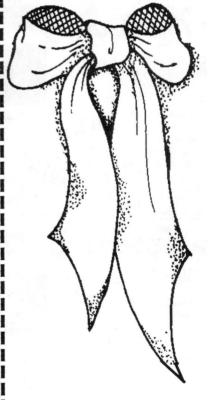

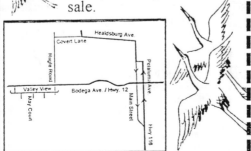

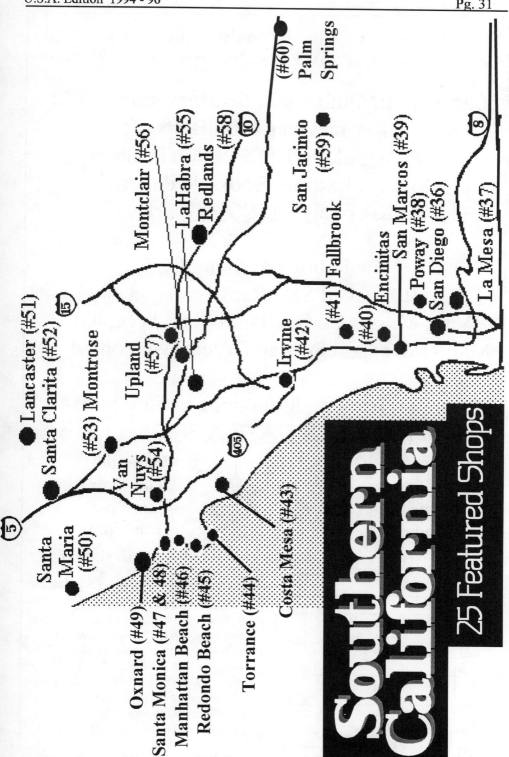

Southern California

25 Featured Shops

San Diego, CA #36 Rosie's Calico Cupboard

7151 El Cajon Blvd. Suite 'F' 92115 (619)697-5758 Owners: Rosie & Vic Gonzalez

Catering to Quilters & Crafters since 1983
Offering Over 4000 Bolts of
First Quality 100% cotton Prints
Notions, Batting, Books & Patterns
At Everyday **DISCOUNT** Prices.

- •New Fabrics Arriving Daily
- •Well Stocked Sale Rack (50% to 75% Savings)
- •Visa, Master Card & Discovery Accepted
- •Mail Orders and Special Orders, Welcomed

Come in, Browse, Meet our Friendly Staff
OPEN SEVEN DAYS A WEEK

Mon.,Tues.,Thurs.,Fri.		**9am-5pm**
Wednesday		**9am-8pm**
Saturday		**8am-5pm**
Sunday		**11am-5pm**

Closed New Years Day, Easter, Thanksgiving and Christmas

I-8	N	7151

70th St. | El Cajon Blvd. | Rosie's | Harbison
71st
Tower
Stanford
University Ave.
Hwy 94

Hwy 8 to 70th St., exit going So. Travel So. for 3/4 mi. to El Cajon Blvd., Turn left (East) onto El Cajon Blvd., travel for a block-and-a-half. We will be on your right hand side, in the College Plaza Center East of the Boll Weevol.
From Hwy. 94, take the Mass, Exit, go No. to Univeristy Ave., turn left, follow to 70th St., turn right, follow to El Cajon Bl., turn Right, and travel for 1 1/2 blocks.

La Mesa, CA #37

Stitch in Time Quilt Shoppe

6119 Lake Murray Blvd.   91942
(619) 466-0977
Owner: Kathleen Wendling
2400 sq.ft.

**Mon - Fri
9:30 - 5:30
Wed til 8
Sat 9:30 - 5**

1800 bolts of 100% cotton. Great selection of solids. Over 400 quilting books plus soft fabric craft patterns too. Notions and classes of course.

Poway, CA #38

The Quilt Shop

12642 Poway Rd. C - 14
(619) 748-2244   92064
Owner: Cindy Minx
Est: 1980   1700 sq.ft.

**Mon - Sat
9:30 - 6
Sun 12 - 4**

Large selection 100% cottons; we specialize in unique and unusual fabrics; complete notions inventory; classes.

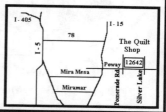

San Marcos, CA #39

Quilt in a Day

1955 Diamond Street   92069
(619) 591-0081 or (800) 777-4852
Owner: Eleanor Burns
Est: 1978   1500 sq.ft.

**Mon - Fri
9 - 5
Tues till 9
Sat 9 - 4**

Education Center, Showroom featuring large selection of 100% Cottons, books, quilting supplies, Video Production Studio.

Encinitas, CA #40

Claire's Collection

3461 Bumann Road   92024-5716
Opened: 1985
Owner: Claire McKarns
(619) 756-5718

Hours By Appt.

Antique Quilts, Tops & Blocks. Old fabrics, buttons, trims. Sewing accessories —old & new— Linens, bedcovers, feedsacks, aprons, handkerchieves, and some antiques. Quiltkeepers.

North of San Diego. From I - 5 take Encinitas Blvd. Exit. Distance is about 7 miles inland (20 min.) Call for exact directions. IT'S AN ADVENTURE !

Cooking and Cleaning—
Activities fit between
designing, sewing,
piecing, applique &
quilting

We Cater to Quilters!

Sharon Walters — Owners — Dolores Coleman

Fabrics   Books

Classes   Supplies

Quilter's Cottage

Light / Mission / Vine / Alvarado / Main / Mission / I-15 / 129 / Quilter's Cottage (Entrance to Parking off Fig) / Fig

Mon - Sat 9:30 - 4:30

(619) 723-3060

129 S. Vine St   92028
Est: 1990   800 sq.ft.

Fallbrook, CA   #41

Irvine, CA   #42

FLYING GEESE FABRICS

14210 Culver Dr. Suite D
92714
(714) 552-3809

Mon - Fri 10 -7
Sat 10 - 6
Sun 12 - 5

Owner: Bonnie Boyd   Est: 1986

Newest Quilt Fabrics, Books, And Patterns. Great Selection of Buttons for Clothing and Quilt Embellishment. Classes

Walnut / 5 Freeway / 14210 / Culver Dr. / 405 Freeway

Flying Geese Fabrics
(In the Heritage Plaza)

The
ole Classic
"Ten Patch" —
give it a try !

Costa Mesa, CA   #43

Piecemakers Country Store

Mon - Fri 10 - 9
Sat 10 - 5:30
Sun 10 - 5:30

1720 Adams Avenue   92626
(714) 641-3112   Est: 1978
Owners: 35 Piecemakers !

Catalog $2.00   12,000 sq.ft.

Complete line of quilting supplies, fabrics, books, notions, dolls, handmade quilts, unique gifts & hundreds of classes every month. Four Craft Fairs per year call for information.

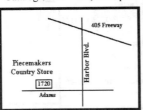

405 Freeway / Harbor Blvd. / Piecemakers Country Store / 1720 / Adams

---

Torrance, CA   #44

Quilts Unlimited

Mon - Fri 10 - 5:30
Sat 10 - 4

2202-F West Artesia Blvd.
(310) 532-9203   90504
Owner: Judy Wood
Est: 1978   2000 sq.ft.

Fabric (all major brands) Books, Patterns, Notions, Classes. Lots of Samples to inspire you !

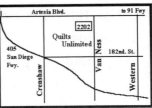

Artesia Blvd. / to 91 Fwy / 2202 / Quilts Unlimited / 405 San Diego Fwy. / Van Ness / 182nd. St. / Crenshaw / Western

Redondo Beach, CA #45

THE COTTON SHOP FINE FABRICS

(310) 376-3518
1922 Artesia Blvd.   90278
Est: 1959   8400 sq.ft.

Mon - Thur
10 - 7
Fri & Sat
10 - 6
Sun 11 - 5

Full Line Fabric
Store with Large
Quilting Dept.
Probably the
Largest Selection
of Hoffman Prints
in Southern
California

Map: to Los Angeles, I-405, Hawthorne Blvd., I-110, Hwy 1, Rosecrans, Cotton Shop, Artesia, 1922

Manhattan Beach, CA #46

Luella's Quilt Basket

1840 N. Sepulveda Blvd.
(310) 545-3436   90266
Est: 1988   1400 sq.ft.
Owners: Luella & Nancy Fournell

Mon - Sat
10 - 6
Sun 11 - 4

We offer a wide
variety of Fabrics,
Classes and
quilting supplies:
3 miles south of
L.A.X.

Map: L.A.X., Rosecrans, Manhattan Village Mall, Sepulveda Blvd., Marine Ave., San Diego (405) Frwy., Hawthorne Blvd., 1840 Luella's Quilt Basket, Manhattan Beach Blvd.

Santa Monica, CA #47

Santa Monica Antique Market

1607 Lincoln Blvd.   90404
(310) 314-4899   20,000 sq.ft.
Featured Dealer: Sandy White Antique Quilts

Mon - Sat
10 - 6
Sun 12 - 5

Recognized as
one of the Top 10
Collectives in
America.
Large Inventory
of Antique Quilts
in a Beautiful
Surrounding.

Map: Lincoln Blvd., Santa Monica Antique Market, 1607, I-405, San Diego Fwy., I-10, Santa Monica Fwy.

Santa Monica #48

McGuire's Quilt & Needlework

521 Santa Monica Blvd.   90401
(310) 395-7753   Est: 1982
Owner: Gerry McGuire
900 sq.ft.

Mon - Sat
10 - 5:30

100% Cotton
fabrics, books,
patterns,
needlework
and notions.

Map: McGuire's Quilt & Needlework, Ocean Ave., 521, 5th St., 6th St., Santa Monica Blvd., 405 Freeway, 10 Freeway

Oxnard, CA #49

Fabric Well

3075 Saviers Road   93033
(805) 486-7826
Owners: Ray & Bev Hicks
Est: 1975   13,200 sq.ft.

Mon - Fri
9:30 - 8
Sat 9:30 - 6
Sun 11 - 5

One of the
Largest
Selections of
Quilting Fabrics
and Supplies you
will find
anywhere.

Map: 101 Freeway, Victoria, Hwy 1, Vineyard, Ventura Rd., Saviers, Oxnard Blvd / Hwy 1, Fabric Well, 3075

Santa Maria, CA #50

Sally's Quilt Quarters

1765 - B South Broadway   93454
(805) 925-1888
Owner: Sally Testa
Est: 1986   950 sq.ft.

Mon - Fri
10 - 5
Sat 10 - 4

Bolts of 100%
Cotton Fabric,
books, notions,
classes and
always friendly
Service !

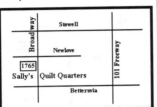

Lancaster, CA #51

Quilters' Cabin

43961 N. 15th St. West
(805) 948-2118   93534
Est: 1988   2400 sq.ft.
Cabin Keepers: Lewis & Gayle
                              Farmer

Tues - Thur
9:30 - 6
Fri 9:30 - 5
Sat 9:30 - 4

Lots of Wonderful
100% Cottons,
Notions, Books,
and Bernina
Sewing Machine
Dealer.

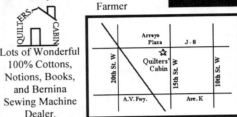

Santa Clarita, CA #52

My Next Quilt

26111 Bouquet Canyon Rd.
(805) 254-1296   91350
Owner: Lois Luera
Est: 1990   1000 Sq.ft.

Tue - Fri
10 - 5
Wed til 8
Sat 10 - 4

Full service quilt shop.
Hundreds of
bolts of cottons,
patterns, books, notions,
classes, &
gift items.
10 minutes from Six
Flags Magic Mountain.

Montrose, CA #53

Quilt 'n' Things

2411 Honolulu Ave.   91020
(818) 957-2287
Owner: Kathleen Pappas
              Donna Senecal   2000 sq.ft.

Mon - Sat
10 - 5

Classes, notions,
books. More than
2000 bolts of
fabric - all 100%
cotton. Expert
Assistance. The
friendliest shop in
Southern Calif.

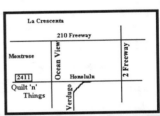

Van Nuys, CA #54

Sandy White Antique Quilts

14936 Gault St.   91405
(818) 988-0575
Est: 1985

By Appointment Only

Lovely Selection of
Appealing Antique
Quilts for both Home
and Office,
For the Collector and
Decorator.

Please Call
for
Directions

LaHabra, CA #55

Calico Corner Quilt Shop

2094 W. LaHabra Blvd.
(310) 694-3384   90631
Owner: Sheila Ingersoll   Est: 1984

Mon - Sat
10 - 5

3500 Bolts of
100% Cotton
Fabric
Notions, Patterns,
Books, Classes,
Friendly Service.

Montclair, CA   #56

Mon - Sat
9:30 - 5

5436 D Arrow Highway
909-985-9000

Marie White
Carolyn Reese
Since 1981

So. California's Largest, Most Complete Quilt Shop
3000 bolts of 100% cotton
300 book titles
More than 1000 craft and quilt patterns
Large selection of notions
Gift items for Quilters and their friends
We do mail order
Use the Central Ave. exit on I-10

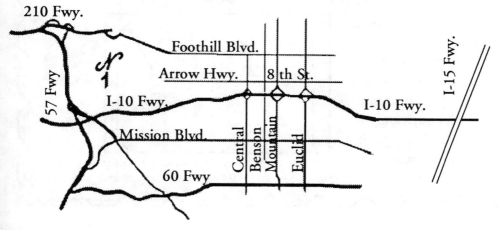

Upland, CA #57

100s of bolts of 100% cotton,
Over 400 titles of Quilting Books

100s of Quilt and Quilt related patterns
Quilt backing in 90 and 108 inches wide,
Hobbs Batting in all sizes on the roll
Complete line of quilting notions, gift items,
finished quilts and more.

Mon - Fri 10 - 6
Sat 10 - 5
May - Dec Open
Thurs til 9 for the
2nd Ave. Market
Street Fair
Open some
Sundays,
please call first

Mail
Order Available

291 N. 2nd. Avenue   91786
Corner of "C" St. and 2nd.
In Old Town Upland
(909) 985-2245
Est: 1984   4600 sq.ft.

Classes for everyone
from the newest
beginner to the
advanced quilter are
offered 7 days a week;
morning, afternoon,
and evening. Both
hand and machine
method.

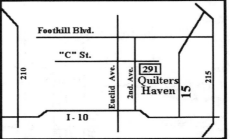

Located 5 minutes from the Ontario International
Airport. From I -10 take the Euclid exit and go North.

Quilting Hoop — Sewing Circle Friend

Redlands, CA   #58

The Calico Horse

Mon - Fri 10 - 6
Sat 10 - 5

461 Tennessee St.   Suite J 92373
(909) 793-5615 or 824-6198
Owners: Debra & Doug Grantz
    Beverly & Bill Dean   Est: 1986   1580 sq.ft.

Large selection of 100% cotton fabrics and supplies. Patterns & Books. Orange crate labels on muslin. Friendly, expert advice. Mail Order Avail.

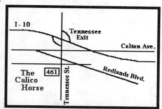

Quilters haven

Classes for Everyone from the beginner to advanced in both Hand and Machine Medthods. Large selection of notions, books, patterns, fabric, gift items and more.

Mon - Sat   11 - 4

2535 S. San Jacinto Ave.
(Farmers Corner Mall)   92583
(909) 925-3488   Est: 1994

San Jacinto, CA   #59

Palm Springs, CA   #60

Creative Expressions of Palm Springs

Mon - Sat 9 - 5

1111 South Palm Canyon Drive
(619) 327-2587   92264
Owner: Priscilla Patencio Gonzales
          Est: 1985

Complete Quilt Shop ! Fabric 100% Cotton ! Largest selection of Southwestern and Indian Prints in the Desert Area. Bead room too !

California Guilds: ADA Quilt Guild, 3460 Wilshire Blvd, Los Angeles 90010
Afro-American Quilters, 22544 Califa, Woodland Hills 91367
Antelope Valley Quilt Association, PO Box 4107, Lancaster 93534
Busy Bear Quilt Guild, PO Box 6513, Big Bear Lake 92315
Cactus Sew-Ables Quilt Guild, PO Box 317, Pioneertown 92268
Camarillo Quilters Assoc., PO Box 347, Camarillo 93011
Canyon Quilters, P.O. Box 22465, San Diego 92192
Citrus Belt Quilters, PO Box 626, Bryn Mawr 92318
Coachella Valley Quilt Guild, 43-761 Towne St., Indio 92201
Coastal Quilters Guild, PO Box 6341, Santa Barbara 93106
Cotton Patch Quilters, PO Box 9944, Bakersfield 93389
Desert Quilters Guild, 410 W. C St., Brawley 92227
Desert Quilters of Nevada, PO Box 28586, Las Vegas 89126
Desert Winds Quilt Guild, PO Box 1989, Victorville 92392
East Bay Heritage Quilters, Box 6223, Albany, 94706
El Camino Quilt Guild, PO Box 1952, Oceanside 92051
Fallbrook Quilters Guild, PO Box 1704, Fallbrook 92028
Flying Geese Quilters, PO Box 19608-154, Irvine 92713
Friendship Quilters, PO Box 1174, Poway 92074
Friendship Square Quilt Guild, PO Box 681, La Habra 90633
Glendale Quilt Guild, PO Box 5366, Glendale 91201
Heart of California Quilt Guild, 415 Camden Way, Madera, 93637
Independence Hall Quilters, PO Box 842,   Arnold, A 95223
Inland Empire Quilt Guild, PO Box 2232, Corona 91718
Legacy Quilters, 9320 Lake Country Dr., Santee 92071
Los Angeles County Quilt Guild, PO Box 252, Norwalk 90651
LA Quiltmakers Guild, 16167 Augusta Dr., Chino Hills 91709
Marin Needle Arts Guild, Box 6015, San Rafael, 94903
Moonlighters, P.O. Box 6882,   Santa Rosa, 95406
Mountain Quilters Guild, Oakhurst Library , Oakhurst
Mt. Tam Quilt Guild, P.O. Box 6192, San Rafael, 94903
Mountain Quilters, PO Box 603, Idyllwild 92349
Night Owl Quilters Guild, PO Box 5019, Upland 91786
Northern California Quilt Council, 3935 Sloat Road, Pebble Beach
Petaluma Quilt Guild , P.O5334, Petaluma, 94955
North County Quilting Assoc., PO Box 982, San Marcos 92079
Orange County Quilters Guild, PO Box 3108, Orange 92665
Orange Grove Quilters Guild, PO Box 453, Garden Grove 92642
Piece by Piece Quilters, 114 Cochrane Road, Morgan Hill, 95037
Porterville Quilters, PO Box 1881, Porterville 93257
Quilters Etc., PO Box 2507, Lumpock 93438
San Fernando Valley Quilt Assoc., PO Box 1042, Reseda 91337
San Jaquin Valley Quilt Guild, PO Box 5532, Fresno, 93755
Santa Clarita Valley QG, PO Box 802863, Santa Clarita 91380
Santa Maria Valley QG, PO Box 2933, Santa Maria 93457
Santa Rosa Quilt Guild, P.O. Box 9251, Santa Rosa, 95405
Schoolhouse Quilt Guild, PO Box 356, Rosemead 91770
Sierra Mountain Quilters Guild   PO Box 1359, Oakhurst, 93644
Seaside Quilt Guild, PO Box 9964, San Diego 92109
Simi Valley Quilt Guild, PO Box 3689, Simi Valley 93093
South Bay Quilters Guild, PO Box 6115, Torrance 90504
Southern CA Council of Quilt Guilds, 2342 W. Avenue N., Palmdale
South County Quilt Guild, PO Box 656, Arroyo Grande 93421
Sunshine Quilters, PO Box 20483, El Cajon 92022
Valley Oak Quilters, PO Box 1093, Tulare 93275
Valley of the Mist QG, 27475 Ynez Rd., Temecula 92391
Valley Quilters, PO Box 2534, Hemet 92545
Valley Quiltmakers Guild, PO Box 589, Canoga Park 91305
Wandering Foot QG, PO Box 9431, Sierra Madre 91025

Other Shops in California:

Auburn	Feathered Nest, 157 Sacramento
Berkeley	Ninepatch, 201 Hopkins
Berkeley	Stonemountain & Daughter, 2516 Shattuck Avenue
Big Bear Lake	Mountain Country Mercantile, 40671 Village Dr.
Burbank	Q is for Quilts, 401 S. Glenoaks Blvd
Burbank	Bearly Stitchin' Fabric Center, 1052 W. Alameda
Cambria	Sew & So, 1602 Main
Campbell	Yardstick, Inc., 2110 S. Bascom Ave.
Carmel	Quilts, Limited, PO Box 7066 93921 Ocean Avenue
Chico	Homey Run Quilters, 1230 Esplanade
Chowchilla	Joan's Notions, 307 Robertson Blvd.
Cypress	Sew and Sew Fabrics, 5949 Ball Road
Davis	The Pincushion Boutique, 825 Russell Blvd.
El Cajon	Calico Junction, 753 Jamacha Road
Fair Oaks	Tayo's Fair Oaks Fabrics, 10127 Fair Oaks Boulevard
Grass Valley	Simply Stitches, 209 W. Main St.
La Mesa	The Country Loft, 8166 LaMesa Blvd.
Lodi	My Favorite Pastime, 1306 Lakewood Mall
Los Angeles	Margaret Cavigga Quilt Collection, 8648 Melrose Ave
Los Gatos	The Makings, 798 Blossom Hill Rd. #12
Lower Lake	Magoon's General Store, 16195 Main
Madera	Quilted Bunny, 1705 Howard Rd
Mendocino	Crossblends, 45156 Main
Monroevia	Material Pleasures, 107 E. Lemon
Montebello	Robbin's Fabrics, Inc., 2524 W. Beverly Blvd.
Montrose	Needle in a Haystack, 2262 Honlulu Avenue
Norco	Quilt n Cross, 2085 River Road
Oakland	Quilt and Quilting Studio, 5369 Foothills Boulevard
Oceanside	Cotton Patch, 307 N. Hill Street
Pacific Grove	The Hand Maden, 18 Grand Avenue
Petaluma	Chanticleer Antiques, 145 Petaluma Blvd. N
Pleasanton	Going to Pieces, 1989 F Santa Rita Road
Redding	Sew Simple, 125 Lake Boulevard
Rocklin	Quilt Connection, 5050 Rockland Rd. #4A
Sacramento	Seams Like Old Times, 5484 Carlson Drive
Sacramento	Sonora Yard Goods, 564 W. Stockton St. #B
Sacramento	The Quilt Rack, 5485 Carlson Drive
San Anselmo	San Anselmo Country Store, 312 Sir Francis Drake
San Anselmo	Hearts and Hands, 241 Sir Francis Drake Blvd.
San Carlos	The Laurel Leaf, 648 Laurel Street
San Diego	Fabriholics, 3944 W. Point Loma Blvd. #H
San Diego	Branch of the Lily, 12873 El Camino
San Diego	Manos Maravillosas, 3683 Midway Drive
San Francisco	San Francisco Fabrics, 1715 Polk Street
San Francisco	Edward's Unusual Fabrics, 80 Geary St.
San Francisco	Mendels' Far Out Fabrics, 1556 Haight
San Marcos	Fabrics Plus, 332 Rancheros Dr. #106
San Marcos	Calico Station, 727 Center Drive #117
San Pedro	Quilt Sails, 312 W. 37th
Santa Ana	Quilting Possibilities, 2207 S. Grand Avenue
Santa Ana	Wild Goose Chase, 1631 Sunflower
Santa Ana	Quilting Time, 912 E. Edinger Avenue
Santa Barbara	B's Country Store, 512 Brinkerhoff Avenue
Santa Clarita	Aunt Ida's Attic, 24251 N. San Fernando Rd.
Santa Monica	Crazy Lady & Friends, 1606 Santa Monica Boulevard
Santa Rosa	Richman Cotton Co., 529 5th St.
Sky Forest	Sew Fun, 28589 Highway 18
Spring Valley	The Quilted Rose, 9621 Campo Road
Spring Valley	Casa Crafters, 9736 Campo Road
Summerland	Sally's Alley, PO Box 876
Valencia	Quilted Heart, 24201 Valencia Blvd. #1371
Vergudo City	Goodwin's Fabrics, P.O. Box 534
Walnut Creek	Creative Needle, 1487 E. Newell Ave.
Walnut Creek	Thimble Creek, 1536 Newell Ave.
Watsonville	Stonemountain & Daughter, 410 Rodriquez
Weaverville	Quilted Treasures, P.O. Box 1830 801 Main Street
Woodland Hills	The Quilt Emporium, 4918 Topanga Canyon Boulevard
Yucca Valley	Stitchin & Quilting, 57365 29 Palms Highway

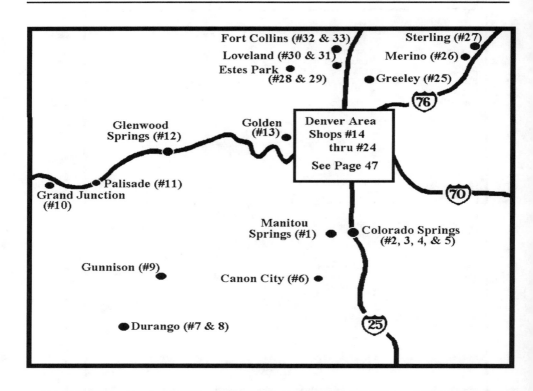

Fort Collins (#32 & 33)
Loveland (#30 & 31)
Estes Park
(#28 & 29)

Sterling (#27)
Merino (#26)
Greeley (#25)

Glenwood
Springs (#12)

Golden
(#13)

Denver Area
Shops #14
thru #24

See Page 47

Palisade (#11)
Grand Junction
(#10)

Manitou
Springs (#1)

Colorado Springs
(#2, 3, 4, & 5)

Gunnison (#9)

Canon City (#6)

Durango (#7 & 8)

COLORADO

33 Featured Shops

Needle —
What I do to
my husband if
he won't take
me to the next
quilt shop.

Colorado Springs, CO #3

High Country Quilts

4771 N. Academy Blvd.
(719) 598-1312   80918
Owner: Barbara L. Blutt   Est: 1983

QUILTING SUPPLIES & INSTRUCTIONS
Large assortment of cotton Fabrics, Books, Patterns, and Notions.

Mon - Fri	10 - 5:30
Saturday	10 - 5
Sunday	1 - 4

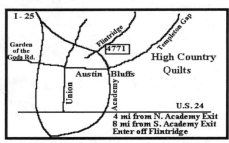

I - 25
Garden of the Gods Rd.
Flintridge
4771
Templeton Gap
High Country Quilts
Austin Bluffs
Union
Academy
U.S. 24
4 mi from N. Academy Exit
8 mi from S. Academy Exit
Enter off Flintridge

Colorado Springs, CO #4

Artistic Antique

Mon - Sat
10 - 5
Or by Appt. in your home

219 West Colorado Avenue   80903
(719) 635-1171   Hm. 599-4278
Owners: Joy Park and Partners
Opened: 1991   1500 sq.ft.

Antique quilts, tops, blocks, vintage fabrics, hooked rugs. From the 1830's to 1940. Photo sales by mail order also.

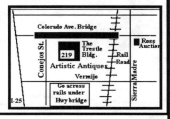

Colorado Ave. Bridge
Conejos St.
The Trestle Bldg.
219
Artistic Antiques
Rail Road
Ross Auction
Vermijo
Sierra Madre
Go across rails under Hwy bridge
I-25

Colorado Springs, CO #5

Nevada Avenue Antiques

Mon - Fri	9 - 5
Sat	10 - 5
Sun	12 - 4

405 S. Nevada Ave.   80903
(719) 473-3351   Est: 1989
Owners: John & Gina Sharp

Over 35 Dealer Mall Quality Antiques & Collectibles.

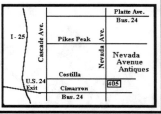

I - 25
Cascade Ave.
Pikes Peak
Nevada Ave.
Platte Ave.
Bus. 24
Nevada Avenue Antiques
U.S. 24 Exit
Costilla
Cimarron
405
Bus. 24

Canon City, CO #6

- Quality Quilting Fabrics
- Notions
- Books
- Patterns
- Supplies
  - Creative Quilting Classes

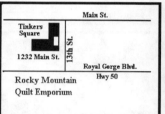

Tinkers Square
1232 Main St.
Main St.
13th St.
Royal Gorge Blvd.
Hwy 50

Rocky Mountain Quilt Emporium

Rocky Mountain Quilt Emporium

Come visit us in colorful Colorado. Canon City is the home of the Royal Gorge and the gateway to the rest of Colorado

13th & Main, Tinkers Square
(719) 269-1577
Owner: Susan Ulrich
1500 sq.ft.

Mon - Sat
10 - 5:30

Durango, CO #7

Forget-Me-Not Fabrics

Mon - Sat
9:30 - 5:30
Sun 1 - 5

144 E. 8th St.   81301
(303) 247-0080
Est: 1982   2250 sq.ft.
Owners: Carolyn Norton & Keira Linterman

We are a full fabric store with heavy emphasis on quilting, Stitchery and speciality yarns.

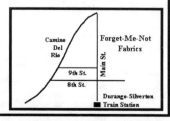

Camino Del Rio
Forget-Me-Not Fabrics
9th St.
8th St.
Main St.
Durango-Silverton
Train Station

Durango, CO #8

Animas Quilts

600 Main Avenue   81301
(303) 247-2582   Est: 1988
Owner: Jackie Robinson
                2600 sq.ft.
"A quilter's paradise" on the western slope of Colorado. 1000 Bolts of wonderful cottons! Publisher of books by Jackie Robinson & other great authors.
Plus more

Summer
10 - 5:30
Winter
10 - 5
Sun 12 - 4

Main Ave.
Animas Quilts
600
Lower Level
6th St.

N.E. corner of
6th & Main
One Block North of
Durango-Silverton
Train Depot

Gunnison, CO #9

E & P Sewing Emporium

135 N. Main St.   81230
(303) 641-0474   (800) 736-4281
Owners: Ellen Harriman & Pat
2000 sq.ft.   Est: 1985   Venturo

Mon - Sat
9 - 5:30
Sun 12 - 4

We are a full-service sewing store offering New Home Sewing Machines, quilting and sewing classes. Home of the Land of the Rainbow Quilt Festival Aug. 10 - 17

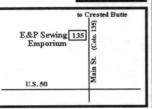

to Crested Butte
E&P Sewing [135] Emporium
Main St. (Colo. 135)
U.S. 50

Palisade, CO #11

Rocky Mountain Quilts

By Appointment

(303) 464-7294
Owner: Betsey Telford   Est: 1986

We own over 250 antique quilts from the late 1700's to the 1940's (80 plus in Colorado). Doll & bassinet size to king size. We also have a cottage industry of 30 ladies doing hand and machine quilting. Special order anything to do with quilts. We restore antique quilts using vintage fabrics. Available 7 day a week by appointment. Dealers and decorators welcome. We are just 12 mi. East of Grand Junction.

Golden, CO #13

Rocky Mountain Quilt Museum

Tues - Sat
10 - 4

1111 Washington Ave.   80401
(303) 277-0377
Non-Profit Self Supporting Museum
Adm: Maureen Peterson   Est: 1990

The only Quilt Museum in the Rocky Mountains. Exhibits change every two months. Send S.A.S.E. for schedule. Admission $1.

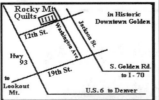

Rocky Mt Quilts [1111]
in Historic Downtown Golden
12th St.
Washington Ave.
Jackson St.
Hwy 93
19th St.
S. Golden Rd. to I-70
to Lookout Mt.
U.S. 6 to Denver

Grand Junction, CO #10

Hi Fashion Fabrics, Inc.

2586 Patterson Rd.   81505
(303) 242-1890
Owners: Arlene & Jeff Vogel
Est: 1965   11,500 sq.ft.

Mon - Sat
9:30 - 5:30

Huge Selection of Quilting Cottons, Books, and Supplies. Complete Line of Other Fabrics: Bridal, Fashion, Outer Wear, Drapery & Upholstery.

Airport
I-70 to Denver
1st St.
7th St.
Horizon Dr.
F Road
[2586]
Patterson Rd.
Near the Corner of 1st and Patterson Rd.
Hwy. 50 to Delta

Glenwood Springs, CO #12

Glenwood Sewing Center

809 Grand Avenue #1   81601
(303) 945-5900
Owners: Bob & Sandy Boyd
Est: 1977
2000 sq.ft.

Mon - Sat
9:30 - 5:30
Sun 12:30 - 4

Treasures for creative people - for quilting - for home decor - for fashion and active wear.

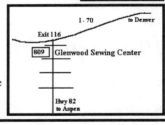

I-70 to Denver
Exit 116
[809] Glenwood Sewing Center
Hwy 82 to Aspen

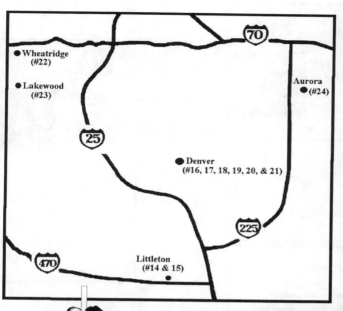

11 Featured Shops

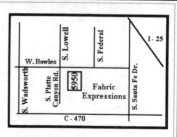

Littleton, CO #15

The Creative Needle

**Mon - Sat
10 a.m.
Sun 12 noon**

6905 South Broadway #113
(303) 794-7312   80122
Owner: Marge Serck
Est: 1978   3500 sq.ft.

One stop for
quilting, cross-
stitch, heirloom
and smocking.
Elna machine
sales and service.
Sister shop in
Denver

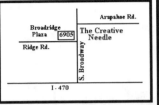

Denver, CO #16

The Creative Needle

**Mon - Sat
10 a.m.
Sun 12 noon**

2553 South Colorado Blvd.   80222
(303) 692-8115
Owner: Marge Serck
        Est: 1992   2400 sq.ft.

One stop for
quilting, cross-
stitch heirloom
and smocking.
Elna machine
sales and service.
Sister shop in
Littleton.

Denver, CO #17

Quilts in the Attic

**Mon - Fri
9:30 - 5:30
Sat.
9:30 - 4:30**

1025 South Gaylord St.   80209
(303) 744-8796
Est: 1972   1200 sq.ft.
Owners: Dyanna Ivy, Joyce Luff,
        Marge Hedges, & Margaret Hill

Fabric - all 100%
cotton - Books,
Patterns, Batting,
Notions. Ideas
and Friendly
Service.

Denver, CO #18

The Country Line
Antiques & Quilts

**Tues - Sat
11 - 5**

1067 S. Gaylord St.   80209
(303) 733-1143
Owner: Genna Morrow
Est: 1988

Antique Quilts
from $20 to $2000
Also—quilt scraps,
pieces, & "cutters"
Gifts made from
Antique quilts our
specialty.

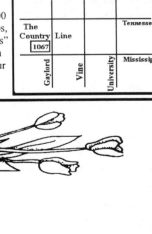

Denver, CO #19

**Wed - Sat
10 - 6
Or By Appt.**

357 Santa Fe Dr.   80223
(303) 623-2710   Est: 1988
Owners: Debra Lunn & Michael Mrowka 9000 sq.ft.
Catalog $13 (Includes $10 coupon)

Hand-dyed and Hand
Painted Cotton and
Silk Fabrics.
Ethnic Textiles
Unusual printed
goods. Buttons,
Beads, Threads and
other good stuff!

Denver, CO #20

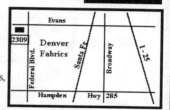

**Mon - Fri
9:30 - 8
Sat 9:30 - 6
Sun 12 - 5**

2309 S. Federal   80219
(303) 934-7415

Denver's Largest
Selection of
Fabrics, Buttons,
Notions, and
Patterns.
Also Quilting Books,
Patterns &
Supplies

Denver, CO #21

Great American Quilt Factory

**Mon - Fri
9:30 - 6
Wed til 8:30
Sat 9:30 - 5
Sun 12 - 5**

8970 East Hampden Ave.   80231
(303) 740-6206   Est: 1981
Owners: Nancy Smith & Lynda
2000 sq.ft.   Milligan

Welcome !
Fabric, 2000 Bolts +
Books, Patterns, Notions.
Home of Dream Spinner
patterns, Possibilities
Books & "I'll Teach
Myself" kids sewing
program.

Machine
Quilting —
Put your foot
down and follow
the curves of
your fancy.

Wheat Ridge, CO #22

Harriet's Treadle Arts

**Mon - Sat
9:30 - 5**

6390 West 44th Ave.   80033
(303) 424-2742   Est: 1981
Owner: Harriet Hargrave   3600 Sq.ft.

Our shelves are
bulging with
beautiful bolts !
Wide variety of
notions.
**Come See
Us ! !**

Lakewood, CO #23

Lakewood Crafts

7777 West Jewell Avenue #1A
(303) 989-9616   80232
Owners: John & Ann Evans
Est: 1987   10,700 sq.ft.

Mon - Thur
10 - 8
Fri 10 - 6
Sat 9 - 6
Sun 11 - 5

Full Line
Craft Store.
Including
quilters'
supplies and
Fabrics.

```
                              I-70
        Lakewood          |
         Crafts           | Wadsworth
         7777             |
  8 miles from I-70    Jewell Ave.
  2 miles from U.S.285
                           U.S. 285
```

Aurora, CO #24

Divine Threads

1930 South Havana #201
(303) 337-9120   80014
Owner: Virginia Wedow
                        Est: 1986

Hours Vary
Please
Call First

I invented and
manufacture
"Measurwings". I
dye rayon threads
for Brazilian
Embroidery and
print my original
designs in books.

```
                          Jewell
          |
  Havana  | 201  Divine Threads
          |      (upstairs)
          |          Iliff
          |      Parker Rd.
 Hampden
```

Greeley, CO #25

Country Crafts & Supplies

903 E. 18th St.   80631
(303) 353-1774   Est: 1983   1200 sq.ft.
Owners: Jean Baker & Sherry Monteith

Mon - Fri
9 - 5:30
Sat 9 - 4:30

Quilters' Heaven
Wide selection of
100% cotton
fabrics, notions,
and lots of critter
and doll patterns.
Mail Orders
Welcome

```
  8th Ave. | U.S. 85 Bypass | 1st. Ave. | Balsam Ave. | Country
           |                |           |             | Crafts &
           |                |           |             | Supplies
           |                |  East 18th St.          |   903
           |                |  (U.S. 34 Bus)
       RR
```

Merino, CO #26

D & J Country Antiques

R.R. #2   P.O. Box 29   80741
(303) 842-5813   Est: 1967
Owners: Dorothy & Jake Leis & Family

By Chance
or By
Appointment
Please Call

Vintage Quilts -
tops - blocks -
Fabric - 30's Feed
sacks - Notions -
Lace - Antique
sewing tools &
machines.

```
                            14
 Antelope Spgs.        Atwood
   Church    R.R.2   Over
                      Pass  Merino
        71    Snyder
                      6
   34                    I-76
          Brush   17 mi. off I-76
   Ft. Morgan     10 mi. W of
                  Merion Overpass
```

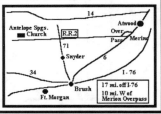

Antiques

Quilts
for Sale

Quilted Clothing —
For people who like
to be warmed by
quilting in the
daytime too.

Sterling, CO #27

Quilts-N-Creations

201 Ash   P.O. Box 991
(303) 522-0146   80751
Owners: Everett & Dorothy Duncan
Est: 1987   Mgr: Leta Propst

**Mon - Sat
9 - 5:30**

Calico Cottons,
Knits, Bridal:
Classes:
Tuxedo Rental:
Authorized
Bernina dealer:
Custom Sewing &
Heirloom Machine
Quilting.

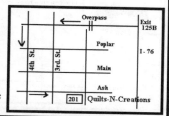

Estes Park, CO #28

Maggie Mae's Quilts 'N

212 Moraine Ave. P.O. Box 4857
(303) 586-4257   80517
Owner: Margaret McCormick
Est: 1990   900 sq.ft.

**Year 'round
10 - 5
Closed Wed.**

Featuring Patterns
by Colorado
Designers.
Kits - Handmade
Wooden Quilt
Racks - Fabrics -
Christmas Projects
& Unique
Wearables.

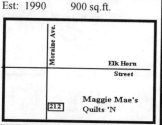

Estes Park, CO #29

Mountain Lady Quilters' School & Supply

475 Fall River Lane, Moraine Rt.
(303) 586-5330   80517
Owner: Connie Westley

**Tues - Sat
10 - 5
or by Appt.**

Everything for
Quilters.
Workshops for
Tourists.
American Made
Quilts.
Kits. Custom Quilting
& Quilts.
Mail Order.
New Home Machines.

Loveland, CO   #30

Treadle Quilts

Tues - Sat
10 - 5:30
Thur til 7:30

205 E. Eisenhower Blvd.
#7 Valley Center   80538
(303) 635-9064   Est: 1993
Owner: Kim D. Garber   1040 sq.ft.

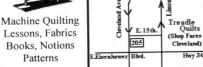

Machine Quilting
Lessons, Fabrics
Books, Notions
Patterns

Cleveland Ave.
E. 15th.
205
E.Eisenhower Blvd.
Lincoln Ave.
Treadle
Quilts
(Shop Faces
Cleveland)
Hwy 34
I - 25

Loveland, CO   #31

Gifts from the Heart

Mon - Sat
10 - 5

1407 West Eisenhower   80538
(303) 669-6820   Est: 1989
Owners: Suzanne Thayne,
Carol McKenna & Mae Lewis

We have quilting
fabrics and
supplies, books,
and patterns. Plus
great handmade
gifts and crafts.

Gifts from
the Heart
1407
West Eisenhower /
Hwy 35
Taft
Approx. 5 miles
from I - 25
I - 25

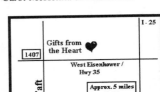

Ft. Collins, CO   #32

Calico Junction

Mon 10 - 7
Tues - Sat
10 - 5

148 W. Oak   80521
(303) 493-0203
Owner: Lorraine Williams
Est: 1985   2000 sq.ft.

'All' the Books
Patterns Galore !
1000 Bolts
(100 Solids)
Beautiful Yarns
Wearable Arts
Quilts, Dolls,
Animals

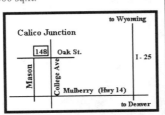

to Wyoming
Calico Junction
148 Oak St.
Mason
College Ave
Mulberry (Hwy 14)
to Denver
I - 25

Ft. Collins, CO   #33

The Fig Leaf

Mon - Sat
10 - 6
Sun 1 - 5

232 E. Monroe   80525
(303) 226-3267
Owners: Rob & Laura Shotwell
Est: 1982   4600 sq.ft.

Over 1600 Bolts of
100% Cotton
Fabrics. Large
Selection of Books,
Patterns and Notions.
Country Furnishings,
Gifts & Accessories.

232 The Fig Leaf
Monroe
College Ave.
Horsetooth
Harmony Rd.
I - 25

Colorado State Guild:
Colorado Quilting Council, P.O. Box 2056, Arvada, 80001-2056
Colorado Guilds:
Arapahoe County Quilters, P.O. Box 5357, Englewood, 80155
Colorado Springs Quilt Guild, Modern Woodman Bldg., CO Springs
Estes Valley Quilt Guild, PO Box 3931, Estes Park, 80517
Colorado West Q. G., 1320 Houston Ave., Grand Junction, 81501
Front Range Cont. Quilters, 7133 Gold Nugget Dr., Longmont, 80503
La Plata Quilter's Guild, P.O. Box 2355, Durango, 81302
Piecing Partners, 1111 Martin Dr., Colorado Springs, 80925
Pride City Quilt Guild, 60 Portero Dr., Pueblo, 81005
Royal Gorge Quilt Council, 1402 1/2 Sherman Ave., Canon City, 81212

Other Shops in Colorado:

Alamosa	Gray Goose, 614 Main
Boulder	Old School House Quiltworks, 4175 Eldorado Springs Dr.
Boulder	Betsy's Natural Fabrics, 2035 Broadway
Buena Vista	Bev's Stitchery, 202 Tabor St. Box 1773
Colorado Springs	Mill Outlet Fabric Shop, 2906 N. Prospect
Englewood	Heritage Quilts and Handcrafts, 10101 E. Caley Ave.
Fort Collins	Calico Country, 4604 Terry Lake Road
Fort Morgan	Quilting Corner, 328 Main
Grand Junction	Quilt Junction & Gallery 412, 412 Main
Greeley	Wild N' Woolly's, 2313 Seventeenth
Hotchkiss	Stitch in Time Quilt Shop, 410 W. Bridge St.
Lafayette	Artistic Creations, 825 Sparta Dr.
Leadville	Mountain Top Quilts, 129 E. Seventh Street
Longmont	The Patchworks, Inc., 700 Florida Avenue
Longmont	Bernina Sewing Center, 510 4th Ave.
Manitou Springs	The Handiworks, 734 Manitou Ave.
Monte Vista	Quilting Hoop, 206 Adams
Ouray	The Quilt Cellar, 700 Main Street
Parker	Chameleons Three, 8916 Mad River Road
Pueblo	Quilt Shop Antiques, 111 E. Abriendo Ave.
Sedalia	Weedpatch Loveables, 3567 N. Winnebago Dr.
Steamboat Springs	Sew What, 437 Oak
Westminster	G&P Trading, 11205 Quivas Loop
Wheat Ridge	B & R's Keepers Cove, 7230 W. 38th Ave.
Yuma	Needle in a Haystack, 212 S. Main Street

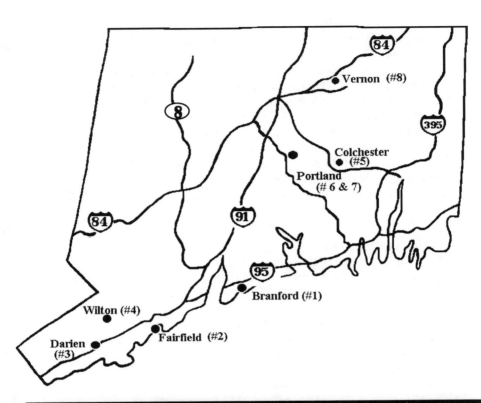

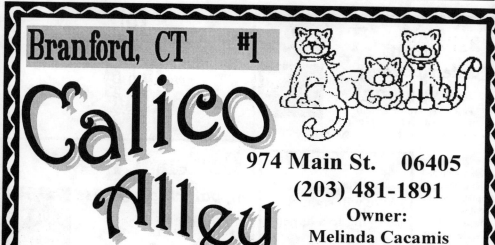

Branford, CT   #1

Calico Alley

974 Main St.   06405
(203) 481-1891
Owner:
Melinda Cacamis
Est: 1992

IT'S WORTH THE DRIVE !

**Unique Designer Fabrics — 100% Cottons
& Authentic Reprints
Quilting Notions & Supplies
Over 500 Patterns & Books
Classes, Sewing Machines, Quilts for Sale
1000's of Fat Quarters**

Mon - Fri 10 - 5   Sat 10 - 4

COME SEE US SOON !

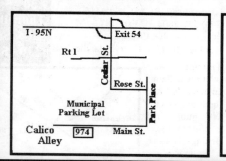

**Within minutes of
Shoreline Trolley Museum
& Thimble Islands.
45 minutes from Mystic Seaport.**
From I - 95 N take Exit 54 (Cedar St)
Take 2nd left on Rose St. Next Right on
Park Place. Take right into Municipal
Parking Lot (1 mile from Hwy)

Fairfield, CT #2

Contemporary Quilting

Mon - Sat 10 - 5

173 Post Road (Moving Soon)
(203) 259-3564   06430   Est: 1984
Owner: Florence Osborne   900 sq.ft.

Over 2000 bolts 100% cotton and all quilting supplies. Inquire about mail order fabric club. "Fabrics of the Month"

Please Call for directions. We will soon be moving to a larger location.

Darien, CT #3

Appalachian House

Mon - Sat 10 - 5

1010 Boston Post Rd.   06820
(203) 655-7885   Est: 1973
6 Rooms in a picturesque House

A non-profit Craft Shop. We provide a Market Place for Mountain Crafts People Dependent on their skill and Talent for their Livelihood.

Directions from I-95 North--Take exit 11--Turn Left--Store is on the Right 1/4th mile on Rt.1
Directions from I-95 South--Take Exit 11--Turn Right--Store is on the right after 1st Traffic Light.

Wilton, CT #4

Yankee Pride Quilt Shop

Tues - Sat 10 - 5

200 Danbury Rd. (Rte. 7)
(203) 762-2620   06897
Owner: Eileen Speight   Est: 1984   1000 sq.ft.

100% Cotton Fabrics, Patterns, Books, Stencils & Quilting Notions. Weekly unadvertised in-shop special sales. Mail Orders Welcome

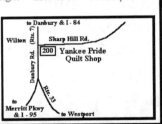

to Danbury & I-84
Wilton (Rte. 7)
Sharp Hill Rd.
Danbury Rd.
200 Yankee Pride Quilt Shop
Rte. 33
to Merritt Pkwy & I-95
to Westport

Connecticut Guilds:
Clamshell Quilt Guild,
    P.O. Box 3, Hartford, 06385
The Greater Hartford Quilt Guild,
    P.O. Box 310213, Newington, 06131
Thames River Quilters,
    New London, 06320
Trumbull Piecemakers,
    34 St. Mary's Lane, Norwalk, 06851
Heart of the Valley,
    Portland, 06480

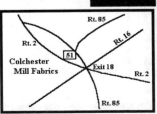

Colchester, CT #5

Colchester Mill Fabrics

**Mon - Fri 9:30 - 5:30
Thur til 8
Sat & Sun 10 - 5**

51 Broadway (Rt. 85)   06415
(203) 537-2004   Est: 1973
Owner: Carolyn Chyinski
10,000 sq.ft. Mgr. Cheryl Marchenkoff

Full line textile outlet specializing in home dec. & quilting. Over 3000 cotton prints & solids in stock. Battings, Books, Notions & Needlework.

Rt. 85
Rt. 2
Rt. 16
51
Colchester Mill Fabrics
Exit 18
Rt. 2
Rt. 85

Portland, CT   #6

Carolyn's Quilting Bee

73 Ames Hollow Rd.   06480
(203) 342-1949
Owner: Carolyn Johnson
Est: 1980

By Appointment

Located in the
Blacksmith Shop of
an 18th Century
Farm.
Visitors are always
welcome.

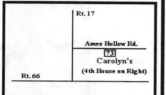

Rt. 17

Ames Hollow Rd.

[73]
Carolyn's
(4th House on Right)

Rt. 66

Portland, CT   #7

Patches & Patchwork

216 Main   06480
(203) 342-4567   Est: 1980
Owner: Jane Wilk Sterry   1200 sq.ft.

**Tues - Fri
10 - 5
Sat 10 - 3**

We carry the
unusual in fabrics.
Latest books,
patterns and
notions. Classes.
Antique quilt
repair!
Commission quilts

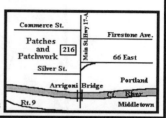

Commerce St.   Firestone Ave.

Patches
and   [216]
Patchwork   66 East

Silver St.

Main St. Hwy 17-A

Portland

Arrigoni Bridge   Ct. River

Rt. 9   Middletown

Vernon, CT   #8

520 Hartford Tpke.   06066
(203) 871-1775
Owner: Kathy Neff
Est: 1955   2800 sq.ft.

**Tues - Sat
10 - 5
Thur til 8**

Kellner's

WINDOW DECORATORS
&
QUILTING SHOP

STAFFED BY QUILTERS!!

Hoffman, P & B, Kona, Fabric
Country, Concord, V.I.P.

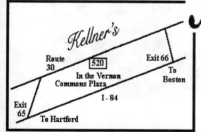

Kellner's

Route
30   [520]   Exit 66
In the Vernon   To
Commons Plaza   Boston

I - 84

Exit
65
To Hartford

Other Shops in Connecticut:	
Avon	Country at Heart, 35 Old Avon Village
Bethel	J. H. Homestead, 79 Putnam Park Road
Brookfield	Carole's Textiles Inc., Brookfield Common
Cheshire	Calico Etc., 116 Elm
Clinton	J & N Fabrics, 55 W. Main
Colchester	Wild Geese, 119 Lebanon Avenue
Cromwell	Fabric Place, 136 Berlin Road
Glastonbury	Close to Home, 2717 Main
New Haven	Quilted Delights, 100 N. Branford Rd.
Orange	Quilt Patch, 541 Boston Post Road
Stamford	Gingham Dog & Calico Cat, 44 Sixth Street
Stanford	Adelles Fabric Center, 918 Washington Blvd.
Torrington	Eleanor's Fabrics, 455 Winsted Road
Torrington	Gingham Rocker, 84 Main
Woodbury	Country Repeats, Box 869 107 Main Street N.

(#1)   Hockessin

DELAWARE

1 Featured Shop

Other Shops in Delaware:
Middletown   Needles & Hoops, Hwy 71 & 301   Summitville Rd.
Wilmington   River Antiques, 4018 Greenmount Road

Traditions Past .... Future Heirlooms

Notions Patterns

Quilt Essentials

Books Classes

Fabric

Hockessin, DE   #1

1304 Old Lancaster Pike #D   19707
(302) 234-9926   Owner: Bonita Kirchart
Opened: 1992   1800 sq.ft.

A complete Quilt Shop with over 2100 bolts of
quilting fabric including calicos, homespuns,
flannels, denims, and wools. We specialize in
the unusual from such makers as Hoffman, RJR,
South Sea and Momen House to name just a few.
Our subspecialty is Sewn Dolls including a
complete selection of Bear making supplies:
Synthetic Furs and Mohairs, joint kits and
other hard to find items.

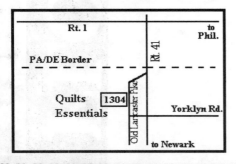

**Mon - Sat
10 - 4:30
Wed & Thur til 8**

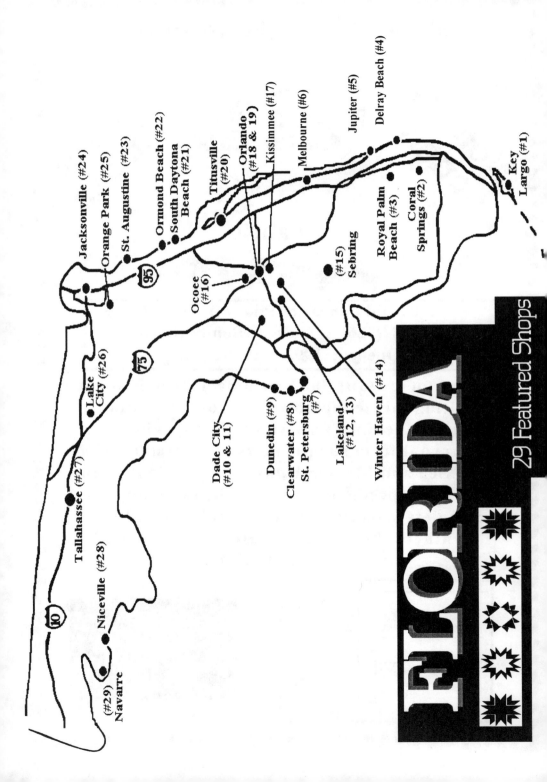

Key Largo, FL   #1

The Cotton Shoppe

Wed - Fri
9 - 12 p.m.
Or By
Appt.

P.O. Box 3168 MM99 U.S. # 1
(305) 453-0789   33037
Est: 1992

Hoffman, RJR, ME Hopkins and more! WE DO MAIL-ORDER !
Send $6 for swatches or $20 to join our Fabric Club.

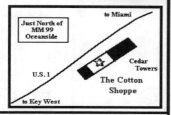

Just North of MM 99 Oceanside

to Miami

U.S. 1

Cedar Towers

The Cotton Shoppe

to Key West

Coral Springs, FL   #2

Country Stitches

Mon - Sat
10 - 5
Thur til 8
Sun 12 - 4

11471 W. Sample Road   33065
(305) 755-2411
Owner: Gayle Boshek
Est: 1982   1600 sq.ft.

Your one stop quilting shoppe.
Over 3000 bolts of fabric and patterns !
You'll be glad you came !

Sawgrass Expressway

11471 | Sample Rd.

Country Stitches

University Dr.

I - 95

I - 595

Royal Palm Beach, FL   #3

Suzanne's QUILT SHOP Inc.

Est: 1988

537 Royal Palm Beach Blvd.
33411
(407) 798-0934
Owner: Suzanne Leimer

Monday - Saturday
10 - 5

Okechobee Blvd.

Royal Palm Beach Blvd. | S.R. 7 / 441 | Suzanne's Quilt Shop in the Royal Plaza | Turnpike | Military Trail | I - 95

537

Southern Blvd.

Lake Worth Rd.

1,500 Bolts of 100% Cotton Fabrics
Books and Patterns for Quilts,
Clothing, and Dolls
Notions, Batting, Stencils
Crazy Quilt Embellishments
Silk Ribbon Embrodiery
Mohair Bear Kits
Classes and Private Lessons,
Quilt Planning

Delray Beach, FL   #4

Quilters Marketplace

Mon - Sat
10 - 5

524 E. Atlantic Avenue   33483
(407) 243-3820
Owner: Marilyn Dorwart
Est: 1987   950 sq.ft.

1200 bolts of
100% cotton.
Complete notion
dept. Many
Patterns and
Books. American
Collectibles, Gifts
and Friendly Staff.

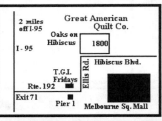

Jupiter, FL   #5

Quilters' Choice

Mon - Fri
10 - 5
Sat 10 - 4

1695 West Indiantown Rd.
(407) 747-0525   33458
Owner: Vivian Irwin   1500 sq.ft.
1000 bolts of   Est: 1992
100% cotton.
Complete
selection of
Notions, Books &
Patterns.
Authorized
Bernina Dealer.
Great classes and
friendly service.

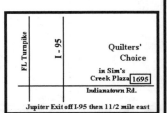

Melbourne, FL   #6

We have
classes
galore. Cotton
Fabrics & Quilting
Supplies.
A GREAT PLACE
FOR FUN,
CHEAPER THAN
A
PHYCHIATRIST.

BERNINA

Mon - Sat   9:30 - 5:30

1800 W. Hibiscus Blvd. #103   32901
Melbourne, Florida   (407) 984-7505
Owner: Barbara Alenci   Est: 1989   1600 sq.ft.   Dealer

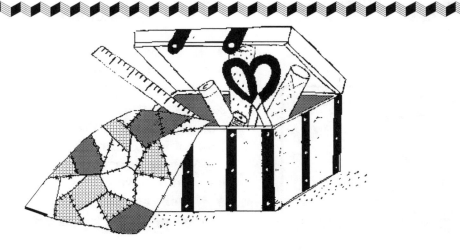

St. Petersburg FL #7

Sewing Circle Fabrics

408 33rd. Avenue N.
(813) 823-7391   33704
Owner: Family Owned &
          Operated
Est: 1961   4500 sq.ft.

**Mon & Tues
9 - 8
Wed - Sat
9 - 5**

200 Quilts on display, both new and antique.

*Home of the
Continuous Quilt Show*

Quilting Supplies

*New Home
Sewing
Machines*

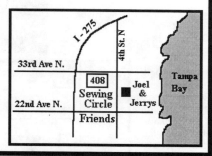

Clearwater, FL #8

Country Quilts 'n Things. Inc.

1810 Drew Street   34625
(813) 461-4171   Est: 1986
Owner: Kathy Handy   600 sq.ft.

Mon 10 - 2
Tues 10 - 8
Wed - Fri
10 - 4
Sat 10 - 2

Friendly quilt shop with 650 bolts of fabric, books, patterns, notions, classes and gift items. Located in The Front Porch

Country Quilts 'n Things
Front Porch
1810 Shopping Center
Drew
3/4 mile west
Hercules
Belcher
U.S. 19
Rt. 60 (Gulf to Bay)

Dunedin, FL #9

Rainbow's End

941 Broadway (Alt 19)   34698
(813) 733-8572   Est: 1982
Owner: M. Facsina
Over 4500 Bolts   6900 sq.ft.
of Cotton Fabric. Complete line of Notions. Over 1000 Books and Patterns. Crazy Quilting, Beadwork & Silk Ribbon Embroidery.

Mon & Fri
10 - 8
Tues, Wed,
Thur 10 - 5
Sat 10 - 4

Broadway
Rainbows End
941
S.R. 580
Main St.
Alt. 19
U.S. 19
S.R. 60
Gulf to Bay

Dade City, FL #10

Quilts Etc.

13230 South Hwy. 301   33525
(904) 567-0444
Owners: Suzanne & Bill Stewart
Est: 1988   4000 sq.ft.

Mon - Sat
10 - 5

Fabric, Quilting Supplies, Books, Patterns, Gifts. Custom machine Quilting & Quilts for Sale.

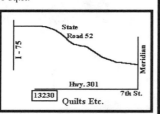

State Road 52
I - 75
Meridian
Hwy. 301
13230
7th St.
Quilts Etc.

Dade City, FL #11

Pioneer Florida Museum Association

15602 Pioneer Museum Rd.
(904) 567-0262   33526
Owned: Pioneer Florida Museum Assoc.
Est: 1975

Tues - Sat
1 - 5
Sun 2 - 5

Handmade items on consignment. Wooden toys & games, T-shirts, cups, cookbooks, books, jelly, candy, postcards, etc.

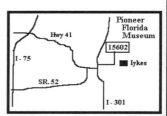

Hwy 41
Pioneer Florida Museum
15602
I - 75
Iykes
SR. 52
I - 301

Lakeland, FL #12

Granny's Trunk

4644 Cleveland Heights Blvd.
(813) 646-0074   33813
Owner: Jean Keene
Est: 1981

Mon & Tues
10 - 7
Wed - Sat
10 - 5

Over 2,000 bolts of quilting fabrics, classes, gifts. Better dress and wearable art fabrics and trims. Many models on display.

to Tampa
Exit 18
I - 4
to Orlando
Memorial Blvd. (Hwy. 98)
Airport Rd.
Highland Dr.
Cleveland Heights
Florida Ave.
4644
Granny's Trunk

Lakeland, FL #13

Fabric Warehouse

3032 North Florida Ave.   33805
(813) 680-1325
Owner: Becky Dody
Est: 1977

Mon - Sat
10 - 5:30

Hoffman Alex. Henry Concord Peter Pan, etc. 90" Sheeting in 8 colors

Hwy 33
L. Hills Blvd.
Post Office
Griffin Rd.
N. Florida Ave.
I - 4
3032 Fabric Warehouse
The New
Home Depot
U.S. 98

Sebring, FL #15

Crafty Quilters

| Tues - Fri |
| 10 - 5 |
| Sat 10 - 4 |

4920 U.S. 27 South   33870
(813) 382-4422
Owners: Dee Dee Bedard &
Est: 1990   Lois Ucciferri

For all your Quilting Needs. Only Brazilian Dealer in Area. Gift items & Classes Available.

Avon Park
Sebring
Lake Shore Mall
U.S. 27
4920
Crafty Quilters
Lake Placid

Rotary Cutter —
The tool for a
quilter on a roll !

Ocoee, FL #16

Herb's Clothesline

| Mon - Fri |
| 9 - 5 |
| Sat 9 - 2 |

114 W. McKay St.   34761
(407) 656-1624
Owner: Joyce Collier
Est: 1966   1500 sq.ft.

100% Cottons
Dress Goods
Silks
Denims
T-Shirt Knits
Notions

Silver Star Rd.
McKay St.
114
Herb's Clothesline
Bluford
State Rd. 50

Kissimmee, FL #17

Queen Ann's Lace

| Mon - Fri |
| 10 - 6 |
| Tues til 9 |
| Sat 10 - 5 |

715 East Vine Street   34744
(407) 846-7998
Owners: Ginny & Tom King
Est: 1991   1400 sq.ft.

1200 Bolts of 100% Cotton plus supplies, notions, & patterns-- **Everything you'll need.** Also many other craft supplies.

to Orlando
Hwy 107 - 92/441
Queen Ann's Lace
in Rainbow Plaza
715
to Disney
Hwy.192   Vine St.   to St.Cloud
Downtown Kissimmee

Orlando, FL #18

Patchwork Cottage Quilt Shop

| Mon - Fri |
| 9:30 - 5 |
| Thurs til 8 |
| Sat 9:30-4 |

2413 Edgewater Dr.   32804
(407) 872-3170
Owner: Rae Harper

100% Cottons, Quilting Supplies, Books, & Patterns. **Good Times to be had here!**

to Daytona
Patchwork Cottage Quilt Shop
Vassar
2413
Vassar
Edgewater Dr.
I - 4
Princeton
to Tampa

#19

Titusville, FL   #20

Factory Emporium

3190 S. Hopkins Avenue
(407) 267-6080   32780
Owner: May Jane Mazurek
Est: 1883   2400 sq.ft.

**Mon - Fri
10 - 5
Sat 10 - 4**

Quilt Shop —
Fabrics,
supplies, books,
patterns, & Notions.
Classes.
90" Sheeting

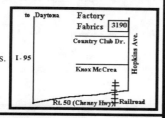

to Daytona   Factory
Factory
Fabrics   3190
Country Club Dr.
I - 95
Knox Mc Crea
Hopkins Ave.
Rt. 50 (Cheney Hwy)   Railroad

YESTERDAY'S QUILTS INC.
ORLANDO, FLORIDA

*Fabric ♥ Books
Patterns ♥ Notions
Supplies*

Half & Full Day Quilt Classes
for the Vacationing Quilter

For information send SASE to:

Yesterday's Quilts Inc.
7036 International Drive
Orlando, Florida 32819

Telephone (407) 354-0107

I – 4
DANSK
Factory Outlet
Sandlake Road
**Yesterday's
Quilts**
Kirkman Road
Pizza
Hut
Long John
Silver's
International Drive

South Daytona, FL   #21

**Mon - Fri
9:30 - 4:30
Thurs til 7:30
Sat 9:30 - 3**

Pelican Needlework Shoppe

**905 Big Tree Road 32119 (Palm Grove Plaza)
(904) 761-8879   Owner: Suzy Komara
Est: 1979   1600 sq.ft.**

**One stop for quilting, needlepoint,
ribbon embroidery & knitting.
Notions & Books!**

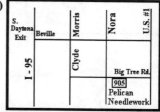

S.
Daytona
Exit   Beville   Morris   Nora   U.S. #1
I - 95   Clyde
Big Tree Rd.
905
Pelican
Needlework

Ormond Beach, FL #22

Grammy's Quilt Shoppe

Mon - Sat 9:30 - 4

489 S. Yonge Street   U.S. # 1
(904) 673-5484   32174
Owner: Mary K. Tate
Est: 1981   1800 sq.ft.

Fabrics -- Notions
Books -- Patterns
Gifts -- Classes
Everything for
the Quilter !

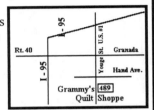

Quilting Thread —
buy only the best
so it won't be the
weakest link
of your quilt.

Saint Augustine, FL #23

Material Things

**Mon 10 -8
Tues - Fri
10 - 5
Sat 10 - 4**

77 Saragossa St.   32084
(904) 829-3778   Est: 1991
Owner: Joyce Snyder
                    1575 sq.ft.

Most beautiful
selection of 100%
cottons in the
area. Over
1,000 bolts.
Wide variety of
books, patterns,
notions and
classes.

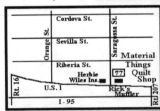

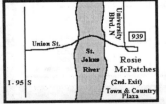

Orange Park, FL #25

Calico Station

**Monday - Thursday
9 - 9
Friday 9 - 5
Saturday 10 - 5
Sunday 12 - 5**

1855-6 Wells Road
32073
(904) 269-6911
Owner: Faye Heyn
Est: 1980 2500 sq.ft.

**The Largest
Quilt Shop in
N.E. Florida**

Over 1500 bolts of 100% Cotton Fabrics.

Classes
Special Orders
Notions
Books and Patterns
Large Selection of
Stencils
Quilts for Sale

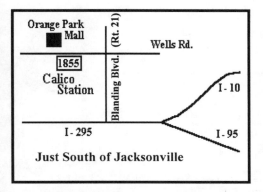

Lake City, FL   #26

Kathy's Quilt Shoppe

328 N. Marion
(904) 755-2907   32055
Mgr: Helen Huckins

**Mon - Fri
10 - 4
Thur 1-
4:30**

Quilting
Supplies,
Frames,
Custom
Ordered
Quilts

Marion
Kathy's [328]
Quilt Shoppe
I - 75
U.S. 90 E
Hwy 41
U.S. 441

Tallahassee, FL   #27

The Needleworks & Quiltery

227 E. 6th Ave. 32303
(904) 222-4458
Owner: Anne Stowell

**Mon - Sat
10 - 5:30**

Quilting,
Needlepoint, and
Cross-Stitch
Supplies.
Quilting Classes.

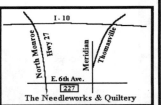

I - 10
North Monroe
Hwy 27
Meridian
Thomasville
E. 6th Ave.
[227]
The Needleworks & Quiltery

Niceville, FL   #28

Strawberry Stitchery

**Mon - Sat
9 - 5:30**

1081 John Sims Pkwy.   32578
(904) 729-1771   Est: 1984
Owners: Linda Burkart, Lynn Burnet
  Bev Schroeder, & Garnet Smith

Complete line
of Quilting
and Cross
Stitch Fabric
and Supplies

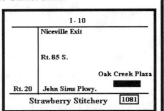

I - 10
Niceville Exit
Rt. 85 S.
Oak Creek Plaza
Rt. 20   John Sims Pkwy.
Strawberry Stitchery   [1081]

Navarre, FL   #29

Sandy Bobbins

8546 Navarre Pkwy.
32566
(904) 939-9338
Owner: L.C. King

**Mon - Fri
10 - 6
Wed 12 - 8
Sat 9 - 4**

Fabric, Books,
Patterns, Notions,
Supplies.
Friendly Chats held
at all Times.
Quilting classes

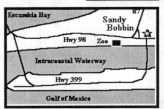

Escambia Bay
Sandy Bobbin
Hwy 98   Zoo
Intracoastal Waterway
Hwy 399
Gulf of Mexico

Florida Guilds:
West Pasco Quilt Guild, 12232 Magnolia Grove Lane, 34667
Gold Coast Quilter's Guild, Box 710, Boca Raton 33429
Manatee Patchworkers, P.O. Box 356, Bradenton, 34206
Central Florida Quilters Guild, P.O. Box 180116, Casselberry, 32718
Creative Quilters of Citrus County, 7165 W. Riverbend Rd., Dunellen, 34433
Palm Patches Quilt Guild, P.O. Box 07345, Ft. Myers, 33919
Citrus Friendship Quilters, 3384 S. Diamond Ave., Inverness, 34452
Florida Keys Quilters, PO Box 1251, Key Largo 33037
Flying Needles, Niceville
Ocean Waves Quilters, 6421 S. Mitchell Manor Circle, Miama, 33156
Pelican Piecemakers, 2636 Sunset Dr., New Smyrna Deach, 32168
Country Road Quilters, P.O. Box 2042, Ocala, 32670
Honeybee Quilters Guild, P.O. Box 0003, Orange Park, 32067
Racing Fingers Quilt Guild, P.O. Box 730544, Ormond Beach, 32173
Cabin Fever Quilter's Guild, 1318 Sweet Briar Rd., Orlando, 32802
Country Stitchers, 2043 Sue Harbor Cove, Orlando, 32750
Saint Andrews Bay Quilters Guild, PO Box 16225 , Panama City, 32406
Pensacola Quilter's Guild, P.O. Box 16098, Pensacola, 32507
St. Augustine Piecemakers, St. Augustine
Pine Needles Quilters, Box 535, Silver Springs, 32688
Ocean Waves Quilt Guild, P.O. Box 43-1673, South Miami, 33243
Possum Creek Quilters, P.O. Box 430, Sparr, 32091
Quilters Unlimited of Tallahassee, P.O. Box 4324, Tallahassee, 32315
Quilters' Workshop of Tampa Bay, 12717 Trowbridge Ln, Tampa, 33624
Stitch Witches, 9020 2-C S.W. 93rd. Lane, Ocala, 34481

Other Shops in Florida:

Auburnville	Quilting, Etc., 1148 U.S. Highway 92 W.
Cocoa	Ma's General Store, Crafts & Gifts, 222 King Street
Cocoa Beach	Needlecraft Junction, 46 N. Brevard Avenue
Ellenton	Country Charm Quilts, 2418 Highway 301
Fort Lauderdale	Annie's Attic, 2339 Wilton Drive
Fort Myers Beach	Quiltique, 6080 Estero Boulevard
Fort Pierce	Tomorrow's Heirlooms, 1840 S. Kings Highway
Gainesville	Quilting Corner, 2441 N.W. 43rd Street #5A
Gulf Breeze	Sew Much More, 2717 Gulf Breeze Pkwy.
High Springs	Apple Creek Mercantile, 55 N.W. First Ave.
Hollywood	Ben Raymond Fabrics, 2818 Hollywood Boulevard
Homestead	Picket Fence Crafts, Inc., 30370 Old Dixie Highway
Jacksonville	Brian's, 7001 Merrill Rd.
Kendall	The Quilt Scene, 9505 S. Dixie Highway
Key Largo	Cotton Gin, 94 1/2 Tavernier North
Live Oak	Quilters Quarters, 129 South St.
Maitland	Sewing Studio, 9605 S. Highway 17-92
Miami	Craft World, 9003 S.W. 107th Avenue
Miami	Quilt Scene, 9505 S. Dixie Highway
Mossy Head	Calico Country Fabrics, P.O. Box 1280
Naples	Fabric Mart, 690 5th Ave South
New Smyrna Beach	Brian's, 1421 S. Dixie Freeway
Ocala	Fabric Plus, 2391 S.W. College Rd.
Orange Park	Country Crossroads, 799-3 Blanding Blvd.
Orlando	Gingersnap Station Limited, 2401 Edgewater Drive
Palm Harbor	Classic Cloth, 34930 U.S. Highway 19 N.
Panama City	Marie's Fabrics & Notions, 1364 West 15th Street
Pembroke Pines	The Quilt Shop, 7161 Pembroke Road
Port Charlotte	Charlotte County Sewing , 3280 Tamiami Trail
Rockledge	Marilyn's Fabrics & Bernina, 886 S. U.S. Highway 1
Sanford	Country Courtyard, 222 E. First Street
Sarasota	Beneva House of Fabrics, 1239 Beneva Road South
Sarasota	Classic Cloth II, 3985 Cattleman
Stuart	Mary Jo's Needles & Pins, 2157 S.E. Ocean Blvd.
Tallahassee	A Stitch in Time, 1950M Thomasville Rd.
Tampa	Necchi Singer Sewing Centers, 104 Fletcher Ave. E.
Tampa	Quilted Sampler, 4109 Macdill Avenue S.
Tampa	Westberry Sewing Center, 14930 N. Florida Avenue
Tampa	American Country, 4802 Gunn Hwy
Venice	Deborah's Quilt Basket, 327 Venice Avenue
West Palm Beach	H. F. Davis Five & Dime, 3901 S. Dixie Highway
Winter Park	Quilts & Country Treasures, 7310 Alona Avenue

10 Featured Shops

GEORGIA

- (#9) Ft. Oglethorpe
- Gainesville (#8)
- Roswell (#7)
- Lawrenceville (#6)
- Tucker (#5)
- Stone Mountain (#4)
- Madison (#3)
- Columbus (#10)
- Savannah (#2)
- St. Simon Island (#1)

St. Simons Island, GA   #1

Stitch N Originals

200 Retreat Village   31522
(912) 638-1390
Owner: Ann N. Steele
Est: 1988   2000 sq.ft.

**Mon - Sat
10 - 5:30**

Speciality Shop
featuring
Needlepoint,
Knitting,
Cross-Stitch &
Quilting
Also visit our other
location in Savannah
at the City Market

Exit 8 - N Golden Isles Pkwy.
U.S. 17
I - 95
Causeway   Demgre
Fredermeard
Exit 6
S. Golden
Isles Pkwy.
Retreat Village S.
Stitch N Originals

Savannah, GA   #2

Colonial Quilts & Crafts

1100 Eisenhower Drive
(912) 352-8061
Owner: Marcia Hammond
2500 sq.ft.

**Mon - Fri
10 - 6
Sat 10 - 4**

Located in historic
Savannah, we offer
a wide array of
fabric, notions,
classes, books and
patterns for quilting,
cross-stitch, French
sewing, smocking,
etc. Complete Jinny
Beyer palette.

Hwy. 516 to I-16
Hwy.26
Hwy. 20
Waters
Derenne
Colonial Quilts
in Eisenhower Sq.
1100
Eisenhower Dr.
Abercorn
Montgomery   Cross
to I - 95

Madison, GA #3

Madison Quilt Co.

Visit a complete Quilt shop located in the town Sherman refused to BURN

Fabrics, books, notions . .

121 South Main St.   30650
(800) 442-8639 or (706) 342-8639
Owner: Melissa Poland   Est: 1991

Mon - Sat
10 - 5:30
Summer
Sun 1 - 5

FABRIC CLUB — Over 400 4" x 4"
samples including RJR, MEH, Hoffman,
A. Henry, P&B — $30.00
(Includes quarterly updates)
Join and receive 10% Discount on
Already Competitive Prices.

Stone Mountain, GA #4

Village Quilt Shop

5348 E. Mountain Street
(404) 469-9883   30083
Owner: Joyce P. Selin
Est: 1981   1200 sq.ft.

Mon - Sat
9 - 5
Thur til 8

A "One-stop
Quilt Shop"
Quilts -- Quilting
Supplies -- Books
Fabrics -- Notions
Class schedule
Available.

Tucker, GA #5

Dream Quilters

2343-A Main Street   30084
(404) 939-8034   Est: 1991
Owners: Pam Cardone & Libby
1250 sq.ft.   Carter

Mon - Fri
10 - 5:30
Thur 12 - 7
Sat 10 - 4

The latest in
cotton fabrics,
books, patterns &
notions.
**A nice place
to visit.
Mail orders
welcome.**

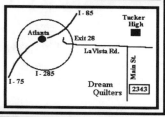

Georgia Guilds: Gala Quilters Guild, 1816 St. Elmo Dr., Columbus, 31901
Hall County Quilt Guild, 5845 Hidden Cove Rd., Gainesville, 30504
N. Georgia Quilt Council, 7292 Cardif Place, Jonesboro, 30236
East Cobb Quilter's Guild, P.O. Box 71561, Marietta, 30007
Calico Stitchers, P.O. Box 13414, Savannah, 31416
Ogeechee Quilters, Savannah
Yellow Daisy Quilters, Box 1772, Stone Mountain, 30086

Lawrenceville, GA #6

Needle Patch

239 East Crogan N.E.   30245
(404) 995-1516
Owner: Dorothy Higbee
Est: 1987   1500 sq.ft.

Mon - Sat
10 - 5
Thur til 6

Everything
for quilting.
Fabric, Craft
Patterns and
all
accessories.

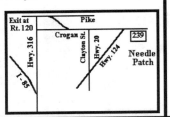

Roswell, GA #7

Calico Quilter

14 Elizabeth Way   30075
(404) 998-2446
Owner: Sharon Dutton
Est: 1983   2000 sq.ft.

Mon
9:30 - 9
Tues - Sat
9:30 - 5

A unique fabric
& notions shop
nestled in the
heart of historic
Roswell,
Georgia

Gainesville, GA #8

Quilted Hearts

2415 G Old Cornelia Hwy.
(404) 536-3959   30507
Owners: Leslie Peck & Sally Babcock
Est: 1991   1300 sq.ft.

Mon
12:30-5:30
Tues - Sat
10 - 5:30

Located North of
Atlanta, we offer
a large selection
of 100% cotton
fabrics, books,
patterns, notions,
classes, and
INSPIRATION!

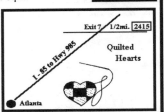

Ft. Oglethorpe, GA #9

Bentley Fabrics

304 LaFayette Rd. (U.S. Hwy. 27)
(706) 866-9619   30742
Owner: Greg Bentley
Est: 1969   3500 sq.ft.

Mon - Fri
10 - 8
Sat 10 - 6
Sun 12 - 5

Dress / Craft
Fabrics,
notions,
quilting supplies.
Liberty Overalls

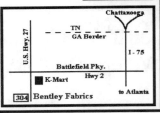

Columbus, GA #10

Southern Sewing Center

2507 Manchester Expressway
(706) 327-1231   31904
Owner: Ann Givens   Opened: 1970   1500 sq.ft.

Mon - Fri
10 - 6
Sat 10 - 5

100% Cotton
Quilt Fabrics,
Quilting Books.
Smocking &
Heirloom Sewing
supplies. Classes
Authorized
Bernina and Elna
Dealer

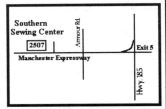

Other Shops in Georgia:
Atlanta, Grannie Taught Us How
        1921 Peach Tree Road N.E.
Atlanta, Cabin Fever Calicos
        1874 Piedmont Avenue N.E.
Augusta, Sewing Gallery, 336 Fury's Ferry Rd
N.
Augusta, Cloth 'N General, 1805 Central Ave.
Blue Ridge, The Cotton Patch, Main Street
Buford, The Country Emporium, 39 E. Main St
Duluth, The Fabric Hut, 3045 Hill Street
Kennesaw, Somewhere in Time
        2940 Dallas Street N.W.
Macon, Calico & Lace, 4357 Forsyth Rd
Rome, The Needle Patch, 2405 Garden Lake
Valdosta, Kathrine's Kraft Kottage
        906 Williams Street

HAWAII

2 Featured Shops

(#1) Honolulu

(#2) Lahaina

Honolulu, HI   #1

Kwilts 'n Koa

Mon - Fri 10 - 6
Sat 10 - 4

1126 12th Avenue   96816
(808) 735-2300
Owners: Kathy Tsark & Tsarkie
Est: 1991   650 sq.ft.

Hawaiian quilting classes, patterns, kits / supplies; Hawaiian gifts & Koa wood.

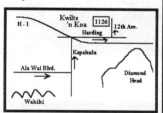

Lahaina, Maui, HI   #2

Quilter's Corner

Mon - Sat 10 - 5

283 Wili Ko Place   P.O. Box 1562
(808) 661-0944   96767
Owners: Kathy & Larry Dunlap
Opened: 1992

Hawaii's Largest selection of finished goods & quilt patterns. We also have gifts, needlepoint & Cross Stitch

Hawaiian Guild:
Hawaii Quilt Guild,
172 Kaopua Loop,
Mililani, 96789

Other Shops in Hawaii:

Hilo	Helen's Fabric Shoppe, 199 Kilauea Ave.
Honolulu	Needles & Bits, Inc., 544 Ohohia Street
Honolulu	Mynah Bird Fabrics, 4715 B Kahala Ave.
Honolulu	Creative Fibers, 3022 Hinano St.
Honolulu	Quilts Hawaii, 2338 S. King
Honolulu	The Calico Cat, 1223 Koko Head Ave.
Kamuela	Upcountry Quilters, P.O. Box 2631
Kihei	The Island, 1178 Uluniu Rd.
Lihue	The Kapaia Stitchery, P.O. Box 1327

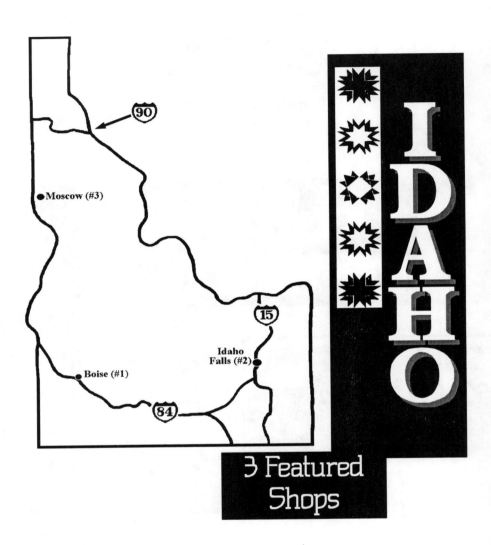

Moscow (#3)

90

15

Idaho
Falls (#2)

Boise (#1)

84

IDAHO

3 Featured
Shops

Idaho Guilds:
Boise Basin Quilters, P.O. Box 2206, Boise, 83701
Seaport Quilter's Guild, P.O. Box 491, Lewiston, 83501
Palouse Patchers, P.O. Box, Moscow, 83843

Boise, ID   #1

The Quilt Crossing

**Mon - Sat
10 - 6
Thurs til 8**

6431 Fairview Avenue   83704
(208) 376-0087
Owner: Patty Hinkel
Est: 1987   3000 sq.ft.

Specializing in
distinctive 100%
cotton fabrics,
classes, books,
gifts & quilt / soft
sculpture
patterns.

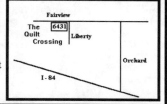

Idaho Falls, ID   #2

KJ's Kreative Treasures

**Tues - Fri
10 - 4
Sat 1 - 4**

1541 East 17th Street   83404
(208) 522-5200   Est: 1990
Owner: Katie Gay   1500 sq.ft.

Friendly "custom"
service - wall/bed
quilts, notions,
frames, books,
patterns and 100%
cotton fabrics.
Also great classes.

Moscow, ID   #3

The Quilt Loft

**Wed - Sat
10 - 4
Thur til 7**

2360 Trail Rd.   83843
(208) 882-3159
Owner: Anne Cosgrove
Est: 1991   800 sq.ft.

1000 bolts of
Quality Fabric,
plus a great
selection of the latest
Books,
Patterns,
& Notions

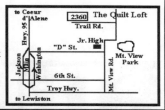

Other Shops in Idaho:

Blackfoot	Country Calicos & Quilts, 391 N. Broadway Street
Boise	Fabric Frolics Sewing Machines Plus, 1226 Broadway Ave.
Coeur d'Alene	Sew What's New, 296 W. Sunset #13
Grace	Fabulous Fabrics, 18 S. Main
Mountain Home	The Gift Box, 115 S. 2nd. E.
Weiser	Calico Corner, 455 State Street

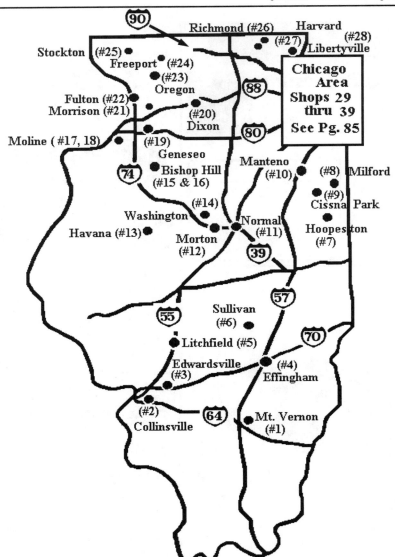

Richmond (#26)   Harvard
                              (#27)   (#28)
Stockton (#25)   Libertyville

Freeport (#24)
        (#23)
    Oregon   Chicago
                                         Area
Fulton (#22)   Shops 29
Morrison (#21)   thru
              (#20)   See Pg. 85
              Dixon
Moline (#17, 18)
              (#19)
         Geneseo
       Bishop Hill   Manteno
       (#15 & 16)   (#10)   (#8) Milford
                                             (#9)
                  (#14)   Cissna Park
   Washington   Normal
Havana (#13)   Morton   (#11)   Hoopeston
                      (#12)   (#7)

                              Sullivan
                               (#6)

                     Litchfield (#5)

           Edwardsville   (#4)
           (#3)   Effingham

              (#2)   Mt. Vernon
           Collinsville   (#1)

ILLINOIS

39 Featured Shops

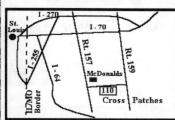

Effingham, IL #4

Dusts' Quilt & Craft Shop

**Mon - Sat
9 - 6**

R.R. #1   Box 310   62401
3 1/2 miles from Rt. 33 turn off
(217) 536-6756

Large selection of
fabrics, books,
pattterns and
stamped textiles for
embroidery.
Notions, laces,
embroidery flosses,
crochet thread
Low Prices.

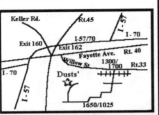

Litchfield, IL #5

Calico Quilts & Frames

**Mon - Sat
8 - 5**

**Located in HE Nursery & Garden
Center in Litchfield**
Or By Mail order from: R.R. #1 Box 5,
(217) 532-2676   Butler, IL   62015-9701
Owner: Judy Tucker

Quilting frames:
Snap Tension,
Klaus Rau,
Q-Snap,
Hinterberg. Many
Speed Cutting
Tools and
Templates, DMC
Pearl cotton, etc.

Sullivan, IL #6

(217) 728-4511

**Mon - Fri
8 - 4:30
Sat By Appt.**

P.O. Box 376   61951   105 E. Jefferson
Owners: Carol & Howard Risley   Est: 1992

Quilts By Carol

**Near Lake
Shelbyville & Illinois
Amish Country**

A Unique Quilt Gallery of
machine quilted, 100%
cotton quilts and other
quilted items for sale.
Custom piecing & Quilting
Dealers Welcome

Hoopeston, IL #7

Hoopeston Fabrics

**Mon - Sat
9 - 5:30
Sun 1 - 4**

222 E. Main St.   60942
(217) 283-7125
DBA: Sewing Boutique
Est: 1980   1800 sq.ft.

Lots of Hoffman's
P&B's, Concords.
Books & Patterns
Classes Galore
Authorized Viking
Sewing Machine
Dealer.
In Downtown
Hoopeston

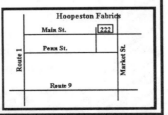

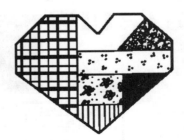

Milford, IL #8

Dixie Cloth Shop

130 East Jones   60953
(815) 889-5349   Est: 1982
Owner: Arlene McKinley
2400 sq.ft.

Mon - Fri
9 - 5
Sat by
Appt.

"Outline" Machine
Quilting a Specialty
90" Preprinted Quilt
Tops. Cheaters
Cloth (Microwave
Quilting)
Backing 90" - 120"
all Colors.
Finished Quilts
Mail Order

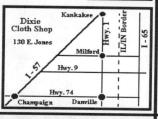

Cissna Park, IL #9

Prairieland Quilts

107 N. 2nd. St.   (Rt.49) 60924
(815) 457-2867
Owner: Suzanne Bruns
Est: 1993

Mon - Fri
9 - 5
Sat 9 - 3

Unique selection
of Fabric, Books,
Patterns, Quilt
Frames and
supplies.
Machine Quilting
Service and
Custom Quilt
Tops available.

Manteno, IL #10

Butler's

5 North Main   60950
(815) 468-8133
Owner: Mary G. Butler
Est: 1934   25,000 sq.ft.

Mon - Fri
8:30 - 5
Sat
8:30 - 1

Largest supply
of 100%
Cottons and
Quilt Supplies
anywhere in
the Midwest.

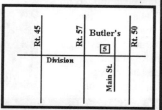

Normal, IL #11

Sewing Studio

1503 W. College   61761
(309) 452-7313   Est: 1983
Owners: Marlene Stearns &
2000 sq.ft.   Margaret Couch

Mon - Fri
9:30 - 6
Sat 9:30 - 5
Sun 12 - 4

Quality quilting and
fashion fabrics.
Quilting & sewing
classes, books.
Quilting & heirloom
supplies & notions.
Bernina / Viking /
White Dealer

Morton, IL #12

The Quilt Corner

2037 S. Main Street   61550
(309) 263-7114
Owner: Karen Ehrhardt
Est: 1988   2000 sq.ft.

Mon - Thur
9:30 - 8
Fri - Sat
9:30-4:30

Complete line of
Quilting Fabrics,
Books, Patterns &
Notions. Large
selection of
Battenburg lace.
Brass & Silver
charms. Classes.

Havana, IL   #13

Grannie Annie's Antique, Stitchery & What-Not Shoppe

128 N. Plum   62644
(309) 543-6827   Est. 1981
2,000 sq.ft.

Mon - Sat 9 - 5

7 Rooms
Quilting Supplies
Lace Curtains
Counted
Cross Stitch
Stenciling
Country &
Victorian Gifts
Antiques

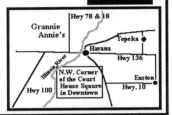

Hwy 78 & 18
Grannie Annie's
Topeka
Havana
Hwy 136
Illinois River
N.W. Corner of the Court House Sqaure in Downtown
Easton
Hwy 100
Hwy. 10

Washington, IL   #14

127 Peddlers Way   61571   1400 sq.ft.
(309) 444-7667   Est: 1985
Owners: Peggy Hessling & Lillian Cagle

Peg & Lil's Needle Patch
"The friendly place for happy Stitchers"

Davenport, IA — Chicago
Peg & Lil's Needle Patch
Washington
Peoria
U.S. 24
Bloomington
I-74
Indianapolis
I-55
Hwy 121
10 miles East of Peoria on the square Downtown
Springfield

FABRICS - 1000 bolts 100% cottons
QUILTING - Large selection of
Books, Patterns, Rotary tools,
Stencils and Classes.
CRAFTERS - Patterns &
Homespun fabrics
Lots of Samples on display.

**Mon 10 - 7
Tues - Fri
10 - 5
Sat 10 - 4**

Bishop Hill, IL   #15

The Prairie Workshop

Box 23   61419
(In the Historic Village)
(309) 927-3367   Est: 1983
Owner: Betty Robertson

**April - Dec
Daily
10 - 5**

Fabric,
Quilting Supplies,
Books,
Handmade Items

In the Historic
Village of Bishop
Hill, Illinois

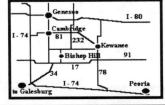

Geneseo
I-80
Cambridge
I-74
81   232
Kewanee
Bishop Hill
91
17
34   78
I-74
Peoria
to Galesburg

Bishop Hill, IL   #16

Village Smithy

309 N. Bishop Hill St.   61419
(309) 927-3851
Owner: Marilyn Nelson
Est: 1984   3200 sq.ft.

**Daily
10 - 4**

Vintage Quilts,
Fabrics, Patterns,
& Books for the
Quilter.
Also old Linens,
Glassware,
Collectibles &
Antiques.

We are Located in
The Historic
Village of Bishop Hill,
Henry County, Illinois

Moline, IL #17

"Quilts By the Oz"

1626 5th Avenue　　61265
(309) 762-9673　Est: 1987
Owner: Harlene Rivelli

1200+ bolts 100%　　2400 sq.ft.
cotton. Large
assortment of
Books, Patterns,
Notions, Bulk
Buttons, Machine
Quilting--White
Sewing Machines
Tri-Chem Paints
Quilts & Quillos

**Mon - Fri
9 - 5
Sat 10 - 2
Or by Appt.**

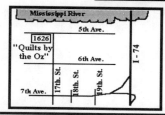

Moline, IL #18

Quilts by Martha

4326 River Drive　　61265
(309) 762-8503
Owner: Martha Thorpe
Est: 1988

Quilts, old and
new, Bought and
sold. Tops, pieces
and old fabric too.
Over 100 Quilts in
a B&B--River
Drive Guest
House.

**Open by
Appt.
or by
Chance**

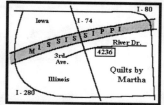

Geneseo, IL #19

Quilt Quarters

100 N. State St.　61254
(309) 944-2693
Owners: Roger & Dianne Peterson
Est: 1992

Satisfying
Quilters and their
needs.
Fabrics, books,
patterns, notions,
and "how to"
classes. Hand
made gifts by
local artists.

**Mon 10 - 4
Tue - Fri
10 - 5
Sat 10 - 3**

Dixon, IL #20

The Quilt Cellar

541 Penrose Road　　61021
(815) 288-5594

**Home Based
Shop**
Hoffman,
Benartex,
Marcus, and other
quality fabrics.
Books, stencils,
quilting supplies
and classes.
**Please
visit soon.**

**Tues - Sat
10 - 5**

Est: 1992
Owner: Sue
Ramage

Morrison, IL #21

CONstantly Stitching N' More

13690 Lincoln Road　61270
(815) 772-2833　Est: 1992
Owner: Connie Barr
Machine　　5000 sq.ft.
Quilting, Fabric,
Notions, Books,
Patterns, Quilt
Classes. Basket
Weaving Classes.
Gift Items
Ready Made
Crafts.

**Mon 10 - 9
Tues - Fri
10 - 6
Sat 10 - 5
Sun 12 - 4**

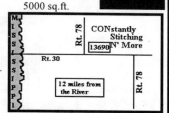

Fulton, IL #22

Calico Creations

1108 Fourth Street　61252
(815) 589-2221　Est: 1986
Owner: Jane Huisingh

Quilting, Crafts,　8,000 sq.ft.
Patterns, Fabric,
Books, Stencils &
Tools.
Professional
Machine Quilting
and Instructors.
Large Class area
and 3 floors of
Antiques.

**Mon - Fri
10 - 5
Sat 10 - 4
Sun 12 - 5**

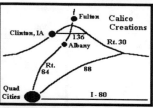

Oregon, IL #23

Holly's Homespun

**Mon - Sat 10 - 5
Sun 12 - 4**

Rte. 2 & 5th St.   500 Gale
(815) 732-4202   61061
Owners: Don & Holly Woodyatt
Est: 1991   1500 sq.ft.

Charming shop with 500 Bolts of Fabric including Lots of Homespun, Plaids, Checks, & Stripes. Also 100's of Patterns & Books for Dolls and Quilts.

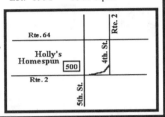

Freeport, IL #24

The Quilter's Thimble

Mon - Sat 10:30 - 5

17 South Van Buren   61032
(815) 235-1892
Owner: Carol Jacobs

Est: 1986   1200 sq.ft.

Classes, Fabrics, Supplies for Quilting. Custom Quilting and designing. Silk Ribbon Embroidery classes & Supplies. Send SASE for Newsletter.

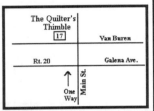

Stockton, IL #25

Patty's Patchwork

**Mon, Thur, Fri, & Sat 10 - 5
Sun 12 - 5
Tues & Wed By Appt.**

8040 U.S. Rt. 20   61085
(815) 947-2862

Owner: Pat Kluckhohn

Located in a white frame country farm home. Fabric, notions, books and patterns. Ready made items and custom work. Classes.

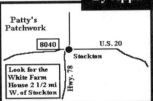

Richmond, IL #26

Sunshine and Shadow Quilt Shoppe

**Mon - Sat 10 - 5
Sun 12 - 5**

10307 Main St.   60071
(815) 678-2603   Est: 1991
Owner: Linda Rullman
In Historic Richmond among Antique & Unique Shops

Purveyor of fine fabrics, books, patterns, quilting notions, doll making items, sundry gifts & Collectibles. Classes Offered.

Harvard, IL #27

Village Peddlar

Mon - Sat 10 - 4

606 North Division   60033
(815) 943-7391   Est: 1989
Owners: Cindy Schultz & Debbie Hollingsworth

Victorian House filled with fabric, 1500 bolts. Notions and Books. Country and traditional atmosphere. Large classroom and quality teachers!

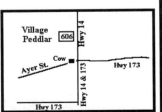

Libertyville, IL #28

Libertyville Sewing Center

**Mon - Thur 9 - 9
Fri & Sat 9 - 5**

326 Peterson Rd.   60048
(Brookside Shopping Center)
(708) 367-0820   Est: 1982
Owners: Linda & Rick Mosier   4500 sq.ft.

Large selection of calicos featuring Hoffman. Quilting Supplies. Sales & Service — Bernina, Viking, Pfaff & Babylock

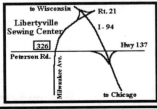

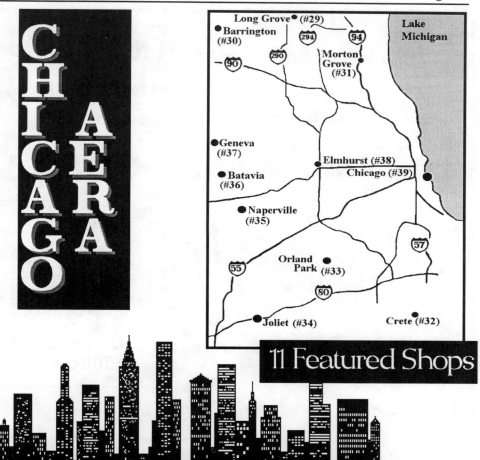

CHICAGO AREA

Long Grove (#29)
Barrington (#30)
Morton Grove (#31)
Lake Michigan
Geneva (#37)
Elmhurst (#38)
Chicago (#39)
Batavia (#36)
Naperville (#35)
Orland Park (#33)
Joliet (#34)
Crete (#32)

11 Featured Shops

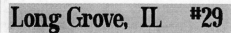

Long Grove, IL   #29

Prints Charming, Ltd.

221 R.P. Coffin Road 60047	**Mon - Sat**
(708) 634-1330 Est: 1978	**10 - 5**
Owners: Joan & Steve Attenberg	**Sun**
1875 sq.ft.	**Noon - 5**

Oldest quilt shop in northwest Suburban Chicago. 100% Cottons, Quilting Notions, Classes. Hundreds of unique craft patterns and supplies.

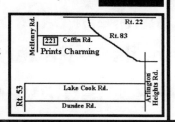

Barrington, IL   #30

A Touch of Amish

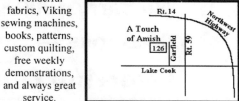

126 Garfield Street	**Tues - Sat**
60010	**10 - 4**
(708) 381-0900	
Est: 1986 1000 sq.ft.	
Owner: Lynn Rice	

Wonderful fabrics, Viking sewing machines, books, patterns, custom quilting, free weekly demonstrations, and always great service.

Crete, IL   #32

1344 Benton   60417
(708) 672-7721

Owners: Nancy Maddrill & Doris Wright
Est: 1990   1000 sq.ft.

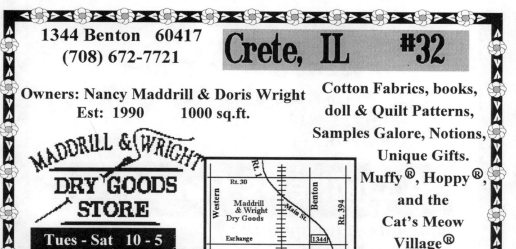

MADDRILL & WRIGHT DRY GOODS STORE

Tues - Sat   10 - 5
Thur til 9

Cotton Fabrics, books,
doll & Quilt Patterns,
Samples Galore, Notions,
Unique Gifts.
Muffy®, Hoppy®,
and the
Cat's Meow
Village®
Collectibles.

---

the Cotton co. (quilters')

Orland Park, IL   #33

Opened: 1988
2000 sq.ft.
Owners: Grace
McCuan &
Donalda Pierik
7046 West
157th Street
60462
(708) 614-7744

Mon 12 - 9
Tues-Sat
10 - 4
Thur til 9

2500+ Bolts of 100%
Cottons —
Alexander Henry,
Benartex, P&B, RJR,
Hoffman, Kaufman, Marcus
Brothers, Spiegel,
Roberta Horton
Homespuns—
Mission Valley,
Red Wagon
Wool & Wool for
rug hooking,
Flannel
250+ Books,
150+ Pattern Companies
Great selection of notions,
Classes, Pfaff Dealer.

Joliet, IL   #34

Roberts Sewing Center

255 North Chicago St.   60431
(815) 723-4210   Est: 1930
Owner: Ken Roberts   2500 sq.ft.

"A Quilter's Paradise"

3000 bolts of top quality
cotton fabric at discount
prices. Pfaff dealership.

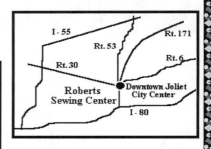

Brother and Singer
Home and Industrial Machines
In-State Sales (815) 723-4210
Out-of-State (800) 273-9111

Mon - Sat   9 - 5

Naperville, IL   #35

Stitches N' Stuffing

790 Royal St. George Dr. #119
(708) 420-7050   Est: 1981
Owners: Beryl & Sarah Coulson
4260 sq.ft.

4000+ Cotton
Fabrics, Homespuns,
Liberty of London.
Patterns, Books,
Notions, Authorized
Bernina sales/service
Smocking, Cross-
Stitch, Heirloom
Supplies. Quilters &
Crafters Heaven

Mon - Sat
10 - 5
Tues &
Thur til 9

Lap — just enough
room for one
quilting hoop and
one cat.

Batavia, IL #36

Quilting Books Unlimited

1911 W. Wilson   60510
(708) 406-0237   Est: 1983
Owners: Darlene & Rob Roberts
                        3000 sq.ft.

**Mon - Fri
10 - 5
Thurs til 8
Sat 10 - 4
Sun 12 - 4**

Boasting a collection of over 1000 quilting books, we are the only resource you'll ever need for hand-made quilts, quilting supplies, 100% cottons, and classes. Country Gifts too.

Rt. 38   to Geneva
Ace Hard.
1911   Quilting Books Unlimited
Randall Rd
Wilson Ave.
Main St.
Batavia Ave.
Fox River
I - 88

Geneva, IL #37

Quilted Fox

322 West Hamilton St.   60134
(708) 232-4888   Opened: 1978
Owner: Sara Buchholz
                        1400 sq.ft.

**Tues - Fri
10 - 5:30
Sat 10 - 4
Sun 12 - 3**

Large selection of unusual & better fabrics: including Liberty—Hoffman Japanese, etc. Pfaff sewing machines. Custom Quilts & Art Clothing.

Rt. 64
Hamilton
Quilted Fox   322
Rt. 38
W. Randall Rd.
4th St.
3rd. St.
Rt. 31
Kirk Rd.
Fox River
I - 88

Elmhurst, IL #38

Fabrics Etc.

111 E. First St.   60126-2888
(708) 530-0230   Est: 1977
Owners: Dorothy Schultze &
3000 sq.ft.   Mary Swanson

**Mon - Fri
9 - 5:30
Mon &
Thur til 9
Sat 9 - 5
Sun 12 - 4**

Fabrics, Classes, Patterns, Books, Notions, Pfaff Sewing Machines and Sergers, with a friendly, knowledgeable staff to help you.

North Ave.   64
Fabrics Etc.
First Ave.   111
290   294
Northwestern Train   West Line
St. Charles Rd.
York Rd.

Chicago, IL #39

The Quilt Cottage Gallery

Lake Shore Drive in Lincoln Park
(312) 404-5500   Est: 1978
Owner: Barbara Marquard Wanke

By Appointment Only

American Antique Quilts in Excellent condition displayed in beautiful home setting. Dealers welcomed. Lincoln Park in downtown Chicago

THE QUILT COTTAGE GALLERY

FOLK QUILTS COUNTRY PATTERNS

PAW

I
L
L
I
N
O
I
S

G
U
I
L
D
S

Mercer County Quilters Guild, PO Box 5, Aledo, 61231
Original Heartland Quilter's Guild, PO Box 1435, Alton, 62002
Northwest Suburban Quilter's Guild, PO Box 146, Arlington Heights, 60006
Hands all Around Quilt Guild, 205 Fairway Drive, Bloomington, 61701
Country Crossroads Quilt Guild, PO Box 214, Butler, 62015
Friendship Star Quilt Guild, 333 Alicia Drive, Cary, 60013
Quiltworks, 2125 Stoner Drive East, Charleston, 61920
Garfield Ridge Quilt Group, 6249 W. 59th Street, Chicago, 60638
Chicago Quilter's Guild, 10406 S. Moody, Chicago Ridge, 60415
Algonquin Quilt Guild, 550 Lochwood Drive, Crystal Lake, 60012
Vermillion Valley Quilters, 616 Bryan, Danville, 61832
Decatur Quilter's Guild, PO Box 415, Decatur, 62
Prairie Green Quilt Club, Box 23, Bishop Hill, 61419
Country Crossroads, Forreston
Geneseo Quilt Guild, Geneseo Community Center , Geneseo,   61254
Petunia City Quilters, 541 Penrose Road, Dixon, 61021
Faithful Circle Quilters, PO Box 9171, Downers Grove, 60515
Loose Threads, 1555 Sherman Ave. #124, Evanston, 60201
Quilters Plus, 480 Butternut Trail, Frankfort, 60423
Geneseo Quilt Guild, Community Center, Geneseo, 61254
Prairie Start Quilters Guild, 33 W. 848 Cherry Lane, Geneva, 60134
Pope County Senior Citizen Quilters, Box 93B, Golconda, 62938
Tri-State Quilters Guild, 338 Park Drive, Hamilton, 62341
Prairie Quality Quilters, 307 Lake Shore Drive, Hanna City, 61536
Village Quilters, PO Box 538, Harvard, 60033
Hinsdale Embroiderer's Guild, PO Box 284, Hinsdale, 60521
Heritage Quilters Guild, 1228 Buell Court, Joliet, 60435
Joliet Quilt Guild, 1121 Alann Drive, Joliet, 60435
So & Sews, 1500 W. Kennedy Road, Lake Forest, 60045
Northern Lake County Quilters Guild, 2121 Old Elm Road, Lindenhurst, 60046
Prairie Piecemakers Quilters, 15850 W. Shady Lane, Lockport, 60441
Illini Country Stitchers, Box 112, Mansfield, 61854
Tuesday-Odd-Thursday Quilters, Box 112, Mansfield, 61854
Kimball Thimble Quilt Guild, 675 Clark Street, Marseilles, 61314
Prairie Quilter's Guild, 802 W. Walnut Street, Mason City, 62664
Country Quilters, 4509 W. Elm Street, McHenry, 60050
Massac Quilt Guild, 201 Oak Drive, Metropolis, 62960
Kaleidoscope Quilters, 59 Hickory Ridge Drive, Morton, 61550
Quilt Sitters Circle, 59 Hickory Ridge Road, Morton, 61550
Cedarhust Quilters, PO Box 341, Mt. Vernon, 62864
Dupage Textile Art Guild, 1200 Yorkshire Drive, Naperville, 60540
Illinois Valley Quilter's Guild, PO Box 1001, Ottawa, 61350
Pieces & Patches, PO Box 184 , Park Forest, 60466
Gems of the Prairie Quilters, 3423 King Henry Court, Peoria, 61604
Heart of Illinois Quilters, 5105 W. Greenridge Ct., Peoria, 61615
Pride of the Prairie Quilt Guild, PO Box 501, Plainfield, 60544
Quinsippi Needleworkers, 202 N. 30th Street, Quincy, 62301
Sinissippi Quilters, PO Box 1556, Rockford, 61110
Itasca Quilt Guild, 516 Avebury, Roselle, 60172
Roselle Quilting Circle, 315 Chatham Lane, Roselle, 60172
Nimble Thimbles Quilt Group, 422 Highnoor Drive, Round Lake Park, 60073
Heritage Quilters of South Suburbia, PO Box 932, S. Holland, 60473
Knot Just Quilters, 280 E. Concord, Sheldon, 60966
Q.U.I.L.T.S., PO Box 7502, Springfield, 62791
Prairie Piecemakers, Box 163, St. Joseph, 61873
DeKalb City Quilters, PO Box 385, Sycamore, 60178
Centennial Quilters, 5808 Wolf, Western Springs, 60558
Salt Creek Quilter's Guild, PO Box 214, Western Springs, 60558
Illinois Quilters, Inc., PO Box 39, Wilmette, 60091
Stagecoach Quilters, 9336 W. Lake Road, Winslow, 61089
Woodstock Quilters, 1664 Eastwood Drive, Woodstock, 60098
Kalico Kwilters Bee, E. Van Emmon, Yorkville, 60560
Prairie Point Quilt Guild, 9103 Ament Road, Yorkville, 60560

Other Shops in Illinois:

Arlington Heights	Linda Z's, 1030 E. Central
Arlington Heights	Hagenbring's, 105 W. Campbell
Arthur	The Calico Workshop, 228 South Vine
Avon	The Clothesline, 102 N. Main PO Box 122
Barrington	Finn's Fabrics, 113 North Cook
Bethalto	Martha's Quilt Shoppe, 3511 Seiler Road
Bloomington	Treadle, 1704 E. Land
Carpentersville	Grist Mill Ends & Things, 39 E. Main
Charleston	Golden Thimble, 940 18th Street
Chicago	Vogue Fabrics, 718 Main Street
Chicago	Fishman's Fabrics, 1101 S. Desplaines Street
Chicago	Jerome Fabrics, Inc., 1750 W. 95th Street
Dunlap	Quilt Crossing, 1719 W. Woodside Dr. Suite B
Edwardsville	Needle Nook, 232 S. Buchanan Street
Edwardsville	Edwardsville Sewing Center, 110 N. Main Street
Effingham	Calico Shoppe, 1108 N. Merchant Street
El Paso	The Corner Cupboard, 37 W. Front Street
Eldorado	Quilts-n-Craft Supplies, 920 4th Street
Equality	Quilt Shop, R.R. #1
Evanston	Wide Goose Chase Quilt Gallery, 1511 Chicago Avenue
Fairview Heights	Quilting Parlor, 94 Kassing Drive
Frankfort	Stitch by Stitch Fabric Shop, 104 Kansas St.
Glen Ellyn	Village Fabrics, 430 N. Main
Glencoe	The Happy Rocker, 342 Park Avenue
Herrin	Quilt & Cottage Crafts, 1221 S. Sixteenth Street
Highland	Rosemary's Fabric and Quilts, 812 Ninth Street
Long Grove	The Patchworks, 223 Robert Parker Coffin Road
Macomb	Everything Nice, 124 North Randolph
McHenry	Granny's Quilts, 4509 W. Elm
Naperville	The Sewing Room, 1272 E. Chicago Avenue
New Lennox	Sew What, 410 E. Joliet
Oak Park	Choices, 1000 Lake
Odin	Mary's Vogue Shop, 105 Green US Hwy 50
Oneida	Country Needle Arts, P.O. Box 322
Paris	Lori's Pins 'N Needles, 109 North Central
Petersburg	Aunt Bea's Calicos & Crafts, 111 E. Douglas
Pittsfield	The Pin Cushion, 510 N. Jackson Street
Princeton	Old Times--Quilter Heaven, 954 North Main
Quincy	Pam's Quilt Shop, 329 Main St.
Rock Falls	Quilt Rack, 1512 Prophetstown Road
Rockford	Quilters Cupboard, 4614 E. State Street
Springfield	A-1 Quilters, 1052 E. Stanford
Washington	Country Mile, 109 Washington Square
Woodstock	Prairie Patchworks Mercantile, Ltd., 106 Cass

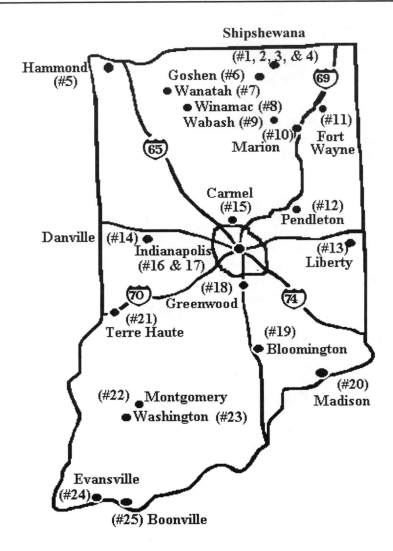

Shipshewana
(#1, 2, 3, & 4)
Hammond (#5)
Goshen (#6)
Wanatah (#7)
Winamac (#8)
Wabash (#9)
(#10)
(#11)
Fort Wayne
Marion
65
Carmel (#15)
(#12)
Pendleton
Danville (#14)
Indianapolis (#16 & 17)
(#13)
Liberty
70
(#18)
Greenwood
74
(#21)
Terre Haute
(#19)
Bloomington
(#22) Montgomery
(#20)
Madison
Washington (#23)
Evansville (#24)
(#25) Boonville

INDIANA
25 Featured Shops

Shipshewana, IN   #1

Spector's Store

Mon - Fri
8:30 - 5:30
Sat 8 - 4:30

305 S. Van Buren (Ind. 5)
P.O. Box 347   46565
(219) 768-4439

Full Line of Fabric
and notions. Quilt
and Craft supplies.
Hand stitched,
quilted items.
Wallhangings &
Quilts. Excellent
Values on Solid &
Printed fabrics.

Map: I-94, Exit 107 I-80/90 Exit 121, Hwy 120, Ind. 13, Spector's Store 305, Ship. Auction, Ind. 9, I-69, Ind. 5, U.S. 20

Shipshewana, IN   #2

Country Creations

Mon - Sat
9 - 5:30

3055 N St. Rd. 5   46565
(219) 768-7045
Owner: Treva Lehman

Est: 1992   1000 sq.ft.

Everything
you've Hoped
for in a Quilt
Shop
plus Hand Quilted
Quilts from our
Amish family
Traditions.

Map: Exit 107 I-80/90 Exit 121, Ind 120, Howe, Ind. 13, Country Creations 3055 in the North Village, Middlebury, Ind. 5, Shipshewana, Ind. 9

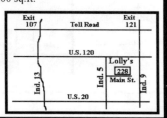

Shipshewana, IN   #3

ENJOY
THE BLEND OF
TRADITIONAL &
CONTEMPORARY

Visit a family tradition that still places
friendly service, quality merchandise
and value as their highest priorities.

FIND THE EVERYDAY & THE UNUSUAL
ALL AT REASONABLE PRICES!

* Largest Selection of Fabrics in the Area

*Over 10,000 Bolts from Calico to Silks

*Many Styles & Sizes of Shoes & Clothing

YODER
DEPARTMENT STORE

Mon - Sat
8 - 5:30

State Road 5   46565
P.O. Box 245
(219) 768-4887
Est: 1946   20,000 sq.ft.

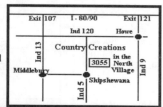

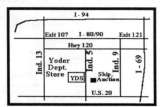

Map: I-94, Exit 107 I-80/90 Exit 121, Hwy 120, Ind. 13, Yoder Dept. Store YDS, Ind. 5, Ship. Auction, Ind. 9, I-69, U.S. 20

Shipshewana, IN   #4

Lolly's Fabrics

Mon - Sat
9 - 5

228 W. Main   P.O. Box 497
(219) 768-4703   46565
Owners: The Alvin Miller Family
Est: 1981   2800 sq.ft.

Superior selection
of quilting
fabrics, stencils,
& notions.

Map: Exit 107, Toll Road, Exit 121, U.S. 120, Ind. 13, Ind. 5, Lolly's 228 Main St., Ind. 9, U.S. 20

Hammond, IN   #5

Carousel Quilt-N-Things

6935 Grand Ave.   46323
(219) 844-8447   Est: 1991
Owner: Boots Crowe

Mon - Fri
9 - 4
Thurs til 8
Sat 9 - 2

New Home Machine—Sales and Service. Fabric, Books, Classes, Quilting Supplies, Patterns, Wood and Q-Snap Frames. Quilts for sale.

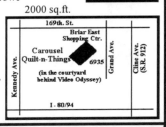

Goshen, IN   #6

Goshen Quilt Shop

66973 U.S. 33 South   46526
(219) 642-4529
Owner: Esther A. Hershberger
          Est: 1986   1200 sq.ft.

Mon - Sat
10 - 4
or by Appt.

Lots of wall hangings & quilts in stock. High quality work. Very few fabrics/notions for retail but lots of inspiration FREE! Catalog $5

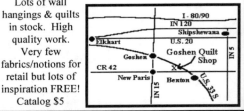

Wanatah, IN   #7

Prairie Point Quilt Shoppe

213 North Main   P.O. Box 383
(219) 733-2821   46390
Owner: Susie Mack   Est: 1989   1000 sq.ft.

Tues- Fri
10 - 5
Sat 9 - 2

Our shop is in an old Victorian House, stocked with over 300 bolts of fabric and a large variety of patterns, books, notions and models. Classes.

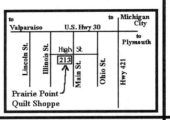

Winamac, IN   #8

The Country Patch

101 East Pearl St.   46996
(219) 946-7799   Est: 1992
Owners: Eddie Ploss & Gladys
                              Knebel

Tues- Sat
9 - 5

New and Unique Quilt Shop featuring 100% cotton 650+ bolts. Springmaid, RJR, Etc.

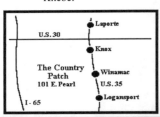

Wabash, IN   #9

Nancy J's Fabrics

1604 South Wabash   46992
(219) 563-3505
Owners: Nancy Jacoby &
Est: 1980   Miriam Peebles

Mon - Fri
10 - 5:30
Sat 10 - 5

The latest & greatest Fabrics. Books and Patterns for quilts, dollmaking & clothing. Plan to spend a day in Historic Wabash!

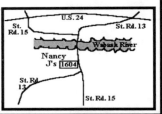

Marion, IN   #10

Sew Biz

3722 South Western Ave. 46953
(317) 674-6001   Est: 1983
Owner: Donelle McAdams
                    3,500 sq.ft.

Mon - Fri
10 - 6
Sat 10 - 5

Viking & White Dealer. 100% cottons, books, patterns, classes, dolls, bears, bunnies, etc. A place to share ideas and get inspired.

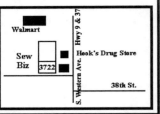

Fort Wayne, IN #11

Patchworks Shop

Mon - Sat
10 - 5:30
Thur til 7

6528 East State Blvd.   46815
(219) 493-1903 or (800) 44PLAID
Owners: Connie & John Benjamin
Est: 1980   3000 sq.ft.

Always new and wonderful cottons. Loads of Homespun, Hoffman, Hortons, Books and Patterns. Specializing in customer service.

Pendleton, IN #12

Needle in the Haystack

Tues - Sat
10 - 5
Sun 1 - 5

132 West State St. (Hwy 38)
(317) 778-7936   46064
Owner: Tammy Vonderschmitt
Est: 1981   1600 sq.ft.

Bernina Dealer & Repair. Fabric, Quilting supplies, Books, Patterns, hand and machine quilting services, Classes. Cross-stitch, craft patterns and supplies.

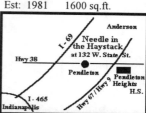

Liberty, IN #13

Stitching Nook

Mon - Fri
9 - 5
Sat 9 - 3

41 W. Union St.   47374
(317) 458-6443
Owner: Diana Bruns
Est: 1982

100% Cotton Fabrics, Quilting Notions, X-Stitch, Framing, Classes, Machine Sales, and Friendly Personal Attention

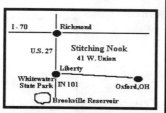

Danville, IN #14

Ventura's Quilting Center

Mon - Sat
9 - 4

35 Lawton Ave. 46122
(317) 745-2989
Owner: Patricia A. Montgomery
Est: 1987   3300 sq.ft.

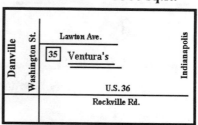

Over 700 bolts of 100% cotton Fabrics. (Hoffmans, Jinny Beyers, VIP's, Etc.) Books, Notions, Batting, Backings, Classes and Samples Galore.

Carmel, IN #15

Quilt Quarters

Mon , Fri, Sat 10 - 5 Tues, Wed, Thurs 10 - 8:30

210 East Main   46032
(317) 844-3636
Owner: Kaye England
                Est: 1989

Over 2500 bolts. Great Selection of unusual prints. 300+ Book Titles.
A fun Place.

Indianapolis, IN #16

Quilts Plus

Mon - Sat 10 - 5 Thurs til 8:30

1748 E. 86th Street   46240
(317) 844-2446
Owner: Linda M. Koenig
Est: 1978   2400 sq. ft.

All sorts of the very best goods for quiltmaking, smocking and rug hooking.

Indianapolis, IN #17

Country Carousel

Tues - Sat 9 - 5

1436 E. Dudley Ave.   46227
(317) 787-1711
Owners: Judy Potter & Lou Kirkhoff   Est: 1988

Complete line of Quilting Supplies, Books, Patterns, Notions. Classes— $15 per Class Machine Quilting

Greenwood, IN #18

The Back Door, Inc.

Mon - Thur 9:30 - 9 Fri 9:30-6 Sat 9:30 - 5

2503 Fairview Place #W   46142
(317) 882-2120
Owners: Kathy Cartheuser & Linda Hale
Est: 1973   2730 sq.ft.

Full line of quilt supplies, bear and dollmaking, tolepainting, counted cross stitch and many many samples. Great place to shop

Bloomington, IN #19

The Quilter's Patch

Mon - Sat 10 - 4

5937 E. State Road 45   47408
(812) 332-8717
Owners: Betty Herman & Bonnie Thickstun

Full service quilt shop. Quilting fabrics and supplies plus books, patterns, notions, classes, and custom designed quilt projects.

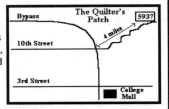

Madison, IN #20

Margie's Country Store

Mon - Fri 10 - 5 Sun 1 - 5

721 W. Main St.   47250
(812) 265-4429
Owner: Marjorie Webb   Est. 1970

For Quality fabrics, books, patterns, country clothing come visit us. Many made-up samples to inspire you. Also gifts and home decorations

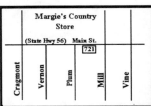

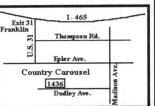

1907 S. 3rd. St.   (U.S. 41)
(812) 232-0610
Owners: Basil & Chris Ave
Est: 1974

Walls of 100% Cotton Fabrics, Quilting Patterns, Books,
Notions, Supplies, Quilting & Sewing Classes
Knowledgeable & Helpful Staff
Custom Monogramming
Craft Patterns
Authorized Pfaff & Bernina Dealer
Service on all makes sewing
machines

		Hullman
		McKeen
1907 Quilts &	More	
		Vorhees
U.S. 41		I - 70

Mon - Fri 10 - 5   Sat 10 - 4

Terre Haute, IN   #21

1 mile North of I - 70 on U.S. 41

Montgomery, IN   #22

David V. Wagler's Quilts

R.R. 1 Box 73   450 E. 200 N.
(812) 486-3836   47558
Owners: David & Anna Wagler
Est: 1980   768 sq.ft.

Mon - Sat
Daylight
Hours

Hand Made Quilts
on display. Quilts
made to order,
applique, pieced, &
wholecloth tops.
100% Cotton
Fabrics, Stencils,
Books, Patterns, Kits

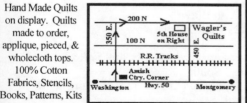

Washington, IN   #23

The Stitching Post

400 East Main Street   47501
(812) 254-6063   Est: 1986
      Southwest   Owner: Mary
Indiana's largest   Dell Memering
selection of   1200 sq.ft.
quality quilting
fabrics--1800
bolts 100%
cottons including
Plaids&Hoffmans.
Quilting supplies,
notions, books, &
patterns.

Mon - Sat
9 - 5
Fri 9 - 6

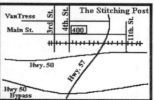

Evansville, IN   #24

Quilter's Barn

Tues, Thurs, & Sat 10 - 4

7915 Marx Rd.   47720
(812) 963-6336
Owner: Bettye J. Sheppard
Est: 1988

Full service shop.
Fabrics, Classes,
Books, Patterns,
Wooden Frames.
Quilt til the cows
come home in a
warm country
atmosphere.

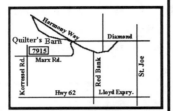

Boonville, IN   #25

The Village Mercantile

Mon - Sat 10 - 5

123 S. 2nd. St.   47601
(812) 897-5687   Est: 1992
Owners: Betty & Steve Cummings   3000 sq.ft.

Turn of the century
charm boasting
100% cottons,
hundreds of
patterns, books,
notions, and
unique gifts for the
quilt enthusiast.

Other Shops in Indiana:

Angola	Calicos & Collectibles, 105 W. Maumee Street
Corydon	Follow Your Heart, 210 N. Elm
Crown Point	Nancy's Needlework Shop, 192 W. Joliet
Elkhart	Quilt Designs, 58371 Hilly Lane
Frankfort	Mary's Crafts and Quilts, 52 W. Armstrong Street
Goshen	Calico Point, 24810 County Road 40
Goshen	Meredith's Sewing Corner, 712 W. Lincoln Ave.
Jeffersonville	Jubilee Gallery, 121 W. Court
Kokomo	Pastime Quilts & Yarns, 4524 Anna Lane
Kokomo	Legacy Quilts, 2217 Avalon Ct.
Kouts	Yours in Stitches, PO Box 348, 207 W. College
Lynnville	Betty's Quilts and Fabrics, 244 West Third Street
Madison	Joan's Quilts & Crafts, 115 E. Main
Metamora	Grannies Calico Sampler, Old Famers Barn, On the Canal
Middlebury	Country Quilt Shoppe, 200 W. Warren PO Box 336
Mishawaka	The Calico Garden, 100 Center
Mitchell	The Quilt Lady, 624 W. Main Street
Monticello	Needles in the Haystack, 116 North Illinois
Muncie	Quilts Etc., 1404 N. Wheeling Ave.
Nappanee	L. J. Wagner Home Interiors, 1200 E. Market
Nashville	Fabric Addict, P.O. Box 620
Nashville	The Quilt Parlor, 173 N. Van Buren
Newburgh	Quilts & Crafts, Inc., 8423 Bell Oaks Drive
North Vernon	Fabric Outlet, RR #1
Oakford	Pastime Quilts & Country Furniture, 1268 E. 400 S. Rd.
Shipshewana	Fabric Outlet, State Road 5 South
Shipshewana	Rebecca Haarer Arts & Antiques, PO Box 52 165 Morton Street
Shipshewana	Quiltmakers, P.O. Box 640
South Bend	Erica's Craft & Sewing Center, 1602 Mishawaka Avenue
South Bend	Heckaman's Quilting & More, 63028 U.S. Route 31
Valparaiso	Jan's Place Needle Art, 2109 N. Roosevelt
West Lafayette	The Country Girl, 1185 Sagamore Parkway W.
West Lafayette	Newalt's Fabric Center, Third & South Street
Woodland	Colonial Outlet, 8 Hadley
Zionsville	Liberty Farmhouse, 25 Cedar Street

Indiana State Quilt Guild, 14 Briar Patch Rd., Bargersville, 46106
Indiana Guilds:
Anderson Evening Guild, 1112 North Drive, Anderson, 46011
Redbud Quilter's Guild, 111 E. 12th Street, Anderson, 46016
Americus Quilting Club, PO Box 312, Battleground, 47920
Quarry Quilters, PO Box 975, Bedford, 47421
Bloomington Quilter's Guild, PO Box 812, Bloomington, 47402
Clay City Calico Quilters, Box 107, Clay City, 47841
Columbus Star Quilter's Guild, PO Box 121, Columbus, 47202
Conner Quilters Guild, 704 W. Third Street, Connersville, 47331
Quilt Patch Quilt Club, 210 Elm Street, Corydon, 47112
Heritage Quilters, PO Box 8, Crown Point, 46307
Love 'N Stitches, 116 S. Muessing, Cumberland, 46229
Heartland Quilters, 55922 Channelview Dri., Elkhart, 46516
Calico Cut-ups Quilt Club, 10013 Teton Court, Fort Wayne, 46804
Crossroads Quilt Club, 3625 Amulet Drive, Fort Wayne, 46815
Qu-Bees Quilt Club, 1512 Irene Avenue, Fort Wayne, 46808
Spring Valley Quilt Guild, 7164 W. Reformatory Rd., Fortville, 46040
Greenfield Guild, 3842 E. 200 S., Greenfield, 46140
Quilt Connection Guild, 2321 Willow Circle, Greenwood, 46143
Hill Valley Quilting, 607 W. Ralston, Indianapolis, 46217
IQ's, 3370 N. Highwoods Dr., Indianapolis, 46222
Quilter's Guild of Indianapolis, PO Box 68853, Indianapolis, 46268
Dune Country Quilters, PO Box 8526, Michigan City, 46360
Hands All Around Quilt Club, 10729 CR 46, Millersburg, 46453
New Paris Puzzle Quilters, 10729 CR 46, Millersburg, 46543
Carolina Quilters, 413 Conduit Road, Mooresville, 46158
Evening Quilter's Guild, 4001 W. State Road 28, Muncie, 47303
Muncie Evening Quilters, 4001 W. State Road 28, Muncie, 47303
Muncie Quilters Guild, 812 W. Cromer, Muncie, 47303
Pioneer Women of Brown County, PO Box 668, Nashville, 47448
Hoosier Favorite Quilters, 1715 Duart Court, New Haven, 46774
Common Threads Quilt Guild, 5811 S. 500 W., New Palestine, 46163
Indiana Puzzle Quilt Club, 68535 CR 23, New Paris, 46553
Raintree Quilters Guild, PO Box 118 , Newberg, 47630
Stitch & Chatter Quilt Guild, 221 W. Seventh Street, Portland, 47371
Piecemaker's Quilt Guild, 211 N. Main Street, Salem, 47167
Sew-n-Sew Quilt Club, 19887 Alou Lane, South Bend, 46637
Randolph County Art Assoc., PO Box 284, Union City, 47390
String-along Quilt Guild, PO Box 2363, Valparaiso, 46384
Indiana State Quilt Guild, 3059 Sullivan, W. Lafayette, 47906
The Old Tippecanoe Quilt Guild, 3059 Sullivan, W. Lafayette, 47906
Spinning Spools Quilt Guild, 4111 CR 16, Waterloo, 46793
Hendricks County Quilters Guild, Senior Center, Danville, 46122
Vigo County Quilters Guild, 1907 S. 3rd Street, Terre Haute, 47802

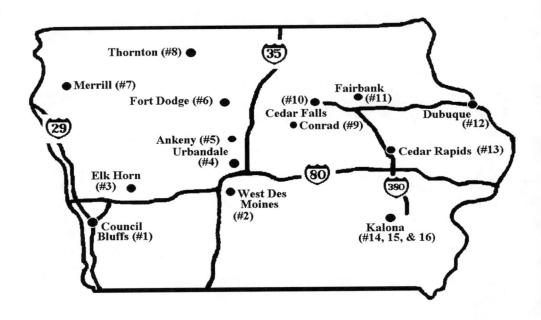

16 Featured Shops

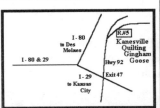

Council Bluffs, IA   #1

Kanesville Quilting
Gingham Goose

Hwy 92E   R.R. #5   P.O. Box 3A
(712) 366-6003   51503
Est: 1990   3000 sq.ft.
Owners: Mavis Hauser & Karen Krause

Mon - Fri
10 - 5:30
Sat 10 - 4

100% Cottons,
Books, Patterns,
Notions, and
Classes.
We do machine
quilting on your
tops.

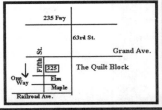

West Des Moines, IA   #2

The Quilt Block

325 5th Street   50265
(515) 255-1010
Est: 1987   3000 sq.ft.
Owners: Marilyn Parks & Mary Miller

M -S 10 - 5
Thur 10 - 7
Sun   1 - 4

Full line quilt
supply store--
fabrics, notions,
books, patterns.
Authorized
Bernina dealer.

Elk Horn, IA   #3

Prairie Star Quilts map

Mon - Sat
10 - 5

Prairie Star Quilts

4132 Main St.   51531
(712) 764-7012
Owner: Julie Larsen
Est: 1986   1500 sq.ft.

We Love Mail Order

Over 700 bolts of 100% cotton fabric.
ALEXANDER HENRY, JINNY BEYER,
MOMEN HOUSE, HOFFMAN, GUTCHEON
The latest in quilting notions, books and patterns.
Largest selection of fabric craft patterns in Western Iowa

Custom Machine Quilting

Urbandale, IA   #4

Living History Farms

Mon - Sat
9 - 5
Sun 11 - 6

2600 N.W. 111th   50322
(515) 278-2400   Est 1969
Non-Profit
Farming Museum

Our farm is a 600 acre, open-air farming museum. We display a portion of our collection of 300 quilts the second week in October. Other gifts and crafts may be purchased in The Gallery

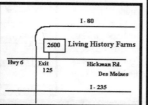

Ankeny, IA   #5

Country Clutter

Mon - Fri
10 - 5:30
Sat 10 - 4
Sun 1 - 4

305 S.W. Walnut St.   50021
(515) 964-2747
Owner: Sue Ites   Est: 1985
Group Appts. Available

Cozy Quilt Shop featuring 500+ bolts of fabric, quilt books, counted cross-stitch, & 100's of doll patterns.
A Quilter's Dream!

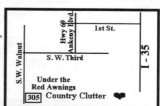

Fort Dodge, IA   #6

Grandma's Quilts, Crafts & Needlework

Mon - Sat
10 - 5
Tues & Thur til 7

1422—1st. Ave. North   50501
(515) 955-1521   Est: 1987
Owner: Mary Consier

In a House built in 1896 with a black wrought iron fence.
We carry crafts, fabric, and lots of books and patterns.
We also carry yarn.

2000 sq.ft.

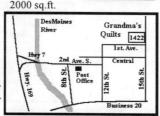

Merrill, IA   #7

The Quiltworks

Mon - Fri
9 - 5
Sat 9 - 12

518 Webster Street
(712) 938-2059   51038
Owner: Mary K. Roder
Est: 1991   875 sq.ft.

Custom Machine Quilting.
Approximately 10 quilts on hand.
Wood quilt racks and shelves.

Map: Main St., 5th. St., Webster St., Hwy. 75, City Park, The Quiltworks

Thornton, IA #8

Quilt Cottage II

Mon - Sat
9:30 - 4
1st Sunday
each month
1 - 4

712 Main St.　50479
(515) 998-2998
Owners: Chuck & Bev Fischer
Est: 1990　500 sq.ft.

Full Service Quilt Shop as well as "Fabric Fix" Swatch Club and Mail Order Service.

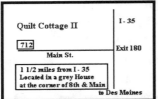

Quilt Cottage II
[712]
Main St.
I - 35
Exit 180
1 1/2 miles from I - 35
Located in a grey House
at the corner of 8th & Main
to Des Moines

Conrad, IA #9

Conrad General Store

Mon - Sat
9 - 5

101 N. Main St. 50621
(515) 366-2043　Est: 1983
Owners: Brenda Shine, Jeannie Zehr, Janice Juchems

Large selection of Quilting Fabrics & Supplies. Country Gift Ware. Heritage Lace, & Nan's Cornhusk dolls in an original store since 1894

Rt.175
Conrad
General Store
Grundy Center
Liscomb
Conrad
Gladbrook
Rt.311
Hwy 14
Marshalltown
Hwy 330
Hwy 30
to Des Moines

Cedar Falls, IA #10

The Quilt Emporium

Tues - Sat
10 - 5

322 Main St.　50613
(319) 277-8303
Owners: Marlys Kauten &
Est: 1993　　Barbara Newcomer

Full Service Shop. Featuring— Fabrics, Notions, Books, Patterns, and Classes.

U.S. 218
Washington
1st. St.
2nd. St.
3rd. St.
4th St.
5th St.
Main St.
State
[322] Quilt
Emporium

Fairbank, IA #11

Jo's Thread & Thimble

Mon - Sat
9 - 5

105 Grove St. 50629
(319) 635-2119　Est: 1974
Owner: Jo Haberkamp　2500 sq.ft.

N.E. Iowa's finest quilt shop. Very large selection of fabrics, notions, patterns, books, and quilting supplies. Quilted Gift Items Also.

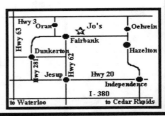

Hwy 3
Oran
Jo's
Oelwein
Hwy 63
Fairbank
Dunkerton
Hazelton
Hwy 281
Hwy 62
Jesup
Hwy 20
I - 380
Independence
to Waterloo
to Cedar Rapids

Iowa Guilds:
East Iowa Heirloom Quilters,
　P.O. Box 1382, Cedar Rapids, 52406
Mississippi Valley Quilters Guild,
　P.O. Box 2636, Davenport, 52809
Des Moines Area Quilt Guild,
　6222 University Ave., Des Moines
Quilting for fun,
　1305 Yewell St., Iowa City, 52240
Northeast Iowa Quilter's Guild,
　Box 43, Monona, 52159
Four Seasons Quilt Guild,
　Box 178, Sloan, 51055

Dubuque, IA #12

Cobblestone Cupboard

Mon - Fri
10 - 5
Sat 10 - 3

3448 Hillcrest Rd. 52002
(319) 583-0534
Owners: Bert & Carol Carney

Expertise Designer Fabric Friendly Service Satisfy all your Quilt Needs plus Heirloom and Personal sewing. Bernina & Elna Machines and Sergers.

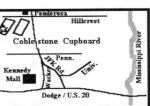

Ponderosa
Hillcrest
Coblestone Cupboard
Penn.
JFK Rd.
Wacker Rd.
Univ.
Mississippi River
Kennedy Mall
Dodge / U.S. 20

Cedar Rapids, IA   #13

The Quilting B

315 Third Avenue S.E. Suite 207
(319) 363-1643   52401
Owner: Beverly Thornton
Est: 1986   750 sq.ft.

**Mon - Fri
10 - 5
Thurs til 7
Sat 10 - 4**

Complete Line of Supplies & Notions. Doll and Santa Patterns Yarns for Santa Beards & Doll Hair. Finished items for sale.

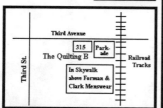

Kalona, IA   #14

Kalona Kountry Kreations

2134— 560th St. S.W.   52247
(319) 656-5366
Owner: Sara M. Miller
Est: 1977   2500 sq.ft.

**Mon - Sat
9 - 5**

We have 5000 - 6000 bolts of fabric, both domestic & imported. Plus quilts, new & antique.

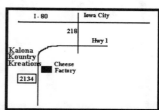

Kalona, IA   #15

Woodin Wheel

515 "B" Ave.   52247
(319) 656-2240
Owner: Marilyn Woodin
Est: 1973

**Mon - Sat
10 - 5**

Over 250 New & Antique Quilts for Sale plus a Private Quilt Museum.

Downtown
Kalona
5 Block off
Highway 1

Kalona, IA   #16

Stitch 'n Sew Cottage

207 4th St. P.O. Box 351
(319) 656-2923   52247
Owners: Dorothy, Cande, & Paul
Est: 1981   Schumann & Niva Burkholder

**Mon - Fri
9 - 5
Sat 9 - 3**

"Where Ma Saves Pa's Dough"

Fabrics, Notions, Quilting Supplies Pillow Forms, Embroidery Supplies, batting

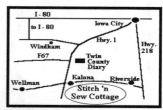

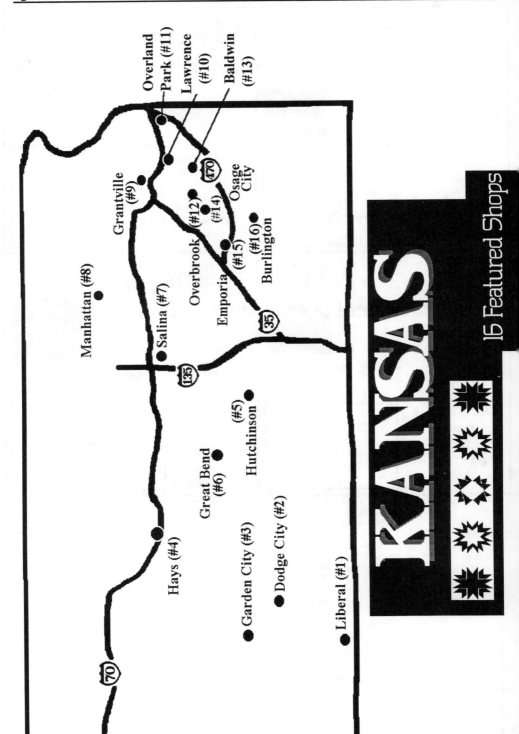

KANSAS

16 Featured Shops

Overland Park (#11)
Lawrence (#10)
Baldwin (#13)
Osage City
Grantville (#9)
Overbrook (#12)
(#14)
Emporia (#15)
Burlington (#16)
Manhattan (#8)
Salina (#7)
Hutchinson (#5)
Great Bend (#6)
Garden City (#3)
Dodge City (#2)
Hays (#4)
Liberal (#1)

Liberal, KS   #1

the Quilt Basket

Mon - Sat
10 - 5:30

608 N. Kansas   67901   (316) 626-5006
Owners: Bruce & Kim Shannon   Est: 1992
(800) 657-8796   Free Newsletter

Quality Fabrics, Notions, Patterns, Books, Custom Quilting, Mail Order Welcome!

Map: The Quilt Basket, 608, Kansas Ave., 7th St., Hwy. 83, Hwy. 54

Dodge City, KS   #2

Roselle's Fabrics

Mon - Sat
9:30 - 6

618 Second   67801
(316) 225-0004
Owner: Roselle Calihan
Est: 1981   1800 sq.ft.

Lots of quilt books, patterns, and quilting aids, 100% cottons and other fabrics.

Map: Boot Hill, Third St., Second St., 618 Roselle's Fabrics, Highway 50

Garden City, KS   #3

Quilt Rack

Mon - Fri
9:30 - 5:30
Sat 10 - 5

519 W. Mary St. #113
(316) 275-8786
Owner: Jeaninne McCarthy
Est: 1987

Quilting & all the Extras!
<u>Cross Stitch</u>
Fabrics
Threads
Patterns
<u>Needlepoint</u>
Threads

Map: Hwy. 83, Quilt Rack 519, Mary St., 8th St.

Hays, KS   #4

Prairie Sampler

Mon - Sat
9:30 - 5:30

1308 Main   67601
(913) 628-2469
Owner: Lois F. Stafford
Est: 1988   700 sq.ft.

Over 650 bolts of 100% cottons, latest books, patterns, quilting supplies, classes and friendly service.

Map: Prairie Sampler 1308, 13th St., Main, Vine St. (Hwy 183), 8th St. (Bus Loop Hwy 40)

Hutchinson, KS   #5

COUNTRY 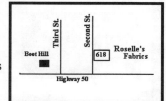 FABRICS

Mon - Sat
9 - 5:30

R. R. #1   6411 W. Morgan Road
(316) 662-3681   67501
Est: 1977
Owners: Janet, Randy, & Leland Headings

100% Cotton Solids and calicos. Quilting Notions, Books, & Batting. Fashion Fabrics, Sewing Notions & Patterns.

Map: Hutchinson, Hwy. 50 / K61 (5 miles West), 6411 Pleasantview Shopping Area Country Fabrics, Hwy 96

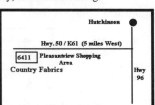

Great Bend, KS   #6

The Calico Shoppe

Mon - Sat
9:30 - 5:30

1415 Main Street   67530
(316) 793-8900   Est: 1987
Owner: Kaye Damm
3750 Sq.ft.

Country Craft Patterns

2000 + Bolts

Classes

Finished Quilts for Sale

```
The Calico           Broadway
Shoppe  1415

                     Courthouse
Forest

         Main St.  Hwy. 281
                     Lakin
```

Salina, KS   #7

Quilting Bee

Mon - Sat
9:30 - 5:30
Thur til 6:30
Sat 9:30 - 5

120 S. Santa Fe   67401
(913) 823-9376
Owner: Shirley Wolf
Est: 1979   4000 sq.ft.

4000 Square Feet
devoted to cotton
quilting fabrics,
notions, books,
and classes. All
major fabrics, lots
of plaids.

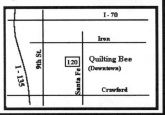

```
            I - 70
            Iron
9th St.  120  Quilting Bee
              (Downtown)
I - 135  Santa Fe  Crawford
```

Manhattan, KS   #8

Ideas Unlimited Quilt Shop

Mon - Fri
11 - 5:30
Thur til 7
Sat 10 - 3

523 South 17th   66502
(913) 539-6759   Est: 1987
Owners: Dorine & Stan Elsea
1000 sq.ft.

Unique fabrics for
quilts & fashions.
Large selection of
books & patterns
for quilts and
pieced garments.

```
                    to K.S.U.
            Poyntz Ave.
   17th St.
Ideas
Unlimited   Mall
Quilt Shop
    523
            Fort Riley Blvd. (KS 18)
```

Grantville, KS   #9

Quilts of Yesterday

Mon, Wed, Fri, Sat 9 - 5

R. R. #1, P.O. Box 24   66429
(913) 246-3544
Owner: Aleta Spreer
Est: 1988   1200 sq.ft.

Quilt Classes - Fabrics - Machine Quilting. Top Quality cotton prints at low everyday prices.

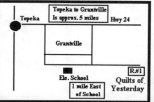

Lawrence, KS   #10

Stitch on Needlework Shop

Mon - Sat 10 - 5:30 Sun 1 - 4

926 Massachusetts St.   66044
(913) 842-1101
Owners: Steve & Leslie Ahlert
Est: 1976   3000 sq.ft.

A full line needlework and gift shop including 100% cottons, books, patterns, and classes.

Overland Park, KS   #11

Wannado

Mon - Fri 9:30 - 5:30 Tue & Thur til 8:30 Sat 9:30 - 4:30

8467 W. 95th St.   66212
(913) 381-5445
Owner: Barbara J. Bruce
Est: 1993   1500 sq.ft.

Quilting & Counted Cross-Stitch Supplies. Classes & Custom Framing. Guild Discounts

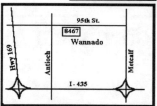

Overbrook, KS   #12

Osage County Quilt Factory

Tues - Sat 10 - 5

400 Walnut   P.O. Box 490
(913) 665-7500   66524
Owner: Virginia Robertson   Est: 1984
2400 sq.ft.

Quilting and Dollmaking books, supplies and notions. 2000 bolt inventory in an old church.

Baldwin City, KS #13

Cygnet Fashions & Fabrics

Mon - Sat 9:30 - 5

713 8th St. 66006
(913) 594-3477   Est: 1986
Quilting supplies,   Owner: Sharon A. Vesecky
  books, patterns,
  fabric—Hoffman,
  Jinny Beyer,
  Springs, Concord.
  Needlework
  supplies. Interlock
  knits, sweatshirt
  fleece, gifts.
  Kansas Products.

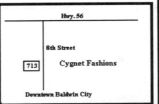

Hwy. 56

8th Street

713   Cygnet Fashions

Downtown Baldwin City

Osage City, KS #14

Calico Cupboard

Tues - Sat 9 - 5

513 Market   66523
(913) 528-4861
Owners: Lewis & Lora Lee Meek
                    Est: 1983
We specialize in
  machine made
  quilts ! Usually
  100 or more in
stock ! **OR** choose
from our 1600 bolt
  inventory for a
  custom order.
Fabric also sold by
  the yard.

5th.   6th.

Market / Hwy 31

Calico   513
Cupboard

30 miles
southwest
of Topeka

Emporia, KS #15

Fabric Corner

Mon - Sat 9 - 6

416 West Sixth Avenue   66801
(316) 342- 3040
Est: 1992   1800 sq.ft.
Owners: Colleen Janssen & Joan Kloppenberg

Quilting classes,
  supplies and
  fabrics -
  Hoffman, RJR,
  Jinny Beyer,
  Springmaid, &
  P&B.

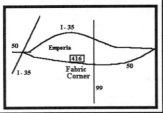

I - 35

50   Emporia

416

I - 35   Fabric
         Corner

50

99

Burlington, KS #16

Silver Threads & Golden Needles

Mon - Sat 9:30 - 5:30 Sun by Appt

321 Neosho   66839
(316) 364-8233
Est: 1985
2000 sq.ft.

Owners: Whitey
& Jerry Anne Hoyt

Top Quality
Fabric $1.99 yd.
& up. Patterns,
Notions, Crafts,
Books, Quilting
Supplies, Craft
Patterns & More
Wholesale/Retail

Topeka   Hwy 75   to Kansas
                            City
                    I - 35
Emporia
         321   Burlington   Neosho
     Silver Threads &
         Hwy 54   Golden Needles
Wichita
         to Tulsa, OK

Kansas Quilters Organization, 1721 Weile, Winfield, 67156
Kansas Guilds:
Silver Needles Quilt Guild, 5500 S. Ohio Rd., Assaria, 67416
Central Kansas Thread-Benders, 1400 Truman, Great Bend, 67530
Big Creek Quilt Guild, 1061 Catherine Road, Hays, 67601
Heart of Kansas Quilt Guild, P.O. Box 271, Hutchinson, 67504
Sunflower Quilter's Guild, P.O. Box 69, Iola, 66749
Quilters Guild of Greater K.C., 1617 W. 42nd Street, Kansas City
Kaw Valley Quilters Guild, 924 Vermont, Lawrence, 66044
Olathe Quilters Guild, 151st Street & Blackbob Rd. Olathe, 66061
Little Balkans Quilt Guild, P.O. Box 1608, Pittsburg, 66762
Miama County Quilters Guild, P.O. Box 453, Paola, 66071
Silver Needles Quilt Guild, Box 1132, Salina, 67402
Walnut Valley Quilters Guild, 1615 East 20th Ave., Winfield, 67156

Other Shops in Kansas:

Council Grove	Quilts & More, 512 E. Main Street
Emporia	Quilts & Yardage Plus, 7 E. Sixth Avenue
Kansas City	Jessie's Quilting, 3316 North 131st.
Kansas City	Grandma Jeans Fabric Shop, 6305 State Ave.
Newton	The Quilt Shop, Limited, 2511 Main N.
Norton	The Sewing Box, 128 S. State PO Box 125
Osawatomie	Calico Quilts and Crafts, 400 Pacific Avenue
Phillipsburg	The Pin Cushion, 747 3rd.
Shawnee	Mission Salt Box Sampler, 4663 Indian Creek
Topeka	The Sewing Nook, 1509 S.W. 6th
Topeka	Bennett's Sewing, 2044 N. W. Topeka Blvd.
Topeka	The Sewing Nook, 1509 S.W. 6th
Topeka	Fabrics Unique, 1517 SW 6th
Topeka	Cozy Craft Corner, 915 NE Hilltop Drive
Wichita	Prairie Quilts, Inc., 5614 E. Lincoln
Wichita	Gramma's Calico Cupboard, 1945 South Hydraulic
Winchester	Winchester Quilting, Rt #1 Box 43

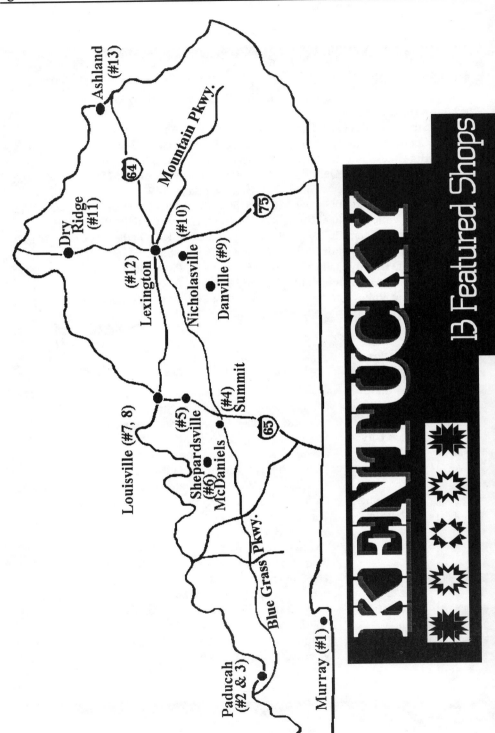

KENTUCKY

13 Featured Shops

Ashland (#13)

Mountain Pkwy.

64

Dry Ridge (#11)

(#12)
Lexington

(#10)
Nicholasville

Danville (#9)

75

Louisville (#7, 8)

(#5)
Shepardsville

(#4)
Summit

McDaniels
(#6)

65

Blue Grass Pkwy.

Paducah (#2 & 3)

Murray (#1)

Murray, KY   #1

The Magic Thimble

Tues - Sat 10 - 5

813 Coldwater Road   42071
(502) 759-4769
Owner: Peggy Smith
                    Est: 1986   1000 sq.ft.

100% Cotton
Fabrics,
Patterns.
Friendly
Atmosphere &
knowledgeable
staff

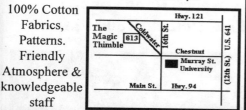

Paducah, KY   #2

Museum of the American Quilt Society

Tues - Sat 10 - 5 April - Oct Sun 1 - 5

215 Jefferson St.

Changing
exhibitions
and
permanent
collection
A Quilter
Must See!

---

(502) 443-5673
420 North 4th St.
42001
Owner: Pat English
Est: 1989

Designer Fabric—Patterns—Classes—Books
Newest Notions - Brazilian Embroidery Supplies
Lace Making - Fabric Painting
Quilter's Jewelry - Tools or Gadgets
We do mail order on all those Hard-to-Finds

Quilter's Alley

Paducah, KY   #3

Mon - Sat 10 - 5

Summit, KY   #4

Quaint Quilts

Mon, Tues, Wed, Fri, & Sat 10 - 5

16117 Leitchfield Rd.   42783
(502) 862-9708   Est: 1985
Owner: Kathryn Richardson
                        672 sq.ft.

Quilts, Curtains,
Machine & Hand
Quilting, Oil
Paintings, Prints,
Basketry, Rugs &
Rug Weaving.
Approx. 100
printed quilt top
fabrics.

Shepherdsville, KY   #5

Quilts by Donna

(502) 955-8673

4214 N. Preston Highway   40165

Owner: Donna Sharp

Est: 1982   1800 sq.ft.

Home of the
original
Quilts by Donna
Calendar.

Come by, pick up a
copy, and take a
look at all of our
wonderful quilts.

Mon 9 - 8
Tues - Fri 9 - 6
Sat 9 - 5

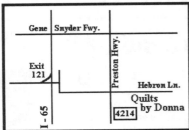

100's of bolts of fabric.
Books & Patterns
Tops, Etc.
Up to 100 +Finished Quilts.

*The Pattern for this Quilt is
included in our Calendar.*

McDaniels, KY #6

Wild Rose Quilt Shop

**Mon - Sat
10 - 4**

Hwy 259 S. 40152
(502) 257-2580

Rt. 1, Box 94
Owner: Merline Long   Est: 1989

100% Cotton
Fabric, Books,
Notions, All
Quilting Supplies,
Quilts and Gifts
AND
Many Happy
Quilters.

Louisville, KY #7

Cotton Patch Quilt Shop

**Mon - Sat
10 - 4**

1734 Bonnycastle Ave.   40205
(502) 458-1617   Est: 1985
Owner: Susan Murphy   1400 sq.ft.

Wide variety of
Fabrics. Quilt
Supplies. Battings.
Novelty Items
Applique, Cross
Stitch, Notions,
Books.
Classes scheduled 4
times a year

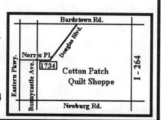

Louisville, KY #8

Happy Heart Quilt Shop

**Mon - Fri
10 - 5
Sat 10 - 4**

7296 - B Manslick Rd.   40214
(502) 363-1171   Est: 1985
Owner: Yvonne Fritze   1200 sq.ft.

Large selection of
fabrics including
Hoffman, RJR,
Jinny Beyer, P&B,
Liberty/London.
Quilt Kits
Extensive line of
books, patterns
and notions.

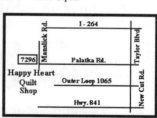

Danville, KY #9

World Wide Fabrics

**Mon - Sat
10 - 6**

104 Man O'War Blvd.   40422
(606) 236-1175   Est: 1976
Owners: Earl & Jean Steinhauer
4000 sq.ft.

Authorized
Bernina Dealer
Calico Cottons
Quilting Books
and Supplies
Bridal Fabrics
and accessories
Complete line of
Notions, Drapery
& Upholstery

Nicholasville, KY #10

Patchwork Peddler

**Mon - Sat
9:30 - 6
Thur
9:30 - 1**

224 Edgewood Drive   40356
(606) 885-6188
Owner: Sandy Bain
Est: 1991   1500 sq.ft.

Quilting Fabrics,
Notions, Hoops,
Frames,
Books + More
Classes
Machine Service

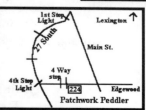

Dry Ridge, KY   #11

The Quilt Box

The Quilt Box is one of Kentucky's nicest Quilt Shops. Its special charm begins on the tree shaded gravel road leading to Walnut Springs Farm where the shop is located - only 3 miles from Exit #159 on I-75 in the scenic bluegrass country - half way between Cincinnati and Lexington.

The Quilt Box opened 12 years ago in a restored 150 year old log cabin - on the farm - and has since been expanded to an adjoining two-story structure.

Truly a one stop Quilting Shop for all of your quilting needs, and a fun place to shop! - staffed by knowledgeable, friendly and helpful people anxious to fulfill all of your quilting needs.

In addition to our broad assortment of quilting related items we are proud of our 2,000+ bolts including the latest designer fabrics at reasonable prices.

Visa and Mastercards are accepted. We welcome mail orders and have a mail-order catalog on request.

We welcome all visitors and always enjoy taking the time to make you feel at home and unhurried. You'll be glad you came and weather permitting, are welcome to enjoy our large patio and deck. Bring and enjoy a picnic lunch, look over the farm animals, and enjoy the scenery.

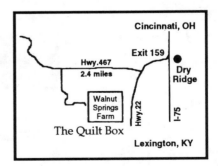

Mon - Sat 9:30 - 5:00
The Quilt Box At Walnut Springs Farm Warsaw Rd.
Dry Ridge, KY. 41035 (606) 824-4007

Lexington, KY #12

Quilter's Square

Mon - Sat
9:30 - 5:30

2416 Regency Road   40503
(606) 278-5010

BERNINA DEALER. All Quilting Supplies, Kits, Repairs, old quilts restoration. Smocking & Heirloom sewing supplies. Large selection of books & patterns.

Owner: Mary Charles
Est: 1982   2400 sq.ft.

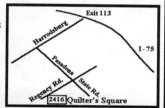

Ashland, KY #13

Craft Attic Quilt Shop

Mon - Sat
10 - 5
Wed 2 - 5

2027 Hoods Creek Pike 41102
(606) 325-1212
Owner: Donnie Maggard
Est: 1982   1500 sq.ft.

100% Cotton Fabrics. Full Line of Quilting Supplies. Books Stencils Classes

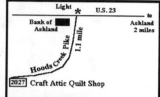

Kentucky Guilds:
Gone to Pieces Q.G., 2027 Hoods Creek Pike, Ashland, 41102
Louisville Nimble Thimbles, P.O. Box 6234, Louisville, 40206
Graves County Piecemakers, Rt. 3, Box 236-2, Mayfield, 42066
Owensboro Quilters Guild, Owensboro, 42301
Murray Quilt Lovers, P.O. Box 975, Paintsville
Licking Valley Quilters, 907 Mary St., Villa Hills, 41017

Other Shops in Kentucky:

Benton	Country Remnants, P.O. Box 172A Route #7
Benton	Needle & Thread, P.O. Box 78
Flatwoods	Monogram & Quilt Cottage, 1402 Brentwood Ct.
Frankfort	Treadleworks, 235 W. Broadway Street
Hopkinsville	Mi Lady's Needlecraft, 1819 S. Walnut
Louisville	Baer Fabrics, 515 E. Market Street
Louisville	Kentucky Art & Craft Gallery, 609 W. Main
Magnolia	Bits and Pieces Fabric Shop, 7396 N. Jackson Highway
Magnolia	Pike View Fabric & Quilt Shop, 1924 Pike View Rd.
Murray	The Busy Bee's Custom Quilt Shop, P.O. Box 195A Route #2
Owensboro	Donna's Stitchery Nook, 2845 Parrish Avenue
Paducah	Hancock Fabrics, 3841 Hinkleville Road
Paintsville	Quilting Shop, Route 87
Pineville	Kathy's Needle & Thread, Route #2
Russellville	Becky's Antiques, 508 E. Ninth
Salyersville	Quilting Shop, East Mountain Parkway PO Box 998
Somerset	Mill Outlet, 4502 S. Highway 27

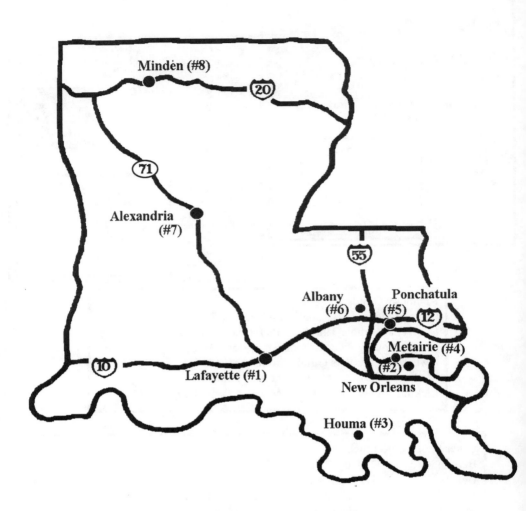

LOUISIANA

8 Featured Shops

Lafayette, LA   #1

Ginger's Needleworks

Tues - Fri
10 - 5
Sat 11 - 3

905 East Gloria Switch Road
(318) 232-7847   70507
Owner: Ginger Moore   Est:1984
450 sq.ft. Quilting   200 sq.ft. Yarns

Quilting fabrics, notions, supplies and quilts for sale. Yarns.

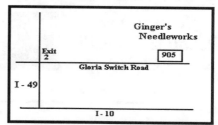

Ginger's
Needleworks
Exit 2
905
Gloria Switch Road
I - 49
I - 10

FREE CATALOG

Send us your name & address,
ATTN: Dept QTC

New Orleans, LA   #2

Mon - Sat   10 - 5

Quilt Cottage   (800) 453-6998

801 Nashville Avenue   70115   (504) 895-3791   Est: 1981
Owners: Carol Schiaffino,
2000 sq.ft.   & Jeanne Lincks

Your Complete Quilt Shop !

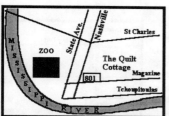

St Charles
State Ave.
Nashville
MISSISSIPPI
ZOO
The Quilt Cottage
Magazine
801
Tchoupitoulas
RIVER

Room full of 100% cotton fabric.
The latest books, notions, &Patterns.
New, Antique, Custom made quilts.
Repair

Send us your name and address
and we'll send you our free
brochure four times per year.

Houma, LA #3

Jo's Cloth Cottage

**Mon - Sat
10 - 5**

206 Bayou Gardens Blvd.
(504) 879-4602   70364
Owner: Joanne Stott
Est: 1982   5000 sq.ft.

Jo's is a creative sewing idea center which specializes in classes, fabrics & supplies for quilting, heirloom sewing, fashion & serger sewing. Lots of models and sewing ideas pack our 5000 sq.ft. store.

Take Hwy. 90 out of New Orleans 55 miles to Hwy 24. Jo's is in the old south square across from the Southland Mall on Bayou Gardens Blvd.

Metairie, LA #4

The Quilting Bee

**Mon - Sat
10 - 5:30**

3537 18th Street #15   70002
(504) 456-2304
Owner: Pamela Mauroner
Est: 1984   500 sq.ft.

100%
Cottons,
books,
patterns and
classes.

Ponchatoula, LA #5

Yesteryear Antiques & Quilts

**Mon - Sat
10 - 5
Sun 12 - 5**

165 East Pine   70454
(504) 386-2741   Est: 1982
Owners: Pat Zieske & Lee Barends

We do Custom Made Quilts !
We have samples and fabrics at the shop for you to look at - you chose your own pattern and colors.

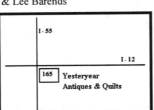

Louisiana Guilds:
Strawberry Patch Quilters
          Albany LA
Red River Quilters, P.O. Box 4811,
          Shreveport, 71134
Jefferson Parish Quilting Guild,
          711 Ridgelake Dr, Metairie
Gulf States Quilting Assoc.,
          P.O. Box 8391, Metairie,
          70011
North Louisiana Quilters, Monroe
Southern Samplers, 165 E. Pine Street
          Ponchatoula, 70454

Albany, LA #6

Patchwork Plus by Vera

**Tues - Fri
9 - 5
Sat 9 - 3**

29937 S. Montpelier Ave. 70711
(504) 567-5269   Est: 1989
Owner: Vera Honea   1100 sq.ft.

Great selection of 100% cotton fabrics, quilter's fat quarters, books, quilting supplies, patterns, notions, silk ribbon. Classes Friendly & Helpful

Alexandria, LA #7

Quilting Quarters

6524 Masonic Drive   71301
(318) 473-9104
Owner: Geraldine Gerami
Est: 1985   1200 sq.ft.

**Mon - Fri
9 - 5
Sat 9 - 12**

We have 1000 Bolts of 100% Cottons ! Also Patterns, books, and notions. ANYTHING FOR QUILTING ! !

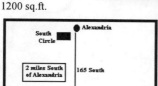

South Circle

Alexandria

2 miles South of Alexandria   165 South

6524   Quilting Quarters

Minden, LA #8

The Little Country Quilt Shop

R.R. #2   Box 20   71055
(318) 377-7630
Owner: Nona Sale   Est: 1983

**Tues - Fri
9 - 5
Sat 10 - 2**

We have approx. 800 - 1000 bolts. All the latest books, patterns, & supplies. Also a variety of classes. Plus we have old and new quilts for sale.

From I - 20 take Exit 49. Go North 3&1/2 miles to the 2nd blinking light. At the light turn right for 1/4 mile to Parish 131. Shop is 1 mile on the left. Watch for Signs ! !

Other Shops in Louisiana:
Baton Rouge   Peaceful Quilter, 12318 Jefferson Hwy
Baton Rouge   The Thimble, 9998 Hooper Road
Bossier City   Fabric Boutique, 1701 Old Minden Rd.
New Orleans   Old Craft Cottage, 816 Decatur St.
New Orleans   The Front Porch, 824 Royal
New Orleans   Partners Pillow Talk, 541 Chartres
West Monroe   Creatively Sew, 2320 Cypress St.

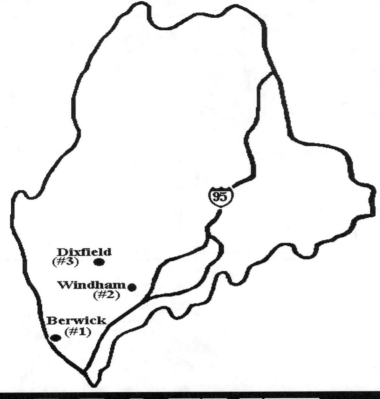

Dixfield
(#3)

Windham
(#2)

Berwick
(#1)

MAINE

3 Featured Shops

Maine Guilds:
Nimble Thimbles, Community Center, Windham, 04062
Pine Tree Quilter's Guild, RD Box 252, Turner, 04282

Berwick, ME #1

Cottage Herbs
Craft & Quilt Shop

**Tues - Sat
10 - 5
Sun 1 - 5**

151 Diamond Hill Road   03901
(207) 698-5507
Est: 1980
Owner: Nancy Riley

**Large Selection
of Calico Fabrics
Dried Flowers
Rowe Pottery
Quilting Supplies**
Baskets, Quilts,
Potpourri, Plants,
Ribbons, Candles,
Grapevines, Dolls
Cross Stitch
Tinware & Crafts

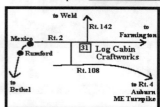

Windham, ME #2

Calico Basket
Quilt Shop

**Mon - Fri
9:30-4:30
Tues til
8:30
Sat 9:30-4**

40 Page Road   04062
(207) 892-5606
Owner: JoAnne Hill
Est: 1982   1300 sq.ft.

Over 2000 Top
Quality Fabrics.
The Latest --
Books, Notions,
Craft Patterns,
and Quilting
Supplies.

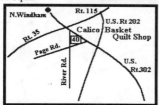

Dixfield, ME #3

Log Cabin
Craftworks

**Tues 9:30-8
Wed - Fri
9:30 - 5
Sat 9:30 - 1**

31 Main   04224
(207) 562-8816   Est: 1981
Owner: Norine Clarke   1200 sq.ft.

Located in the
foothills of
Western Maine
we offer a variety
of Fabrics,
Current Books,
Tools and
Notions.

Other Shops in Maine:

Bangor	Brewer Fabric Shop, 570 Stillwater
Bar Harbor	Sewing by the Sea, RFD #1
Cape Elizabeth	Elizabeth's Parlor & Pantry, 539 Ocean House Road
Columbia Falls	The Calico Cupboard, Inc. Rural Route 1
Freeport	Quilt & Needlecrafts, 22 Main St.
Lisbon Falls	Mill Fabric Center, 2 Ridge
North Edgecomb	On Board, Booth Bay Rd.
Portland	Design Cotton Fabrics, 399 Fore
Rumford	The Pin Cushion, 94 River Street
Saco	Patchwork Boutique Quilt Shop, 304 Beach
Searsport	Cat's Meow, Rural Route 1
Waterboro	The Right Stitch, Highway 202
West Gardiner	Main-ly Quilts N' Crafts, Hallowell Road
Wiscasset	The Marston House, PO Box 517

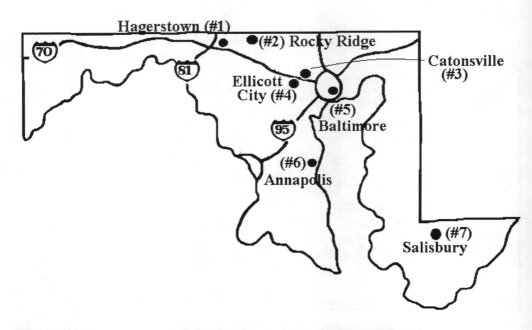

Maryland

7 Featured Shops

Quilt Show Today

Hagerstown, MD #1

TRADITIONS AT THE WHITE SWAN

June - Aug
Tues - Sat 10 - 5
Sept - May
Mon - Sat 10 - 5
Sun 1 - 5

16628 National Pike   21740
(301) 733-9130
Owners: Dick & Wendy Shank   Est: 1985   1700 sq.ft.

Authorized Bernina Dealer

Largest Quilt Shop in the area with
everything for the quilter—
beginner thru advanced.
1200 bolts of fabric including—
Hoffman, RJR, P&B, Mary Ellen
Hopkins, Benartex, Spiegel, Marcus
Brothers, Gutcheon, Springs, Concord,
Peter Pan, VIP. Notions, Books, Patterns,
Stencils, & Classes

In an historic stone
house (c. 1812)
3 miles West of town

Rocky Ridge, MD #2

Dolls & Quilts Barn

9459 Longs Mill Rd.   21778
(301) 898-0091
Owner: Yvonne Khin
Est: 1990   3500 sq.ft.

Tues - Sat
10 - 3

Revolving exhibits of
Dolls and Quilts with
changing seasons.
Special consultations
for Dolls or Quilts by
Appt. Only
Admission: $2.50
Seniors $2.00

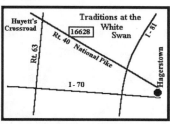

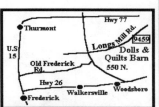

Catonsville, MD #3

Seminole Sampler

71 Mellor Ave.   21228
(410) 788-1720   Est: 1981
Owner: Kaye Pelovitz
3800 sq.ft.

Mon - Sat
10 - 5
Mon &
Thur til 8

2000+ gorgeous
and unusual bolts
(cotton). Call for
group discount
information.
3 interesting shop
neighbors:
Stitching Post,
Weaver's Place,
& Basketworks.

Ellicott City, MD #4

Winter
Sun.&Tue 12-5
Wed - Sat 10 - 5
Summer
Sun&Mon 12 - 5
Tues - Sat 10 - 5

8167 Main St.   21043   (410) 465-7202
Owner: Inge Stocklin   Est: 1989

Quilts, Pillows, Wall-
hangings. Quilt Racks,
Hangers, & Frames.
Clothing, Jewelry,
Cards. Restoration,
Appraisals,Lectures.
Fabric, Supplies &
Classes. Gifts too.

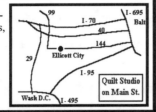

Baltimore, MD #5

Creative Needle Magic, Inc.

8600-F Harford Rd.   21234
(410) 882-0222   Est: 1988
Owners: Phyllis Pitarra &
800 sq.ft.   Lauraine Buccheri

Tues, Thur,
Fri & Sat
9:30 - 4
Wed 12:30 - 8

Fabric, Notions,
Books, Patterns,
and Classes.
Specializing in
Quilting, Smocking
& Heirloom French
Machine Sewing.

Annapolis, MD #6

Cottonseed Glory

4 Annapolis St.   21401
(410) 263-3897
Owner: Pat Steiner
Est: 1978

Mon - Sat
10 - 5
Sun 1 - 4
Fall & Winter

3000 bolts
from over 40
manufacturers.
Books,
Gourmet Notions,
PATTERNS,
PATTERNS,
PATTERNS !

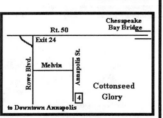

Salisbury, MD #7

Jenny's Sewing Studio

311 Civic Avenue   21801
(410) 543-1212
Owner: Jennifer Friedel
Est: 1982   3200 sq.ft.

Mon, Wed,
& Fri 10-8
Tue, Thur,
& Sat 10 - 6

Full service quilt
shop & sewing
machine dealer.
(Bernina, New
Home, Pfaff,
Singer) Over
1000 bolts of
fabric and approx.
30 classes offered.

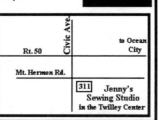

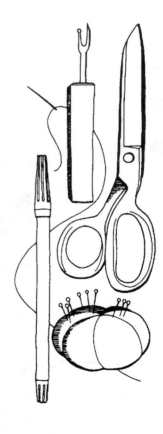

Maryland Guilds:
Annapolis Quilt Guild, 98 Spring Valley Dr., Annapolis, 21403
Baltimore Heritage Quilters' Guild, P.O. Box 66537, Baltimore, 21239
Faithful Circle Quilters, 5012 Lake Circle West, Columbia, 21044
Friendship Star Quilters, P.O. Box 8051, Gaithersburg, 20898
Eternal Quilter, 346 Chalet Dr., Millersville, 21108

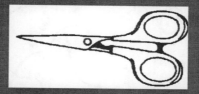

Other Shops in Maryland:

Arnold	Fabric Corner, 1500 Pine Bluff Way
Boonsboro	Old School Fabrics, 230 Potomac
Chevy Chase	Kathryn Berenson Quilts, 7206 Meadow
Easton	Dover Street Booksellers, 8673 Commerce Dr. #13
Easton	American Pennyroyal, 5 N. Harrison Street
Frederick	Sisto's Sewing Studio, 1560 Opossumtown Pike
Frederick	Quilters Heaven, 310 E. Church Street
Potomac	Stella Rubin Antiques, 12300 Glen Road
Prince Frederick	Calvert Home & Sewing, Old Salomons Rd
Rockville	G Street Fabrics, 11854 Rockville Pike
Sevema Park	Cathy Smith Antique Quilts, PO Box 681
Upper Marlboro	Stitches & Sew On, 9020 Trumps Hill Road

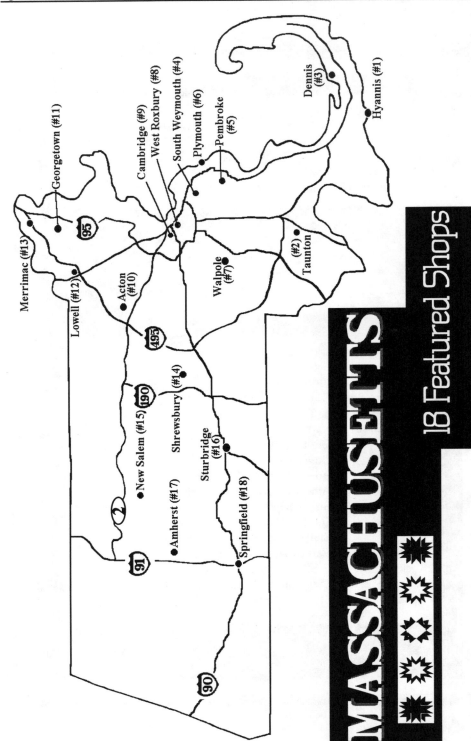

MASSACHUSETTS

18 Featured Shops

Hyannis (#1)
Dennis (#3)
Taunton (#2)
Georgetown (#11)
Cambridge (#9)
West Roxbury (#8)
South Weymouth (#4)
Plymouth (#6)
Pembroke (#5)
Merrimac (#13)
Lowell (#12)
Acton (#10)
Walpole (#7)
Shrewsbury (#14)
New Salem (#15)
Sturbridge (#16)
Amherst (#17)
Springfield (#18)

Hyannis, MA   #1

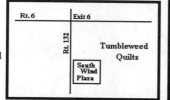

Tumbleweed

Southwind Plaza   Rte. 132
(508) 778-2434   02601
Est: 1985   3000 sq.ft.

**Mon - Sat
10 - 5:30
Sun 12 - 5**

Fabric, Books,
Notions, Batting
and Gifts.
We carry almost
every popular brand
of Fabric.
Reading Area.

Rt. 6	Exit 6
Rt. 132	Tumbleweed Quilts
South Wind Plaza	

Taunton, MA   #3

*The Sewing Room
Quilt Shop*

**Tues - Sat
12 - 5**

80 Alfred Lord Blvd. 02780-2002
(508) 824-9452   Est: 1981
Owner: Nina M. Bollivar   1400 sq.ft.

Fabrics -- Books
Patterns.
All the newest
quilting notions.
Classes --
morning and
evening.

Dennis, MA   #2

612 Route 6A Main Street   02638
(508) 385-2662   Est: 1982
Owner: Barbara Prue   1050 sq.ft.

**Fabric!
(100% Cottons)
Quilts!
Supplies - Books -
Lessons
Yarn - Needlepoint
We do mail order,
give us a call.**

**Mon - Sat   10 - 5
Year Round
Sundays in the summer 12 - 5**

Ladybug Quilting Shop in Olde King's Grant		
Route 6A	612	
	Exit 8	Exit 9
Route 6 Sandwich		Dennis
Yermouthport		

Cape Cod Canal Bridge

South Weymouth, MA #4

"A SHOP DEDICATED TO QUILTERS. WHERE CUSTOMERS ARE PATRONS AND PATRONS BECOME FRIENDS"

We carry a complete line of Quality Fabrics.
Including: Hoffman, RJR (Jinny Beyer),
American Classic (Jeff Gutcheon), Hi-Fashion of New York,
Alexander Henry, Fabric Country, Benartex, P&B,
and many other famous brands.
All 100% cotton--Over 1,800 Bolts to pick from.

Other merchandise includes:
Batting, books, patterns,
stencils, and templates.
100% Egyptian cotton threads
for quilting/piecing.
A complete line of notions and
Metrosene and Sulky thread for
machine embroidery and hand work.

**Mon - Fri
9:30 - 9:30
Saturday
9:30 - 6:00**
During July & Aug.
Close Fridays at 6

WE DO SPECIALTY WORK AND
CONSIGNMENT ITEMS ARE ALSO
AVAILABLE

**1500 Main Street
(Route 18)   02190-1306
(617) 340-1351
Est: 1989**

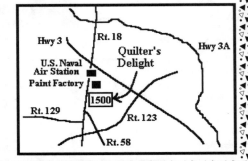

Pembroke, MA #5

**Mon - Sat
10 - 5:30
Sun 12 - 5**

158 Center St.   02359
(617) 293-6400
Est: 1973   1000 sq.ft.

Large selection of fabrics, hundreds of books, notions, batting & more. In a pre-civil war house.

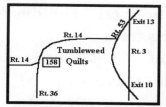

Plymouth, MA #6

Sew Crazy

**Mon - Fri
9 - 5:30
Sat 9 - 5
Sun 12 - 5**

5 Main St. Extension   Rt. 3A
(508) 747-3019   02360
Owner: Dottie Krueger
Est: 1977

Bernina, elna, & New Home Sewing Machines. Over 800 bolts of fabric and more coming. Notions & Lots of Patterns.

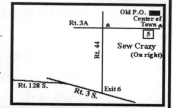

Quilting Bee —
Somewhere
between
Quilting A and Z

Walpole, MA #7

Quilts Ltd.

**Mon - Sat
10 - 5
Wed &
Thur til
8:30**

1428 Main St.   Bristol Square Mall
(508) 668-0145   02081
Est: 1983   1800 sq.ft.
Owners: Phyllis Nixon, Louisa Smith
& Mary Cisternelli

We carry Beautiful Cotton Fabric, Stencils, Notions, Unique Cards, Books, Specialty Items. Classes A.M. or P.M. Gift Certificates

West Roxbury, MA #8

Quilter's Nook

**Mon - Sat
10 - 4
Thur eve
7 - 9**

1766 Centre   02132
(617) 325-5633
Owner: Fran Monahan
Est: 1988   800 sq.ft.

Quilter's Nook is a very warm and friendly shop. We have over a thousand bolts of fabric, lots of books and classes too!

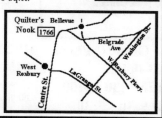

Cambridge, MA #9

Cambridge Quilt Co.

**Mon - Sat
10 - 6
Sun 12 - 5**

14 A Eliot St.   02188
(617) 492-3279   Est: 1975
Owner: Cathy Berry
1000 sq.ft.

Our shop maintains 1200 bolts of fabric and over 400 current quilt books, plus the latest in quilting supplies and classes!

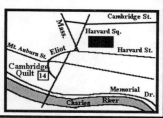

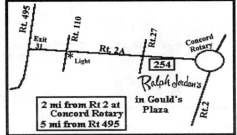

Georgetown, MA #11

The Crazy Ladies at The Quilted Acorn Shoppe

10 East Main Street   01833
(508) 352-7419   Est: 1983
Owners: Susan Nagle, Cynthia Erekson, & Sandra Schauer

Tues - Sat
9:30 - 4:30

Unique combination of Folk Art Painting, Quilting Supplies, Fabrics and Classes specializing in an "Antique Look". Many Homespuns Doll Patterns, too!!

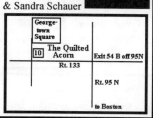

George-town Square

10   The Quilted Acorn
Rt. 133

Exit 54 B off 95N

Rt. 95 N

to Boston

Lowell, MA #12

The New England Quilt Museum

Boott Mills at the foot of John Street

Please Call for Current Information

(508) 452-4207
P.O. Box 7076
01852

Central St.

Lowell Connector from Rt. 495

Merrimack St.

Park

John St.

New England Quilt Museum

Boott Mills

Merrimac, MA #13

Red Barn Sewing & Yarn Center

90 West Main St.   Rte. 110
(508) 346-9292   Est: 1978
Owners: Helen Gosselin & Linda Ouellette   2000sq.ft.

Mon - Fri
9 - 5
Tues &
Thur til 7
Sat 9 - 4

100% cotton fabrics, quality yarns, patterns, books, supplies. Authorized New Home Sewing Machine Dealer Quilting, Knitting & Sewing Classes.

Red Barn Sewing & Yarn Center

Rte. 110   Exit 58
90   I - 495
I - 95
Exit 52

Shrewsbury, MA #14

Calico & Co.

Rt. 140   01545
(508) 842-2455
Owner: Joanne & Richard Erenius
Est: 1984   1000 sq.ft.

Tues - Fri
10 - 5
Wed til 6
Sat 10 - 4
Sun 1 - 5

Helpful & Friendly Service & Supplies for your every Quilting & Cross Stitch need. Classes to inspire your creativity.

Rt. 140 N.

Rt. 9 E.

Shrewsbury Center

CC   Calico & Co.

UPS

Rt. 20 E.

New Salem, MA #15

Fiber Naturals

#710 Route 202 Daniel Shays Hwy.
(800) FIBER 07 - (800) 342-3707
Owners: Karen & John Wallman

**Tues - Sat
9 - 6
or by
Appt.**

Largest selection of
Organic Cotton
Fabrics in the U.S.
Buy & sell quilts
made from all
natural fibers
(Including batting
and thread)
Quantity Discounts
& Mail Order

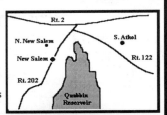

Sturbridge, MA #16

The Quilt and Cabbage

P.O. Box 534   01566
                          538 Main St.
                          (508) 347-3023

**Mon &
Wed - Sat
9:30 - 4:30
Sun 11 - 4
Closed Tues**

Quality fabrics
with an extensive
variety of quilting
stencils, books, &
supplies. Custom
quilts & pillows.
Woolen throws,
capes, caps &
Scarves.
Gift Items.

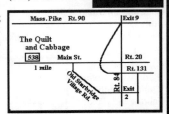

Amherst, MA #17

My Favorite Quilt Shop

65 University Dr.   01002
(413) 549-6009   Est: 1986
Owners: Marion Newell & Yvonne Berman
                          1000 sq.ft.

**Tues - Fri
10 - 5:30
Sat 10 - 4**

Everything for
quilters--batting,
books, classes,
cutters, hoops,
mats, needles,
patterns, rulers,
over 500 bolts of
fabric plus
friendly service.

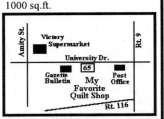

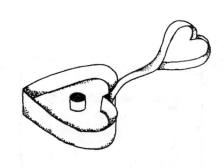

Springfield, MA #18

Double J Quilt Shop

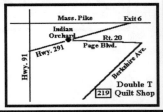

219 Berkshire Ave.
(413) 737-9605   01109
Owner: Jean Thibodeau   Est: 1983

**Mon - Sat
10 - 4**

We carry a wide
stock of fabrics
from Hoffman,
A.Henry, RJR,
Libas, MEH,
P&B, Bali and
Guatemalan
types. Plus Books
and Notions.

Massachusetts Guilds:
Quilter's Connection, 12 Monadnock Rd., Arlington, 02174
Plymouth Cty. Cranberry Quilters, P.O. Box 149, Carver, 02330
Chelmsford Quilters Guild, P.O. Box 422, Chelmsford, 01824
Merrimack Valley Quilters, P.O. Box 1435, Haverhill, 01831
Bayberry Quilters of Cape Cod, P.O. Box 1253, Orleans, 02653
New England Quilters Guild, Box 7136, Lowell, MA, 01852
Yankee Pride Quilt Guild, P.O. Box 833, Pittsfield, 01201

Other Shops in Massachusetts:

Auburn	Apple Tree Fabrics, 59 Auburn Street
Beverly	Colors, 132 Dodge Street
Bourne	Quilts 'n Things, 676 B Macarthur Blvd.
Brewster	The Yankee Craftsman, 230 Route 6A West
Chelsea	Golden Thimble, 345 Broadway
Cummaquid	The Picket Fence, Route 6A
Dover	Mehlco Crafts, 129 Centre
East Brookfield	Calico Crib, 108 Howe Street
East Longmeadow	Thimbleworks, 56 Shaker Road
Florence	Calico Fabrics, 52 Main Street
Great Barrington	Studio 83, 83 Main
Greenfield	Bear's Paw Quilts & Country Crafts, 1182 Bernardston Road
Holden	The Fabric Nook, 1087 Main
Medford	Going to Pieces, 420 Salem
Medway	Sisters, 97 Summer
Orleans	Pineapple Pantry, Rt 6A, Oracle Square
Pocasset	Quilts & Things, 674-B MacArthur Blvd.
Rehoboth	The Crafty Lady, 285 Winthrop
Rockport	Rocky Mountain Quilts, 2 Ocean Avenue
South Hamilton	Cranberry Quilters, 161 Bay Road
Southampton	South Hampton Quilts, P.O. Box 364
Southbridge	Stitch in Time, E. Main
Vineyard Haven	The Heath Hen Yarn & Quilt Shop, Tisbury Market Place
Wakefield	Susie Kate's Quilt Shop, 1117 Main
Wakefield	Sunburst Quilt & Yarn Shoppe, 27 Turtle
Wellesley	The Gifted Hand, 32 Church

Michigan's Upper Peninsula
Shops #54 thru #56   See Page 152

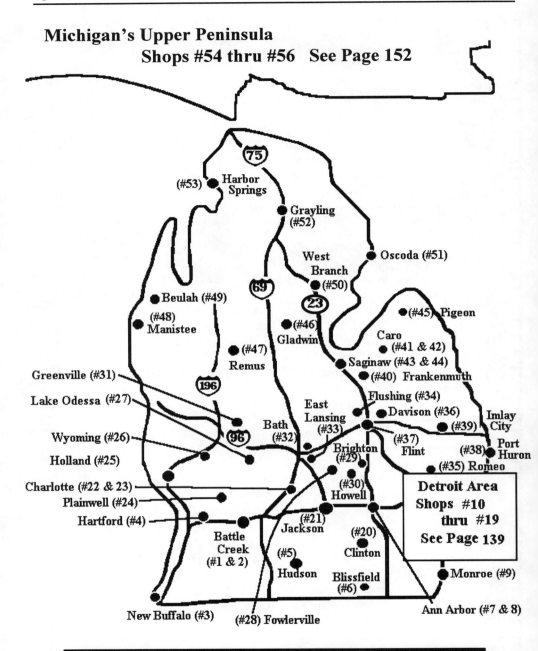

(#53) Harbor Springs

Grayling (#52)

Oscoda (#51)

West Branch (#50)

Beulah (#49)

(#48) Manistee

(#46) Gladwin

(#45) Pigeon

Caro (#41 & 42)

(#47) Remus

Saginaw (#43 & 44)

(#40) Frankenmuth

Greenville (#31)

Lake Odessa (#27)

Flushing (#34)

East Lansing (#33)

Davison (#36)

Imlay City

(#39)

Wyoming (#26)

Bath (#32)

Brighton (#29)

(#37) Flint

(#38)

Port Huron

Holland (#25)

Charlotte (#22 & 23)

(#30)

(#35) Romeo

Plainwell (#24)

Howell

Hartford (#4)

(#21) Jackson

(#20)

Detroit Area Shops #10 thru #19 See Page 139

Battle Creek (#1 & 2)

(#5) Hudson

Clinton

Blissfield (#6)

Monroe (#9)

New Buffalo (#3)

(#28) Fowlerville

Ann Arbor (#7 & 8)

MICHIGAN
56 Featured Shops

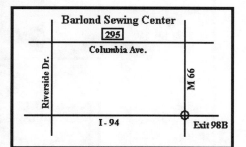

The Quiltery

1540 East Columbia Ave. 49017
(616) 965-2116   Est: 1981   2500 sq.ft.
Owners: Patty Pastor & Lynne Evans

Battle Creek, MI   #2

Visit us in our NEW location !

HUGE selection of quality 100% cottons by Hoffman, RJR, Jinny Beyer, P&B, Benartex, Red Wagon, Gutcheon, Roberta Horton, Chapel House, and others; Complete line of notions, books, patterns; Custom framing; Unique handmade gifts; Classes in quiltmaking and needle arts; Counted Cross-Stitch and other fancy embroidery supplies are ALWAYS 20% off suggested prices. Call for a free newsletter listing classes and sales.

Map:
- E. Columbia
- Columbia Ave. Exit
- M-66
- Main St.
- 1540 The Quiltery
- Exit 98B   Exit 100
- I-94

Tues - Fri
10 - 5
Sat 10 - 1

New Buffalo, MI   #3

The Quilt Cottage

By Appointment Only

Off Route 12 (Michiana)
(616) 469-0505 weekends
or (312) 404-5500 to set appt.
Owner: Barbara Marquard Wanke
Est: 1978

American Antique Quilts in Excellent condition displayed in enchanting cottage setting overlooking a stream in the dunes by Lake Michigan.

THE QUILT COTTAGE

Hartford, MI   #4

Sue Ellen's Quilt Shop

Tues- Fri 10 - 5

59591 Jerrdean Dr.   49057
(616) 463-5622   Est: 1980
Owner: Ruth Howader

100% Cotton Fabrics Books, Patterns, Notions, Custom Hand Quilting, Quilt Making, and other Quilting services. Cloth doll patterns and findings.

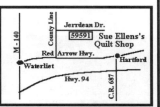

Map:
- County Line
- Jerrdean Dr.
- 59591 Sue Ellens's Quilt Shop
- M-140
- Red Arrow Hwy.
- Waterliet
- Hartford
- Hwy. 94
- C.R. 687

Hudson, MI   #5

Needles & Threads Quilt Shop

Mon - Fri 9 - 5
Sat 9 - 4

227 W. Main St.   49247
(517) 448-5901   Est: 1989
Owners: Bob & Maridell McKnight   1500 sq.ft.

A large assortment of 100% cotton fabrics. Quilting books, patterns, notions, classes & Custom Machine Quilting.

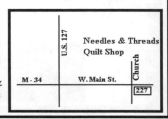

Map:
- U.S. 127
- Needles & Threads Quilt Shop
- M-34   W. Main St.
- Church
- 227

Blissfield, MI   #6

The Cotton Patch

115 W. Adrian St.
49228
(517) 486-2722

**Tues - Sat
10 - 5
Sun 12 - 5**

A Quilt and Gift Shop. Large selection of fabric, patterns, books, and quilting supplies. Gifts, crafts, and Amish dolls.

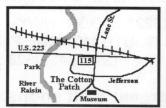

What's The Next Great Quilt Pattern? It's right at your Finger Tips.

Ann Arbor, MI   #7

THE LOOKING GLASS QUILT SHOP

1715 Plymouth
N. Campus Plaza
48105

**Mon - Thur
10 - 6
Fri & Sat
10 - 4**

(313) 662-2228
Carla Aderente

A full line quilt shop with wonderful fabrics, books, patterns, and notions. Come Say Hi !

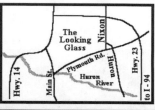

Viking Sewing Center

5235 Jackson Rd.   48103   (313) 761-3094
Owner: Dale Houghtaling   Est: 1968   4000 sq.ft.

**Mon - Fri 10 - 6
Sat 10 - 4**

Over 2000 Bolts 100% Cottons, Battings, Q-Snap frames, Classes, Books, Patterns, Notions, Heirloom Supplies, Unique threads. Viking, White & Bernina Machines

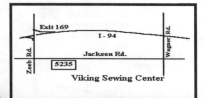

Ann Arbor, MI   #8

Monroe, MI   #9

GERWECK'S

HOMESPUN FABRICS

15221 S. DIXIE HWY.   48161
SOUTH MONROE PLAZA
(313) 242-9528

**One of Michigan's largest quilt shops.
with 4,000 sq. feet of quilting!**

Over 3,000 bolts of fabrics
1,500 plus of books and patterns
Complete supply of notions
100's of samples to inspire you
Gift items for quilters & Sewers
Complete line of PFAFF sewing
machines
Classes
Personal, helpful, and friendly service
Quality machine quilting service
7 years experience
Backings & battings available
up to 120" wide

**Hours: Mon-Sat 10:00-5:00
(fall & winter) Tues 10:00-9:00
Closed Sundays
Bus Tours
Welcome**

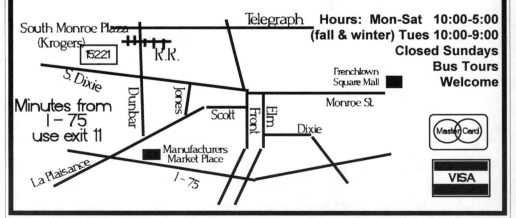

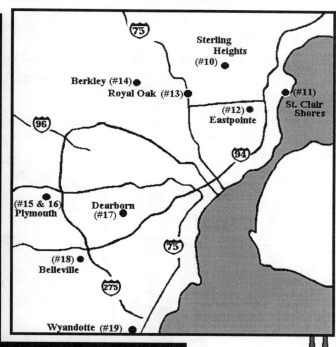

Sterling
Heights
(#10) ●

Berkley (#14) ●
Royal Oak (#13) ●

(#11) ●
St. Clair
Shores

(#12) ●
Eastpointe

(#15 & 16) ●
Plymouth

Dearborn
(#17) ●

(#18) ●
Belleville

Wyandotte (#19) ●

10 Featured Shops

Sterling Heights, MI   #10

Quilt-n Friends

4090 17 Mile Road   **48310**   **(313) 979-7422**
Owner: Gretchen L. Tatge   Est: 1983   1200 sq.ft.

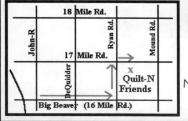

Mon - Fri 9 - 5   Sat 9 - 3
Mon & Thurs Eve til 8:30

100% Cotton
Fabrics

Notions ... Books ... Patterns ... Gifts
Classes Year Round ... Machine Quilting
Newsletter every 2 months ... Friendly Staff

"The Complete Quilt Shop"

St. Clair Shores, MI #11

The Quilters Patch

31380 Harper   48082
(810) 293-1999   Est. 1981
Owner: Beverly Maxvill
                    1200 sq.ft.

**Mon, Tues,
Fri 10 - 6
Thur 10 - 7
Sat 10 - 5**

Author of Victorian
Patchwork &
Embroidery
Meredith
Books—many
original designs
available for Quilts
& Blocks. Fabrics-
Notions-Books.

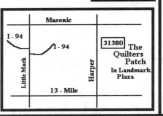

Eastpointe, MI #12

Mountain Clan Quilt Shoppe

22216 Gratiot Ave.   48021
(810) 772-8792   Est: 1993
Handmade goods   Owner: Peter Kue   800 sq.ft.
by Hmong Artists.

**Mon - Fri
10 - 6
Sat 10 - 4**

Custom made
Quilts.
Ready made Hand
applique Tops.
Special Orders
Welcome.
Hand Quilting at
reasonable prices.

Royal Oak, MI #13

Sew Quick

510 South Washington   48067
(313) 542-7174
Est: 1969   2500 sq.ft.
Owners: Ella Hafferkamp & Fay Munzinger

**Mon - Sat
9:30 - 5
Thur til 8**

Unique collection of
Fabrics, notions, &
Classes. Quilt fabrics
by Hoffman, RJR,
Alex. Henry, Kona &
more. Also smocking,
heirloom, knits,
suitings, lingerie.

Berkley, MI #14

Guildcrafters

2790 West 12 Mile Rd.   48072
(810) 541-8545
Owner: Jo Merecki
Est: 1982   2,500 sq.ft.

**Mon - Fri
10 - 6:30
Sat 10 - 5**

Largest Quilting
Fabric, Notion,
Stencil & Book
supply in the
area.
Classes,
Gifts.
Friendly Service.

Village Patchwork

Owner: Kitty Cole
& Jan Williams
(313) 453-1750
Est: 1989
1400 sq.ft.
100% Cotton Fabrics up to
108" wide.
Hoffman, P&B, RJR, Spiegel,
Concord, VIP, and many
more. Notions, Books,
Classes & Quilts.

Plymouth, MI #15

**WE SHARE THE SAME SHOP
900 Starkweather Street   48170**

**Mon - Fri 10 - 5 Sat 10 - 3
July & Aug   Mon - Fri 10 - 4**

Creative Quilting

Owner: Jean
Coleman
(313) 455-6155
Est: 1990
A unique machine
quilting service
individually tailored to
enhance your pieced top.
Choose from a variety
of border and
block designs.

Plymouth, MI #16

Dian's Quilt & Fabric Shop

Mon -Fri 10 - 5:30 Sat 10 - 4

794 S. Main   48170
(313) 459-3630
Owner: Dian Barnard
Est: 1982   1800 sq.ft.

A full service quilt shop
With 100% cotton fabrics, a variety of books, battings, patterns & lots of classes.

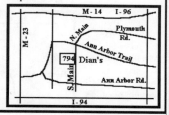

Dearborn, MI #17

Quilting Supplies Lessons, Books, Patterns, Fabrics

BERNINA
Authorized Dealer
Sales, Service & Repair
1033 Mason   48124
(313) 278-8681
Owners: Julie & Hazel Hollowell
Est: 1981

Mon - Sat 10 - 5   Tues & Thur til 8

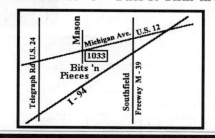

Belleville, MI #18

Sue's Quilt Shop

Mon - Fri 10 - 5 Sat 10 - 4

48120 Harris   48111
(313) 461-6540
Owner: Sue Crain
Est: 1989   504 sq.ft.

Fabrics, supplies, books and classes available. Quilts for Sale. Hand quilting service and custom orders taken. Reasonable prices

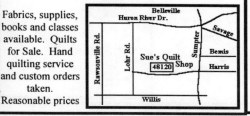

Wyandotte, MI #19

Quilt Basket

Mon - Sat 10 - 5

3359 Third Street   48192
(313) 282-5074
Est: 1983   1500 sq.ft.
Owners: Barbara Gunterman & Barbara Gorno

Fabrics--45", 90", 108". Books, Patterns, Counted Cross-Stitch. Classes in Applique Patchwork, & Quilting by Hand or Machine Handcrafted Gifts.

Clinton, MI #20

Tangled Thread Fabric Shop

114 1/2 Jackson St.   Box 438
(517) 456-4875   49236
Owner: Peg Voll
Est: 1993

**Mon & Fri
10 - 4
Tues-Thur
10 - 5
Sat 10 - 3**

We carry 100% cotton fabrics, an assortment of Battings, Patterns, Books. Always adding to our supplies. DMC Floss is available and some ready-made crafts for sale.

U.S. 12

Tec-Clinton St.

Fire Station

Hotel

Jackson St.

Tangled Thread

114

Jackson, MI #21

Hearts All Around

2614 Kibby Road   49203
(517) 789-8228   Est: 1983
Owner: Barbara Henderson
2,000 sq.ft.

**Mon - Fri
10 - 5:30
Tues &
Thur til 8
Sat 10 - 4**

Fabrics, books, patterns, quilt "gadgets", classes! Machine quilting services. Authorized Pfaff sewing machine dealer.

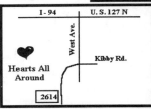

I - 94   U.S. 127 N

West Ave.

Hearts All Around

Kibby Rd.

2614

Charlotte, MI #22

Hen House of Charlotte

211 S. Cochran 48813
(517) 543-6454
Owner: Nancy Conn
Est: 1974

**Mon - Sat
10 - 5:30**

A craft shop specializing in quality materials including 100% cotton and homespun fabrics, Stenciling, X-Stitch, Tole Painting and Basket Supplies

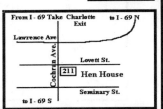

From I - 69 Take Charlotte Exit

to I - 69 N

Lawrence Ave

Cochran Ave.

Lovett St.

211 Hen House

Seminary St.

to I - 69 S

Charlotte, MI #23

J. B. Wares

136 S. Cochran   48813
(517) 543-2222
Owner: Beverly Rakowski
Est: 1991   3000 sq.ft.

**Mon - Fri
10 - 6
Sat 9 - 5**

Fabric, Quilting supplies, quilt frames, quilts, handcrafted wood items, wall hangings. We offer basting, binding & finishing services.

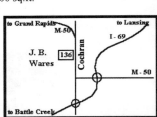

to Grand Rapids   to Lansing

M-50

I - 69

J. B. Wares   136

Cochran

M - 50

to Battle Creek

Plainwell, MI #24

Quilts, Etc.

211 Bannister   49080
(616) 685-9074   Est: 1990
Owners: Denise DeDoes &
1000 sq.ft.   Kathleen Edwards

**Tues - Sat
10 - 5**

Fabrics: Large Selection of 100% Cottons. Books, Patterns, Notions, Everything for the Quilter. Classes Quilts for Sale, Custom Orders.

211
Quilts Etc.

M - 131

Bannister

Main

Anderson

M - 89

Holland, MI #25

Field's World of Fabrics

281 East 8th
(616) 392-4806
Owner: Jack Veldman
Est: 1953   9000 sq.ft.

**Mon - Sat
9 - 9**

Packed with Fabrics ! Many Unique Prints.

Windmill Island

Field's

Historic Downtown

281

Chicago Dr.

BR. 31

Holland

Lincoln Ave.

U.S. 31

Mon - Fri 10 - 8
Sat 10 - 5

Wyoming, MI   #26

Caryn's Country Closet

73 — 54th St. S.W.   49548
(616) 538-6466

Est: 1991   3000 sq.ft.

- **Beautiful Fabrics**
- **MANY Books and Patterns**
- **Cross Stitch**
- **Stamp Art**
- **Custom Framing**
- **Gifts**
- **Lots of Classes**
- **Decorative Painting Books & Supplies**

Lake Odessa, MI   #27

Katie's Stitch 'N' Stuf

Mon - Sat 9 - 5:30

1017 4th Avenue   48849
(616) 374-8535   Est: 1986
Owner: Kathleen Stuart
1200 sq.ft.

Quilting Fabrics,
Large Selection
of Templates,
Books, Craft
Supplies, Yarn,
Counted Cross
Stitch, Crochet
Threads, Classes
Available.

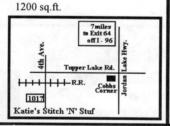

Fowlerville, MI   #28

Forgotten Arts

Mon - Fri 10 - 5
Sat 10 - 3

Friendliest Little Quilt Shop in
Livingston County
124 E. Grand River   48836
(517) 223-7992 Owner: Marsha West
Silk Ribbon   Est: 1993   1700 sq.ft.
Embroidery. Large
selection of 100%
cottons. Full line of
P&B Solids, Books,
Notions, Classes.
Antique Reproduction
sewing accessories for
your chatelaines.

Brighton, MI   #29

The Quilter's Shoppe

Mon - Fri 11 - 6
Sat 10 - 4

213 W. Main, Suite #4
(810) 220-0434   48116
Owner: Christine Laginess

A cozy quilt shop
carrying a large
selection of 100%
cotton fabric, books,
patterns, hand dyed
fabric and notions.

Howell, MI   #30

The Stitchery

1129 E. Grand River Ave.
(517) 548-1731   48843
Owners: Marci & Bill
Middaugh
Est: 1980   4000 sq.ft.

Mon - Fri 9 - 6
Sat 9 - 5   Sun 12 - 4
Call for Summer
Hours May - Aug

100% Cotton Prints including
Hoffman, RJR, J. Beyer, P&B,
Hopkins, Horton, Marcus, VIP,
Concord, Peter Pan, Spiegel,
Chapel Hill, Dan River,
Lunn Tiedye & Airbrush, Springs,
Gutcheon,Timeless Treasures etc.

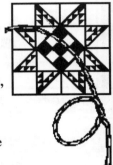

Silk Ribbon Embroidery Supplies
Over 100 Widths/Colors to choose
from plus other specialty ribbons
Books, Supplies, Notions, & Classes

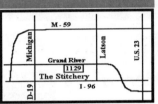

Livingston County's Largest Quilt Shop & Sewing Machine Center

Greenville, MI   #31

Janie's Button Box

218 S. Lafayette St.   48838
(616) 754-5544
Owner: Gail L. Besemer
Janie's Button Box is   Est: 1994
a quaint retail fabric   4000 sq.ft.
and craft supply
shop. We have a
large quilting
department with over
400 bolts of quality
fabric and hundreds
of quilting notions.

Mon - Fri
9 - 9
Sat 9 - 6
Winter
Sun 12 - 5

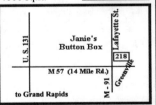

Bath, MI   #32

Quilting Memories
My Mother's Dream

13630 B. Main St.   48808
(517) 641-6522
Owner: Laurie Gass
Est: 1994   1500 sq.ft.

Mon, Thur, Fri
11 - 6
Tues, Wed 12 - 8
Sat 10 - 4
Sun 12 - 4

Complete supplies
for quilters.
Silk Ribbon
Brazilian Embroidery
Offer weekend and
evening classes.
Great assortment of
quilters cottons.

Quilter's Will —
being of
sound mind ? ?

East Lansing, MI　　#33

VISIT MICHIGAN'S LARGEST QUILT SHOPPE

Country Stitches has a full line of quilting books, quilting stencils, notions, basketweaving supplies, quilt related gifts and much more. We have over two thousand bolts of the most beautiful calicoes and solids available anywhere. Year round we have over a hundred quilts (both large and small) hanging on the walls. We have Viking, White, Bernina and New Home sewing machines and will have someone ready to answer your questions. Of course, we teach over a hundred classes in quilting, sewing, basketweaving, crafts and more. Our friendly, helpful staff is looking forward to your visit.

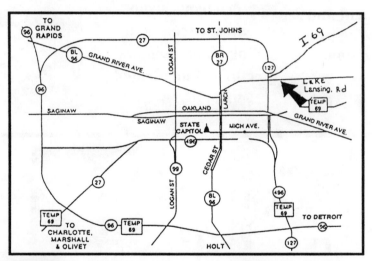

 # Country Stitches

Coolidge Court, across from Meijer
2200 Coolidge Rd at Lake Lansing Rd.,
East Lansing, MI 48823
(517) 351-2416 or
1-800-572-2031
Mon.- Fri. 10 a.m.-9 p.m.
Sat. 10 a.m.-6 p.m.

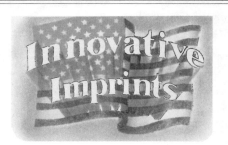

Innovative Imprints
10264 Beecher Road
Flushing, MI 48433-9728
(810) 659-9606

Stitch an heirloom quilt of treasured memories. Let us imprint your photographs to fabric.

Orders accepted by Mail or if you're in the area call for an appointment and see this amazing process in action.

We will imprint your photographs, color or black and white, to fabric, leaving a generous seam allowance. Your originals will be returned unharmed.

Flushing, MI   #34

Romeo, MI   #35

Country Girl Fabrics

67370 Van Dyke at Frontier Town
(810) 752-9600   48095
Owner: Cheryl Bittner
Est: 1986   1200 sq.ft.

Mon - Sat
10 - 6
Sun 11 - 6

Large selection of 100% cotton. Books, notions, and classes. Cross stitch also. Always friendly service and lots of fun.

Davison, MI   #36

Davison Fabrics

231 North Main Street   48423
(313) 653-2641
Owner: Donna Fritts
Est: 1975   1850 sq.ft.

Mon - Sat
9 - 5:30
Mon til 8
Fri til 6

We specialize in 2,800 bolts of calico prints, which are top of the line companies. Thousands of Craft Patterns!

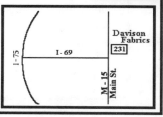

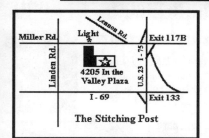
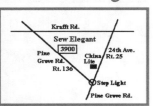

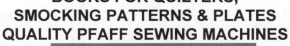

Imlay City, MI #39

The Pincushion

Mon - Thur
9:30 - 5:15
Fri 9:30 - 6
Sat 9:30 - 5

113 East Third Street   48444
(313) 724-7065   Est: 1971
Owner: Joyce Schihl

1800 sq.ft.

Quilting Fabrics & Supplies, Notions, Many Books, Patterns, Large Button Selection, Small Town Friendly Service. Our Customers are our Friends.

```
M 21  (Imlay  City Rd.)
                    The
                    Pincushon
          Almont Ave.  113      M - 53
                    3rd. St.
          I - 69
```

Frankenmuth, MI #40

Frankenmuth Woolen Mill

Winter 10 - 5
Summer
9 - 9
364 days a year

570 S. Main Street   48734
(517) 652-8121

Est: 1894

Look for our ad on the next page

We manufacture & sell wool filled comforters and accessories. We carry a full line of cotton fabrics and quilting supplies.

```
                    Geyer St.
   Zehnders    Cass St.       T
                              u
                    Frank.    s
   Bavarian   570   Woolen    c
   Inn        Main St. Mill   o
        CASS RIVER            l
                             a
```

Caro, MI #41

Quilt Talk Antiques

Tues - Thur
10 - 5:30
Fri 10 - 8
Sat 9 - 2

209 N. State St.   48723
(517) 673-7997 Res. 673-6115
Owner: Marilyn Van Allen
Est: 1990   1700 sq.ft.

Quilts and Tops 1890-1970. Some new Quilted Items. Antique furniture peices, Attic Treasures — old and enjoyable. Quilt Classes

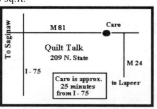

```
        M 81        Caro
To Saginaw
        Quilt Talk
        209 N. State      M 24
I - 75                  to Lapeer
        Caro is approx.
        25 minutes
        from I - 75
```

Caro, MI #42

Ruby's Yarn & Fabric

Mon- Wed & Sat 9-5:30
Thur & Fri 9 - 7

124 N. State   48723
(517) 673-3062
Owner: Ruby Reid   Est: 1966

Complete line of Quilting Fabrics & Supplies. Classes in Machine Quilting, Crazy Quilting, Applique, Wearable Art, Designing, and Silk Embroidery.

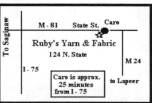

```
        M - 81    State St.  Caro
To Saginaw
        Ruby's Yarn & Fabric
        124 N. State        M 24
I - 75                    to Lapeer
        Caro is approx.
        25 minutes
        from I - 75
```

7402 Gratiot Rd.   48609
(517) 781-1202
Est: 1993   2000 sq.ft.

Owners:
Sally Morley & Pam
Mikkola

Saginaw Quilted Apple

Mon - Sat 9:30 - 5:30
Tues til 8

EVERYTHING FOR THE QUILTER &
SEWING ENTHUSIAST
Quality Fabrics, Books, Patterns, Notions
and many classes.   **BERNINA**

Saginaw, MI   #43

Saginaw, MI   #44

Calico Junction

2115 Bay Street   48602
(517) 793-6854   Est: 1982
Owners: Ann Bender, Pauline Duby
1200 sq.ft.   & Gail Kohlschmidt

Mon - Fri
10 - 5:30
Sat 10 - 4
Summer:
M- Sat 10 - 4

Classes, fabrics,
notions, books,
craft and quilt
patterns, stencils,
quilt frames and
gift certificates.
Personalized
Service.

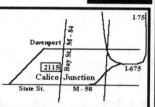

Pigeon, MI   #45

Pigeon River Mercantile & Wool Co.

40 S. Main 48755
(517) 453-2311   Est: 1992
Owners: Ed & Wanda Eichler

Mon - Fri
9 - 5:30
Fri til 8
Sat 9 - 5

Over 1000 bolts
100% cottons,
wool batts, custom
comforters, cross
stitch & knitting
supplies.
Country Gifts
and Toys.

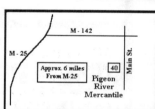

Gladwin, MI   #46

The Log Cabin Fabric Shoppe

663 East Cedar Avenue   48624
(517) 426-2772   Est: 1990
Owner: Cherie Thornton
2300 sq.ft.

Tues- Fri
10 - 4
Sat 10 - 3

We specialize in:
100% cotton fabrics
Books, Patterns,
Q-snap frames and
over 200 quilting
stencils. Classes
offered year 'round

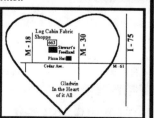

Remus, MI   #47

Towne Fabrics, Gifts, & Crafts

135 W. Wheatland Ave. 49340
(517) 967-8250
Owners: Ann Jensen and Jann Parks
Est: 1989   2300 sq.ft.

Mon - Fri
9 - 5:30
Sat 9 - 4

Quilts supplies from
fabrics to frames.
Also reed and cane
supplies. Our staff is
knowledgeable &
caring. Quilt show
July 22-23, 1994

Towne Fabrics

Just west of the
corner of M66
& M20. Half
way between
Mt. Pleasant
and Big Rapids

Manistee, MI   #48

The Quilted Heart

Mon - Sat
10 - 5

607 Parkdale   49660
(616) 723-7069
Owner: Judy Dunlap

Est: 1989   700 sq.ft.

Complete Line of
Quilting Supplies.
Fabrics, Books,
Notions, Craft
Patterns,
Handmade Quilts
Dolls, Unique
Gifts, Classes in an
old Farm House

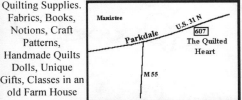

Beulah, MI   #49

Margie Ann's Quilt Shop

Mon - Sat
10 - 5
Call for
Summer Hrs.

194 South Benzie Blvd.   49617
(616) 882-4024
Owner: Marjorie Nelson
Est: 1980   2500 sq.ft.

Complete line of
quilting supplies.
Fabrics, Books,
Classes, Cross
Stitch, Handmade
Quilts and gifts.
Always helpful
and friendly.

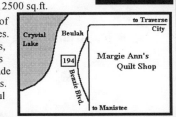

West Branch, MI   #50

Button Hole

Mon - Fri
9 - 6
Sat 9 - 5

208 West Houghton   48661
(517) 345-0431
Owner: Darlene Jones

Est: 1981   2000 sq.ft.

We have
Everything for
the Quilter ! !
Located in a
Victorian,
downtown
West Branch on
Business
Loop I - 75

Oscoda, MI   #51

Loose Threads Quilt Shop

Mon - Sat
10 - 5
Summer
Sundays
12 - 4

208 S. State St.   48750
(517) 739-7115   3500 sq.ft.
We Accept Visa, MC & Discover

Over 3500 sq.ft. of
Quilters Heaven !
More than 1200
Bolts of Fabric by
Benartex, Hoffman,
Spiegel, Jinney
Beyer, P&B, & More
250 Quilt Books.

Grayling, MI   #52

The Ice House Quilt Shop

Mon - Sat
10 - 5

509 Norway Street   49738
(517) 348-4821
Owner: Jill Wyman
Est: 1980

A unique shop for
the person
seeking quality in
all quilting
supplies.
Bernina Dealer.
Gifts--Gourmet
Foods.

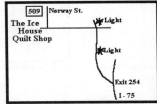

Harbor Springs, MI   #53

Quilting Barn

Mon - Sat
10 - 5
Year -
round

1221-A West Conway Road
(616) 347-1116   49740
Owners: Dolores P. Boese &
Karen Boese Schaller
Est: 1978   850 sq.ft.

Emmet County's
Complete Prof.
Quilting Store.
We have over
2000 bolts of
100% cotton fabric
and 19 years of
experience.

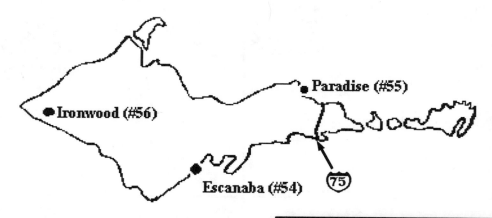

Paradise (#55)

Ironwood (#56)

Escanaba (#54)

(75)

3 Featured Shops

MICHIGAN'S UPPER PENINSULA

Escanaba, MI   #54

The Sewing Room

| Mon - Fri |
| 10 - 5 |
| Sat 10 - 3 |

1215 Ludington Street   49829
(906) 789-9595
Owner: Carmel Edgar
Est: 1988

Specializing
in quilt classes
and supplies.
Also Cross-
Stitch and
special orders.

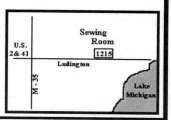

U.S. 2 & 41

Sewing Room

1215

Ludington

M - 35

Lake Michigan

Paradise, MI   #55

Village Fabrics & Crafts

| Summer |
| Daily 10-7 |
| Winter |
| 10 - 6 |
| Closed Tue |

Hwy M-123 W.   P.O. Box 254
(906) 492-3803   49768
Owner: Vicki Hallaxs   Est: 1986

Quilting, Counted
Cross Stitch,
Plastic Canvas,
Unique Crafts.
Hundreds of
Books and
Patterns—Many
of Area
Attractions. Gifts

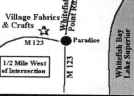

Village Fabrics & Crafts

Whitefish Point Rd.

M 123

Paradise

1/2 Mile West of Intersection

M 123

Whitefish Bay Lake Superior

Stitch in the Ditch —
Hidden Handiwork

Ironwood, MI   #56

The Fabric Patch

Owners: Arlene Wanink, Ruth Potter,
& Joanne Kuula

121 N. Lowell St. 49938   (906) 932-5260
Opened: 1981   1000 sq.ft.

Mon - Thur
9:30 - 5
Fri 9:30 - 6:30
Sat 9:30 - 4

Quilting and Craft
Headquarters of the North
Largest Selection in
The U.P. and Northern
Wisconsin

Choose from over
3500 Bolts of Quilting Fabrics
Huge Selection of
Quilting Books and Craft Patterns

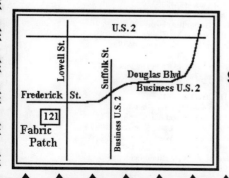

Authorized Dealer for
Viking and White
Sewing Machines & Sergers

Mail Order
Available

Michigan Guilds:
Trinity Piecemakers, 9077 Allen Road, Allen Park, 48101
U of M Faculty Women's Quilters, 2481 Trenton Court, Ann Arbor, 48105
Michigan Quilt Network, PO Box 339, Atlanta, 49709
Thunder Bay Quilters, Box 960 , Atlanta, 49709
McKay Library Quilters, 105 S. Webster Street, Augusta, 49012
Berrien Towne & Country Quilters, 4218 E. Tudor Road, Barrien Springs, 49103
Cal-Co Quilters' Guild, PO Box 867, Battle Creek, 49016
Bay Heritage Quilters Guild, 321 Washington Ave., Bay City, 48708
Pieceable Friends, 1991 E. Lincoln, Birmingham, 48009
Needlework & Textile Guild, 3219 Woodside Court, Bloomfield Hills, 48013
Brighton Heritage Quilters, 10281 Carriage Drive, Brighton, 48116
Casual Quilter's, 5418 Ethel, Brighton, 48116
North Star Quilters, 8436 E. 48th Road, Cadillac, 49601
Rivertown Patchworkers, 1849 Richmond, Cheboygan, 49721
West Michigan Quilters Guild, 13646 48th Avenue, Coopersville, 49404
Thumb Thimbles Quilt Guild, 5140 English Road, Clifford, 48727
General Dearborn Quilting Society, 915 Brady Road S., Dearborn, 48124
The Monday Night Quilters, 79939 40th Street, Decatur, 49045
St. Raymond's Quilters, 20212 Fairport , Detroit, 48205
The Crazy Quilters, 51106 Glenwood Rd., Dowagiac, 49047

Victorian Quilters Guild, PO 149, Empire, 49630
Bay deNoc Quilt Guild, P.O. Box 567, Escanaba, 49829
Care & Share Quilters, 4052 Fairgrove Rd., Fairgrove, 48733
Crazy Quilters, 7870 Peninsula, Farwell, 48622
Evening Star Quilters, 5327 Hopkins Flint, 48506
Genesee Star Quilters, 614 S. McKinley Road, Flushing, 48433
Rumpled Quilts Kin, PO Box 587, Frankfort, 49635
Tall Pine Quilters, 2073 Baldwin, Fremont, 49412
North Country Piecemakers, PO Box 10, Glennie, 48737
Au Sable Quilt Guild, PO Box 198, Grayling, 49738
Claire County Crazy Quilters, 5189 Hamilton, Harrison, 48625

Tulip Patch Quilting Organization, 600 Woodland Drive, Holland, 49424
Composing Threaders, 144 N. Trybom Drive, Iron River, 49935
Pieces & Patches Quilt Guild, Box 6294, Jackson, 49202
Log Cabin Quilters, 6632 Woodlea , Kalamazoo, 49004
West Michigan Quilter's Guild, PO Box 8001, Kentwood, 49518
Capitol City Quilt Guild, 7131 Willow Woods Cr., Lansing, 48917
Lansing Area Patchers, 3305 Sunnylane, Lansing, 48906
Anchor Bay Quilters, 5757 N. River Road, Marine City, 48039
Marquette County Quilters Assoc., PO Box 411, Marquette, 49855

Midland Mennonites, 364 E. Gordonville, Midland, 48640
Quilters Squared Quilt Guild, 2715 Whitewood Dr., Midland, 48640
Patchers at the Lake Shore, 926 Wellington Court, Muskegon, 49441
Niles Piecemakers, 1347 Louis Street, Niles, 49120
Greater Ann Arbor Quilt Guild, 22452 Meadow Brook, Novi,   48375
Calico Patch Quilters, 1550 W. Drahner Rd., Oxford, 48371
Little Traverse Bay Quilters Guild, PO Box 2022, Petoskey, 49770
Pinckney Quilting Sisters, 11383 Cedar Bend Dr., Pinckney, 48169
Island City Quilters, 180 S. Sherwood, Plainwell, 49080

Plymouth Piecemakers , 11768 Turkey Run, Plymouth, 48170
Portage Quilt Guild, 6278 Redfern Circle, Portage, 49002
Loose Threads, 37550 Hebel Road, Richmond, 48062
Oakland County Quilt Guild, 282 Rose Briar Drive, Rochester Hills, 48309
Piece to Peace Quilting Club, 3914 Mission, Rosebush, 48878
Friendship Ring Quilt Guild, 305 E. Harrison St., Shelby, 49455
Wyandotte Museum Quilters, 13407 Pullman, Southgate, 48195
Piecemakers Quilt Guild, 202 Jay Street, St. Charles, 48655

Tri County Quilt Guild, 4619 Hatherly Place, Sterling Heights, 48310
Sunrise Quilters, 318 N. McArdle Road, Tawas City, 48763
Eton Center Quilters, 7946 McKinley, Taylor, 48180
Trenton Quilters, 3398 Norwood Dr., Trenton, 48183
Cass River Quilters' Guild, 6977 Sohn Road, Vassar, 48768
Northern Lights Quilt Guild, 1315 Dewey, Wakefield, 49968
Greater Ann Arbor Quilt Guild, 29807 Autumn Lane, Warrren, 48093
Metro Detroit Quilt Guild, 6148 28 Mile Road, Washington, 48094
Barrien County Coverlet Guild, PO Box 529, Watervliet, 49098
Quilt-N-Friends, 6332 Aspen Ridge Blvd., West Bloomfield, 48332
OTLB Quilters, 2831 Highland Drive, West Branch, 48661

Other Shops in Michigan:

Bad Axe	The Country Goose, 255 E. Huron
Belding	The Cloth Cupboard, 304 W. Main
Boyne City	Apple - Bee Coterie, 111 N. Park
Cadillac	Julie Ann Fabrics, 111 S. Mitchell
Caledonia	Rainbow's End Variety, 9343 Cherry Valley Ave.
Chassell	Einerlei Shop, 422 Wilson Memorial Drive
Commerce	Quilt Corner, 8275 Cooley Lake Rd.
Essexville	Marjorie's, 1602 Woodside
Fairview	Creative Corner Quilt Shop, 1526 N. Abbe Rd
Ferndale	Traurig's Quilt & Pillow Shop, 22050 Woodward
Grand Haven	The Stitching Post Plus, 944 Robbins Rd.
Grand Rapids	Wild Goose Chase, P.O. Box 1166
Grand Rapids	Owen Smith Quilting Centers, 4051 Plainfield N.E.
Grand Rapids	The Daisy Den Stitchery, 2290 44th S.E.
Hillsdale	Country Fabrics, 2831 N. Osseo
Hillsdale	My Favorite Things, 33 N. Broad
Ishpeming	Nancy's, 322 S. Lake
Jenison	Country Needleworks, Inc., 0-584 Chicago Avenue
Lambertville	Village Fabrics & Crafts, 8019 Summerfield Rd.
Mason	Keans Hallmark & Variety, 406 S. Jefferson
Michigan Center	Ardie's Boutique, 5459 Page
Middleton	Calico Cupboard, 5409 S. Ely Highway
Midland	Material Mart, 86 Ashman Circle
Montrose	Country Novelties, 14274 Marshall Road
Niles	Down Under Quilts, 16 South 12th Street
Norway	Northern Expression, 640 Main
Omer	Quilt Patch Antiques, 429 E. Center Street
Paw Paw	The Vintage Sampler, 51599 Ct. Rd. 653
Petosky	Calico Crafts, 1691 Spring P.O. Box 2390
Port Sanilac	Country Magic II, 56 S. Ridge
Portland	Quilters Gallery, 1419 E. Grand River
Prudenville	Chris' Frabrics, West M - 55
Riverdale	Country Clip N Sew, 11995 W. Monroe Road
Saline	Cross Roads Fabric & Quilt Shop, 141 E. Michigan
South Haven	Calico Creations, 265 Center St.
Spring Lake	Purple Turtle Quilts & Gifts, 17567 Valley City
Traverse City	BJ's Cozy Quilts, Etc., 229 E. Front Street
Traverse City	Boyd's and Sew Much More, 1105 S. Garfield Ave.
Vassar	One of a Kind Crafts & Gifts, 108 Goodrich St.

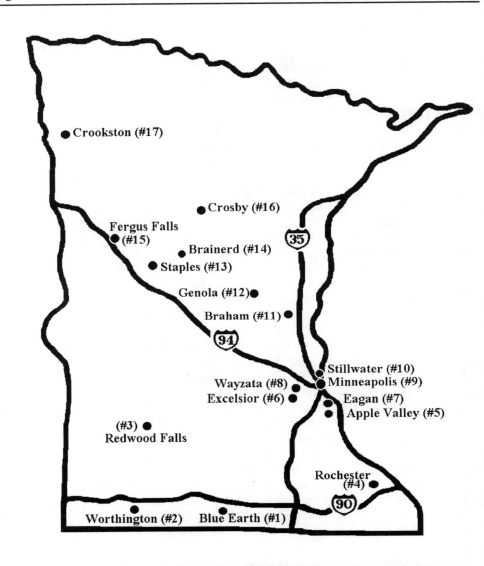

17 Featured Shops

Blue Earth, MN   #1

Quilt Company

Mon - Sat
9 - 5
Thur til 8

120 S. Main   56013
(507) 526-2647
Est: 1988   1300 sq.ft.
Owners: Lola Hendrickson, Jolyn Olson,
    & Tracy Peterson

Complete line of Quilting Needs. Fabric, Patterns, Notions, Classes, Service. Also Custom Quilting.

```
           I - 90
        County Rd. 16
        6th St.
    120  Quilt          U.S. 169
    Main St. Company
        7th St.         County Rd. 16
```

Worthington, MN   #2

CRAFTY CORNER
Quilt & Sewing Shoppe

Mon - Thur
9 - 5:30
Fri 9 - 9
Sat 9 - 4

1820 Oxford St.   56187
(507) 372-2707
Owner: Zuby Jansen
Est. 1982   2600 sq.ft.

We sell 100% cotton fabrics. 1500 bolts in stock. Many Patterns Bernina Sewing Machine sales & Service Quilting Supplies!

```
              I - 90
   Hwy 59 S        Northland Mall        Hwy 60 S
   Burlington Ave.
        Grand Ave.
              Omaho
                Milton
                  Douglas   Oxford
                        1820  Crafty Corner
```

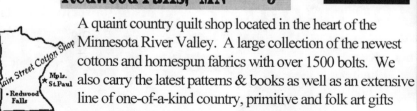

MAIN STREET
COTTON SHOP

Owner: Jean Lepper

141 E. 2nd St.   Redwood Falls, MN   56283
(507) 637-5221 or (800) 624-4001

Mon - Fri
9 - 5
Thurs 9 - 8
Sat 9 - 4

Redwood Falls, MN   #3

A quaint country quilt shop located in the heart of the Minnesota River Valley. A large collection of the newest cottons and homespun fabrics with over 1500 bolts. We also carry the latest patterns & books as well as an extensive line of one-of-a-kind country, primitive and folk art gifts

Colored mail-order catalog available
Call (800) 624-4001   24 hrs. day
Same day mail order service

```
Main Street Cotton Shop
        Mpls.
      * St.Paul
  • Redwood
    Falls
```

Rochester, MN   #4

Patchwork & Pinafores

324 Elton Hills Drive N.W.
(507) 288-2040   55901
Owner: Susan Dillinger   Est: 1990
2375 sq.ft.

1300 + Bolts of fabric, books, patterns. notions, gifts, classes.

**Mon - Sat
9 - 5
Tues &
Thur til 9**

Apple Valley, MN   #5

Fabric Town

7655 West 148th St.   55124
(612) 432-1827
Owner: Barbara Sherman
Est: 1981   3000 sq.ft.

**Mon - Fri
9:30 - 8:30
Sat 9:30 - 5
Sun   12 - 5**

Approx. 1000 bolts of 100% cottons, books, patterns. Crafts and cross-stitch. Classes, Friendly Knowledgeable Staff.

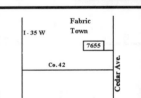

Excelsior, MN   #6

The Sampler

**Quilting, Wall Stencils,
Smocking, Cross-Stitch.
Lots of Patterns & Gifts.**

314 Water Street   55331   (612) 474-4794

Owner: Karol
         Plocher

Est: 1977   1450 Sq.ft.

**Mon - Fri
9:30 - 6:30
Saturday
9:30 - 5:30
Sunday
12 - 4:30**

Directions: Take Highway 494 to Highway 7 West - go to 7th Stop Light Turn Right at first street. Turn Right, approx. 1 1/2 blocks on left. We're in the Excelsior Mill

Eagan, MN   #7

Country Needleworks

1284 Town Centre Dr. #119
(612) 452-8891   55123
Owner: Sandy Quam   Est: 1989
1200 sq.ft.

| Mon - Thur |
| 9:30 - 8 |
| Fri & Sat |
| 9:30 - 5 |

A Country Shop offering the finest in cotton fabrics, books, patterns and quilting supplies. Classes available.

Minneapolis, MN   #9

Eydie's Country Quilting

2822 West 43rd. Street   55410
(612) 929-0645
Owners: Eydie & Tim Happel
Est: 1986   900 sq.ft.

| Mon - Sat |
| 10 - 5 |
| Sun 12 - 4 |

100% Cotton Fabrics, Patterns, Books, Supplies. Located in a Vintage House !

35 W to Crosstown
West to Xerxes Exit
North on Xerxes to 43rd.
Right on 43rd St. for
2 1/2 blocks.

Wayzata, MN   #8

Wayzata Quilting Emporium

| Mon - Wed |
| 9 - 6:30 |
| Summer 9 - 5 |
| Thurs Always |
| 9 - 8:30 |
| Fri & Sat 9 - 5 |

927 East Lake Street   55391
(612) 475-2138
Owner: Darlene Myers
Est: 1980   1650 sq.ft.

... country gifts
... dolls and quilts
... books and patterns
...quilting supplies
... over 1500 bolts of cotton
... classes year round
... a friendly staff to serve you
... call or stop in for our class brochure

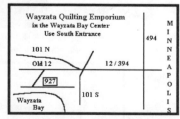

Twenty minutes west of Minneapolis
— over 1500 bolts of cotton —
A complete quilt shop !

Quilter's Children — Chips off the ole Block

Stillwater, MN #10

And Sew On

1672 S. Greely St.   55082
(612) 430-9441   Est: 1990
Owners: Deborah Gangnon &
Roanne Axdahl

100% cotton   2000 sq.ft.
quilting fabrics,
knit fabrics,
notions, patterns,
books, classes and
Viking / White
sewing machines.
Lots of great
samples !

Mon & Wed
9:30 - 6
Tue & Thur
9:30 - 8
Fri 9:30 - 5
Sat 9:30 - 4

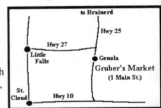

Braham, MN #11

Rosemary's Quilts & Baskets

103 W. Central Dr.   55006
(612) 396-3818   Est. 1988
Owner: Rosemary Brabec
1500 sq.ft.

Quilting Fabrics,
patterns, notions
and large selection
of books. Classes
year 'round.
Friendly, expert
service. Also
basketry supplies
and classes.

Mon - Thur
9 - 5
Fri 9 - 6
Sat 9 - 4
Closed July Sats

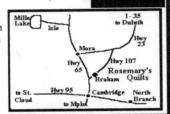

Genola, MN #12

Gruber's Market

#1 Main Street   56364
(612) 468-6435   Est: 1936
Owners: Sue Poser & Paul Gruber
8000 sq.ft.   Free Catalog

The most unique
Quilt Shop
you'll ever enter.
5000+ Bolts
Cotton. A true
General Store with
German sausages,
meats and more!

Daily
7 - 10

Staples, MN #13

QUILTING MEMORIES

216 2nd. Ave.   56479   (218) 894-1776
Owners: Lorna Wiens & Sue Caquelin

Mon - Fri
10 - 5:30
Sat 10 - 3

Custom Machine
Quilting,
Fabric,
Quilting Supplies,
Patterns, Classes
and Friendly
Service.

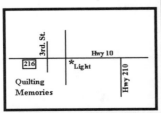

Brainerd, MN #14

Country Fabrics & Collectibles

**Mon - Sat
10 - 5
Thur til 8**

909 S. 6th St.   56401
(218) 829-7273
Owner: Lou Rademacher   Est: 1971

Our 1800
Mercantile
is filled with the
latest craft patterns,
fabrics, & gifts.
Stop in for a
cup of cider.

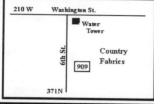

Fergus Falls, MN #15

The Quilter's Cottage

**Tues - Fri
10 - 5
Sat 10 - 3
Closed
July Sats**

715 Pebble Lake Rd.   56537
(218) 739-9652
Owner: Cheri Steenbock
Est: 1988   1500 sq.ft.

Everything
you need for
quilting
including help
and a friendly
smile.

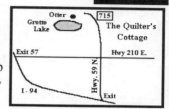

Crosby, MN #16

Quilter's Country Store

**Mon - Fri
10 - 5
Sat 10 - 2**

129 W. Main St.   56441
(218) 546-7166   Est: 1992
Owner: Rae A. Kittelson   2800 sq.ft.

Fabulous fabrics,
books, patterns.
Custom machine
Quilting. Classes
and great service.
Quilt Club
meeting Tuesday
evenings.

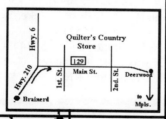

Crookston, MN #17

Z Place

**Mon - Sat
9 - 5:30**

101 N. Main St.   56716
(218) 281-5218
Owners: Fred & Jan Ziegler
Est: 1989   2500 sq.ft.

Fabric and Supplies
for the Beginner
and Advanced
Quilter.
Classes Available
Custom Quilts
Made.

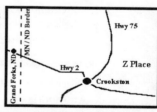

Notes

Minnesota State Guild:
Minnesota Quilter, Inc., 8616 Darnel Rd., Eden Prairie, 55344
Minnesota Guilds:
Lakes Area Quilters, 1219 S. Nokomis, Alexandria, 56308
Hands all around Quilters, PO Box 329, Braham, 55006
Pine Tree Patchworkers, P.O. Box 935, Brainerd, 56401
Quilters along the Yellowstone Trail, Box 261, Buffalo Lake, 55314
Chaska Area Quilt Guild, P.O. Box 44, Chaska, 55318
Loon Country Quilters, 4646 Hwy. 2 E., Grand Rapids, 55744
Rochester Quilters' Sew-Ciety, P.O. Box 6245, Rochester, 55903
Thief River Falls quilter's Guild, Box 121, Thief River Falls, 56701

Other Shops in Minnesota:

Alexandria	Quilt Shop, 1903 City Rd. 22
Angora	Country Crafts, 8719 Highway 53
Champlain	The Quilting Duck, 10914 Noble Ave. N.
Hayward	Calico Hutch, P. O. Box 51
Minneapolis	Glad Creations Inc., 3400 Bloomington Ave. S.
Morris	R & R Fabric, 1001 Atlantic Avenue
Oklee	The Oklee Quilt Shop, 128 S. Main
Rochester	Linda's Quiltery, 2806 Northern Valley Dr. NE
St. Cloud	Granny's Legacy, 25284 Lake Rd.
St. Paul	Country Needleworks, 1284 Town Centre Drive
St. Paul	The Country Peddler, 2242 Carter Ave.
Staples	Fabric Center, 216 End. Ave. N.E.
Wells	The Creative Needle, 135 S. Broadway

Mississippi

Mississippi State Guild:

      Mississippi Quilt Association, 909 N. 31st Ave., Hattiesburg, 39401

Shops in Mississippi:

Clinton	Olde Towne Stitchery, 301-A E. College Street
Hattiesburg	The Quilted Heart, 1901 Hardy St.
Jackson	Joy's Busy Hands, 2565 Mcfadden Road
Laurel	Magnolia Blossom Fabrics, North Laurel Shopping Center
Lucedale	The Fabric Barn, 125 E. Main
Maben	Springer's Dry Goods, 124 Highway 15
Meridian	The Craft Cottage, 2928 N. Hills Street
Tupelo	Heirlooms Forever, 1413 W. Main Street
Vicksburg	Stitch - N - Frame Shop, 2222 S. Frontage Road

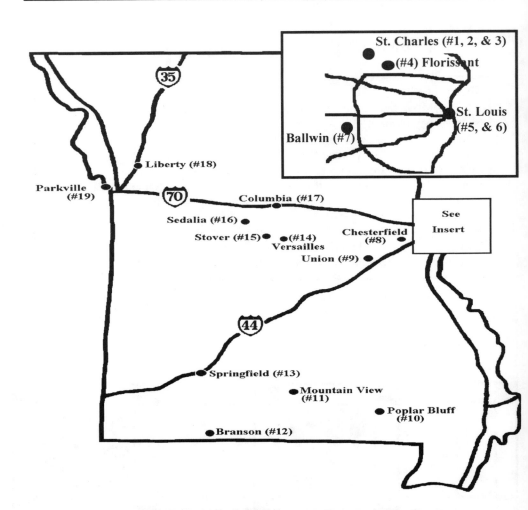

19 Featured Shops

St. Charles, MO   #1
Huning's Quilt Fair

334 North Main Street   63301
       (314) 946-5480   Est: 1860
Owner: Monica Vandeven   5200 sq.ft.

HANDMADE QUILTS
Pillow Cases
Pillow Case Doll Kits
Quilt Tops
Quilt Blocks (Bucilla & Tobin)
Flosses (DMC & J & P Coats)
Quilt Stencils & Frames
Quilt Backing, Books & Patterns
Largest Selection of Fabrics in town
Nancy Frock Dresses
Nursing Home Dresses
Hospital Gowns
Magic Lady Panty Girdles
Exquisite Form & Platex Bras
Dearform Slippers
    VISA MASTER DISCOVER

Mon - Sat
9 - 5:30
Sun
11 - 5

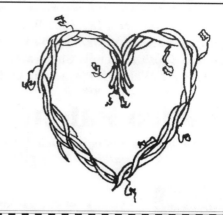

Wedding Ring —
A symbol or love,
whether jewelry
or grandma's quilt.

St. Charles, MO   #2
Patches Etc. Quilt Shop

337 South Main   63301
(314) 946-6004
Owner: Ann Watkins
Est: 1979   850 Sq.ft.

Mon - Sat
9:30 - 5
Sun 11 - 5

Quilts, Fabric
and Patterns --
Certified
appraisals by
Ann Watkins.
Also visit out
Craft Center and
Button Shoppe

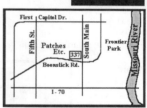

Historic
Saint
Charles

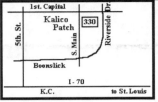
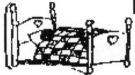

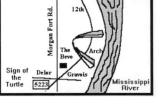

Ballwin, MO   #7

In Stitches

Mon - Sat
9:30 - 4:30
Tues, Wed
& Thur til 8

14664 Manchester Rd.   63011
(314) 394-4471
Owner: Pam Bryan
Est: 1988

We carry over 2600 bolts of fabric including designer fabrics.

In Stitches is located just west of St. Louis 4 1/2 miles west of I - 270 on Manchester Rd.

Chesterfield, MO   #8

Dotty's Quilt Shop

Mon - Fri
7 - 4
Sat 10 - 2

769 Spirit of St. Louis Blvd.
(314) 532-7300   63005
Est: 1968
Owners: Lester E. & Dortha L. Wheatley

Machine & Hand Quilting, Calico Fabrics, Craft Patterns and Items.

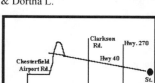

Union, MO   #9

Material Things

Mon - Fri
9 - 5:30
Sat 9 - 3

204 East Main   63084
(314) 583-1767
Owner: Janet Niermeyer
Est: 1991   1000 sq.ft.

Quilts, Pillows, Fabric, Books, Patterns, QSnap™ Frames.

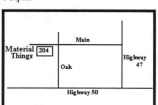

Poplar Bluff, MO   #10

Quilters Craft Shop

8:30 - 5:30
Except Fri.
close @ 5

1302 South 11th   63901
(314) 785-6514
Owner: Mary L. Hoeinghaus
Est: 1984   800 sq.ft.

100% cottons, books & Patterns specialize in Quilts, quilt racks and many other crafts.

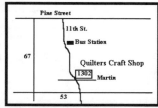

Mountain View, MO   #11

Calico Cupboard

Mon - Fri
10 - 5
Sat 10 - 3

221 Oak St.   65548
(417) 934-6330   Est: 1981
Owner: Darlene Godsy
1500 sq.ft.   Catalog $2.00

600 bolts of cotton fabrics, lots of patterns, books, notions, counted cross stitch books and supplies plus friendly Ozarks service.

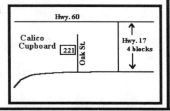

Branson, MO   #12

Quilts & Quilts

Summer
8 - 8 Daily
Winter
9 - 6 Daily

1137 West Hwy. 76   65616
(417) 334-3243
Owner: Marlys Michaelson
Est: 1981   8,000 sq.ft.

Largest and most complete quilting shop in the 4 state area. Handmade Quilts. Over 4000 bolts of Calico and Gifts !

Springfield, MO #13

The Quilt Shoppe

**Tues - Fri
9:30 - 5:30
Sat 10 - 4**

2762 South Campbell   65807
(417) 883-1355
Owners: Rosalie Carey & Gilda
Est: 1978   2100 sq.ft.   Young

2000 Bolts of
100% cotton,
books, patterns,
notions, Q-snap
frames, 120" wide
lining, classes,
x-stitch supplies.

Map:
- Sunshine
- Bass Pro
- Campbell
- National
- Gleanstone
- The Quilt Shoppe 2762
- Battlefield Mall
- Battlefield

Versailles, MO #14

Clark's Fabrics

**Mon - Sat
9 - 5**

West Vue Shopping Center
Hwy 5 & 52 W.   65084
(314) 378-5696   Est: 1964
Owner: Kirk Chapman   1800 sq.ft.

Great selection of
all types of fabric,
including quilting,
clothing and home
decorating.
Buttons, Buttons,
Buttons !

Map:
- Clark's Fabrics
- West Vue Shopping Center
- Hwy. 5 & 52
- Hwy.52
- Hwy. 5
- Versailles

Stover, MO #15

Nolting's Longarm Mfg.

**Mon - Fri
7:30 - 4
Sat & Sun
By Appt.**

Hwy. 52 East R.R. #3   Box 147
(314) 377-2713   65078
Fax: (314) 377-4451
Owner: Frederick D. Nolting
Est: 1984

Five sizes of
longarm quilting
machines and
tables. Quilting
being done
everyday !

Map:
- Nolting's Longarm Manufacturing
- R.#3 Stover   Cole Camp
- Hwy. 52 East
- Hwy 65

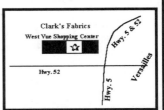

Machine
Quilting —
Requires a big
heart and a
long arm.

Sedalia, MO #16

Quilt Crazy
Ye Olde Fabric Shoppe

**Mon - Fri
9:30 - 5:30
Sat 10 - 5**

2302 West Broadway   65301
(816) 826-9055
Owner: Dorothy Bartley
Est: 1990   1400 sq.ft.

100% Cottons,
Books, Patterns,
Counted Cross-
Stitch, Quilting
Supplies. Your
one-stop quilt
shop.

Map:
- Quilt Crazy - Ye Olde Fabric Shoppe
- Fairview Center   2302   Broadway   50
- State Fair Blvd.
- 65
- "Y" - 16th St.
- Missouri State Fair

Columbia, MO #17

Silks & More
Fine Fabrics

**Mon - Thur
10 - 7
Fri & Sat
10 - 5**

2541 Bernadette Dr.   65203-4674
(314) 446-2655   5200 sq.ft.
Owner: Millie Kaiser   Est: 1985

Large selection of
beautiful 100%
cotton prints and
solids, designer
fabrics, books,
patterns, and notions.
Come see us!

Map:
- I - 70
- Silks & More   2541
- Bernadette
- Stadium Blvd.
- Ash
- Worley

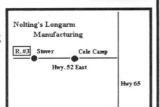

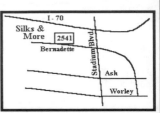

Liberty, MO #18

Liberty Quilt Shop

131 South Water   64068
(816) 781-7966
Owner: Kathleen Glasco
Est: 1988   1500 sq.ft.

**Mon - Sat
10 - 5**

Over 2000
bolts of 100%
cotton. Books,
patterns, and
friendly,
helpful staff !

```
Kansas (Hwy 152)

Water St.    Mill St.    Lightburn (Hwy 33)

Liberty Quilt
131  Shop
```

Parkville, MO #19

Peddler's Wagon

115 Main   64152
(816) 741-0225
Owners: Teri Hahs
Est: 1982   3400 sq.ft.

**Tues - Sat
10 - 5**

Quilts, Smocking
Supplies, Quilting
supplies, Fabric,
Primitive Rug
Hooking, Country
Gifts, Ladie and
Friends Dolls.

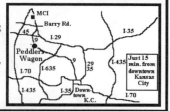

Missouri State Quilter Guild, Rt. 1, Box 1060, Cassville, 65625
Missouri Guilds:
Booneslick Trail Quilters' Guild, P.O. Box 542, Columbia, 65205
Flower Valley Quilting Guild, P.O. Box 9002, Florissant, 63032
Nitetime Needlers, P.O. Box 28731, Kansas City, 64118
Northland Quilters' Guild, P.O. Box 46654, Kansas City, 64118
Quilters Guild of Greater Kansas City, P.O. Box 22561, Kansas City, 64113
Country Patchworkers, P.O. Box 365, Marshall, 65340
Ozark Piecemakers Quilt Guild, P.O. Box 4931, Springfield, 65808

Other Shops in Missouri:	Augusta	Tips 'N Trix Shop, 5625 High
Branson	The Cotton Patch Quilt Shop, 2420 W. Hwy. 76	
Cape Girardeau	Uniquely Sew, 1141 N. Kingshighway	
Cape Girardeau	Linda's Quilt Place, 1626 New Madrid	
Carrollton	Quilted Thimble, 14 N. Main Street	
Columbia	Tina Fabrics, 615 East Broadway	
Farmington	Old Village Quilt Shop, 113 S. Jackson Street	
Florissant	Helen's Hen House, 180 W. Dunn Rd.	
Fredericktown	Carolina Fabric Center, 130 E. Main	
Hannibal	The Hickory Stick, 326 N. Main Street	
Joplin	Bernina of Joplin, Inc., 610 Main	
Lebanon	H & H Fabric and Quilt Center, 326 W. Commercial Street	
Lees Summit	Browning's Fabrics & Notions, 321 South Main	
Mt. Vernon	Grannie's Patchworks, 105 E. Dallas Street	
Osceola	Quilts and Crafts, 312 Second Street	
Sedalia	D & T Quilt Shop, Route 6 #232	
Springfield	A-1 Sewing Machine Co., 908 North Glenstone	
Springfield	Gloria's Quilts Etc., 3847 W. Driftwood	
St. Joseph	Heartland Quilt Company, 1824 Sacramento	
St. Joseph	Bits & Pieces, 3606 Beck Road	
Ste. Genevieve	Monia's Unlimited, 316 Market	
Ste. Genevieve	Quilted Treasures by Huber Crafts, 199 North Main	
Thayer	Merendi's Quilts & Crafts, 204 Chestnut Street	
Waynesville	Sampler Basket, 123 N. Benton Street	

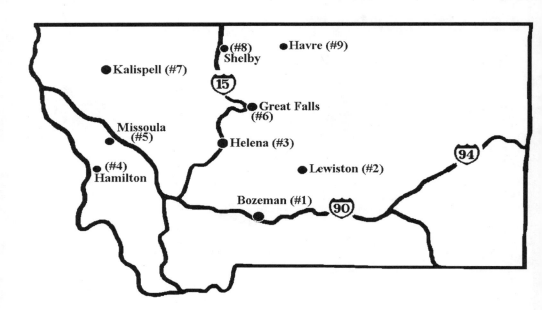

MONTANA

9 Featured Shops

WHEN LIFE GETS HECTIC DON'T FORGET TO MAKE TIME FOR QUILTING

Bozeman, MT #1

The Patchworks

126 East Main   59715
(406) 587-2112
Owner: Margo Krager
Est: 1976   3500 sq.ft.

**Mon - Sat
9:30 - 5:30
Thurs til 8
Sun 12 - 5**

We have over 1900 Bolts of Fabric
and specialize in reproduction
cottons of 4 time periods from the
early 1800's until 1945.

Helena, MT #3

Calico Cupboard

601 Euclid Ave. # C   59601
(406) 449-8440
Est: 1989   2000 sq.ft.
Owners: Ivy Crawford & Dianne Ducello

Specialize in fine
100% cotton
Fabric, unique
patterns, quilting
books, notions,
classes and gifts.

**Mon - Sat
10 - 5**

I Quilt
Therefore I Am

Lewistown, MT #2

Megahertz

223 W. Main St.   59457
(406) 538-8531
Est: 1992   3300 sq.ft.

**Mon - Sat
9 - 5:30**

Fabrics, Notions,
· Antiques.
Authorized Pfaff
Dealership.
Custom Embroidery,
Quilt and Sewing
Classes. Stop in and
see the Historic
Megahertz Builting.

In the Center of
♥ Lewistown
Montana

Hamilton, MT #4

The Fabric Shop

201 S. Second   59840
(406) 363-3471   1200 sq.ft.
Owner: Rosalie Reinbold
Featuring over 700   Est: 1972
bolts of prints & Solids
   Hoffman
Alexander Henry
Concord, Marcus
   Peter Pan
Wamsutta+More
Quilting Supplies
& large selection
   of books.

**Mon - Sat
9:30 - 5:30**

to Missoula
45 Miles
3rd. St.   2nd. St.   Hwy 93
201
The Fabric Shop   1st. St.

Missoula, MT #5

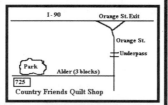
Country Friends Quilt Shop

Mon - Sat 10 - 5

725 West Alder   59802
(406) 728-7816
Est: 1988   4,200 sq.ft.
Owners: Anna Mae Cheff, Elaine Ployhar, &
   Cherie Jacobsen

Books, Patterns,
100% Cotton
Fabric, Quilts,
Quilting Classes,
Wonderful
Country
Handcrafted Gifts

Map:
I-90 — Orange St. Exit
Orange St.
Underpass
Park — Alder (3 blocks)
725
Country Friends Quilt Shop

Great Falls, MT #6

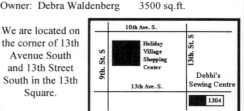
Debbi's Sewing Centre

**Mon - Thur 9:30 - 7
Fri & Sat 9:30 - 5:30**

1304 13th Ave. S   59405
(406) 452-7222   Est: 1988
Owner: Debra Waldenberg   3500 sq.ft.

We are located on
the corner of 13th
Avenue South
and 13th Street
South in the 13th
Square.

Map:
10th Ave. S.
9th. St. S
Holiday Village Shopping Center
13th. St. S
13th Ave. S.
Debbi's Sewing Centre
1304

Kalispell, MT #7

Quilt Gallery

**Mon - Fri 9:30 - 5:30
Sat 9:30 - 5**

1710 Hwy. 93 S.   59901
(406) 257-5799   Est: 1983
Owner: Joan P. Hodgeboom
Over 2000 Bolts of   4700 sq.ft.
100% Cotton Fabric.
Large supply of
books, notions,
patterns. Large
selection antique,
handquilted,
Chippewa, Novelty,
and machine Quilts.
Mail Orders

Map:
U.S. Hwy 2 E.   Hwy 93
County Courthouse
11th St.
Quilt Gallery
Airport Rd.
1710
18th St.

Shelby, MT #8

THE Creative NEEDLE

Mon - Sat 9 - 5:30

225 Main St.   59474
(406) 434-7106
Owner: Shelby Creative Investment

Complete Quilt
Shop.
Fabric, Notions,
Pfaff Sewing
Machines. Plus we
do commercial
quilting and ship
anywhere.

Map:
I-15
U.S. 2   Front St.
Butterys
225   U.S. 2
Main St.
Bank
The Creative Needle
I-15

Havre, MT #9

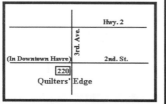
Quilters' Edge

220 3rd. Ave.   59501
(406) 265-1191
Owner: Patricia Haas
Est: 1993   1500 sq.ft.

Mon - Sat 9 - 5

Books, Patterns,
Notions, Stencils,
Batting & Fabric.
Authorized Pfaff
Sewing Machine
Dealer.
Mail Order
Available

Map:
Hwy. 2
3rd. Ave.
(In Downtown Havre)   2nd. St.
220
Quilters' Edge

Notes

Montana Guilds:
Yellowstone Valley QG, 3114 Country Club Circle, Billings, 59102
Quilters Art Guild of the N. Rockies, PO Box 4117, Bozeman, 59772
Helena Quilter's Guild, P.O. Box 429, Helena, 59624
Flathead Quilters Guild, PO box 3227, Kalispell, 59903
Central Montana Fiber Arts Guild, Lewiston
Missoula Quilter's Guild, 6323 Woods Rd., Missoula, 59802
Triangle Squares Quilt Guild, 124 Sixth Avenue S., Shelby, 59474

Other Shops in Montana:

Billings	Pin Cushion, 2646 Grand Avenue #9
Billings	Flynn Quilt Frame Co., 1000 Shiloh Overpass Rd.
Billings	Bernina Sewing & Fabric Center, 527 24th St. W.
Billings	Quilting Bug, 2675 Central Ave.
Great Falls	Pincushion Fabrics, 313 Central Avenue
Libby	The Stitchin Shoot, 305 California Avenue
Seeley Lake	Kathy's Cloth, PO Box 647
Twin Bridges	Mary R. Originals, 204 South Main
West Yellowstone	Busy Bee Fabrics, 405 Hwy 20
Whitefish	The Patchwork Junction, 550 First Street

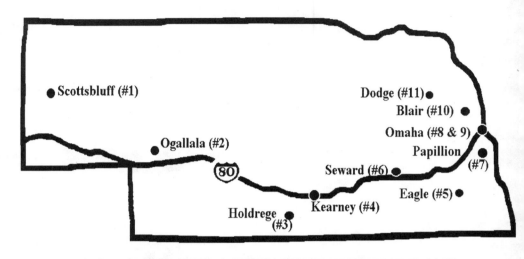

NEBRASKA

11 Featured Shops

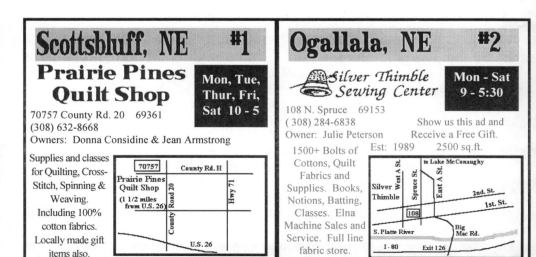

Scottsbluff, NE #1

Prairie Pines Quilt Shop

Mon, Tue, Thur, Fri, Sat 10 - 5

70757 County Rd. 20   69361
(308) 632-8668
Owners: Donna Considine & Jean Armstrong

Supplies and classes for Quilting, Cross-Stitch, Spinning & Weaving. Including 100% cotton fabrics. Locally made gift items also.

Ogallala, NE #2

Silver Thimble Sewing Center

Mon - Sat 9 - 5:30

108 N. Spruce 69153
(308) 284-6838
Owner: Julie Peterson
Show us this ad and Receive a Free Gift.

Est: 1989   2500 sq.ft.

1500+ Bolts of Cottons, Quilt Fabrics and Supplies. Books, Notions, Batting, Classes. Elna Machine Sales and Service. Full line fabric store.

Holdrege, NE #3

Quilter's Delight

Over 1500 bolts of 100% Cotton fabric. Plus everything you need to finish your project:
Books, Patterns, Notions.
Also some novelty items.

Hwy 6 & 34

Hwy. 183

West Ave.

323 Quilters' Delight

6 blocks from the intersection of 6 / 34 & 183

323 West Ave.   68949
(308) 995-2728
Owner: Janet Kugler
Est: 1991   1400 sq.ft.

Mon - Fri 9:30 - 5:30
Thurs til 8   Sat 9:30 - 5

Kearney, NE #4

Quilter's Emporium

Mon - Sat
10 - 5

2202 Central Ave.
(308) 236-0799   68847
Owner: Mary Bennett
Est: 1991   (In the Old Kaufmann Centre)

We have everything for the quilter: Fabric, Books, Patterns, and Notions. Also a wide variety of gifts.

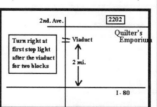

2nd. Ave. | 2202
Turn right at first stop light after the viaduct for two blocks | Viaduct | 2 mi. | Quilter's Emporium
I - 80

Eagle, NE #5

Country Quilts

Mon - Sat
10 - 5

541 South 4th Street   68347
(402) 781-2557
Owner: Ginny Hill
Est: 1990   1200 sq.ft.

Country Victorian Quilt Shop: Fabrics, Notions, Books, Patterns, Beautiful Custom Machine Quilting.

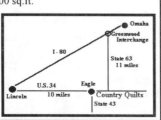

Omaha
Greenwood Interchange
I - 80
State 63 11 miles
U.S. 34   Eagle
Lincoln   10 miles   Country Quilts
State 43

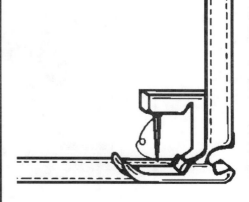

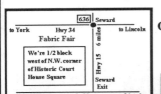
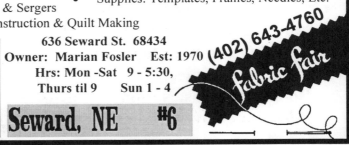

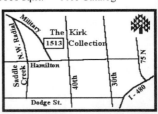

Blair, NE   #10

Topstitch

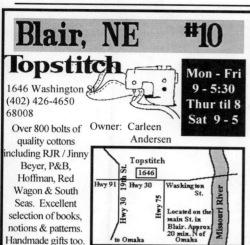

1646 Washington St.
(402) 426-4650
68008

Mon - Fri
9 - 5:30
Thur til 8
Sat 9 - 5

Owner: Carleen Andersen

Over 800 bolts of quality cottons including RJR / Jinny Beyer, P&B, Hoffman, Red Wagon & South Seas. Excellent selection of books, notions & patterns. Handmade gifts too.

Topstitch
1646
Hwy 91 19th St. Hwy 30 Washington St.
Hwy 30 Hwy 75 Located on the main St. in Blair. Approx. 20 min. N of Omaha
to Omaha Omaha
Missouri River

Dodge, NE   #11

Vogies Quilts & Treasures

Mon - Sat
9 - 5:30

2nd & Oak St.   P.O. Box 367
(402) 693-2230   68633

Owner: June Vogltance

Over 1000 bolts of quilting fabrics, books, patterns, and supplies for all quilting needs. Also: Giftware, Jewelry, and Accessories.

Hwy 275
Norfolk
Hwy 91
Dodge Omaha
at 2nd & Oak Lower Level of Marv's Grocery Vogies Quilts & Treasures

---

Nebraska State Quilt Guild, 6325 Tanglewood Lane, Lincoln, 68516
Nebraska Guilds:
Cottonwood Quilters, Box 27, Elkhorn, 68022
Prairie Piecemakers, P.O. Box 1202, Fremont, 68025
Prairie Pioneer Quilters of Grand Island,Box 675, Grand Island, 68802
Hastings Quilters Guild, P.O. Box 442, Hastings, 68901
Lincoln Quilters Guild, P.O. Box 6861, Lincoln, 68506
Blue Valley Quilters, 636 Seward Street, Seward, 68434

Other Shops in Nebraska:

Curtis	Penny's Quilt Korner, PO Box 378
Fremont	Stitchers, 445 E. 6th St.
Grand Island	The Patch Works, 205 North Locust Street
Heming Ford	Pat's Creative Stitchery, RR #1 Box 47
Holbrook	Heartland Quilts, 416 Centre
Kearney	Craft-o-Rama, P.O. Box 63
Lincoln	The Craft Store, 48th & Leighton
Lincoln	The Calico House, 5221 S. 48th
Lincoln	Attic Basket & Calicos, 1537 N. Cotner
Norfolk	Golden Needle, 509 Norfolk Ave
Papillion	Quilt Boutique, 546 N. Washington St.
Syracuse	The Needle's Eye, 55 5th St.
York	Countryside Fabrics, 718 Lincoln Avenue

3 Featured Shops

NEVADA

Nevada Guilds:
Desert Quilter of Nevada, P.O. Box 28586, Las Vegas, 89126
Truckee Meadows Quilters, Box 5502, Reno, 89513

Other Shops in Nevada:
Henderson	Betty's Fabrics & Crafts, 740 S. Boulder Hwy.	
Incline Village	The Cotton Needle, 868 Tahoe Blvd. PO Box 7985	
Las Vegas	Maudie's Antique Cottage, 3310 E. Charleston Blvd.	
Las Vegas	Heddy's Fabrics, 5640 W. Charleston Blvd.	

Reno, NV #1

Windy Moon

- **Fabrics**
- **Traditional Quilts**
- **Notions**
- **Classes**
- **Gifts**

611 Kuenzli St.
Creamery Bldg.
(702) 849-0195
Est: 1994
4300 sq.ft.

Mon - Sat 10 - 6

Also visit our other shop in Tahoe City, CA See page 22

**Nestled high in the Sierra's, Windy Moon quilts makes quilting easy for the mountain visitor. 1 hour classes give both the novice and experienced quilter tips on new techniques and ideas.
Doll Classes and Accessories also Available.**

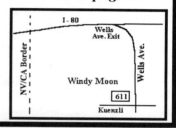

Reno, NV #2

The Cloth Cottage

221 Vassar St.   89502
(702) 348-0086
Owner: Gail Cram
Est: 1988   1600 sq.ft.

**Tue - Fri 10 - 5:30
Sat 10 - 5**

Over 2000 bolts of fabric — all 100% cotton. Fat quarter bundles. Above all — The Friendliest shop in Nevada!

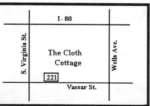

Quilt Show Deadline — Tightening the Tension

Las Vegas, NV #3

Fabric Boutique

4717 Faircenter Pky   89102
W. Charleston at Decatur
(702) 878-0068   6000 sq.ft.
Owner: Darleen Ros   Est: 1991

**Mon - Fri 10 - 8
Sat 10 - 6
Sun 12 - 5**

3000 bolts of Quilting Fabric Huge Book Selection Classes We also carry Fashion Fabric

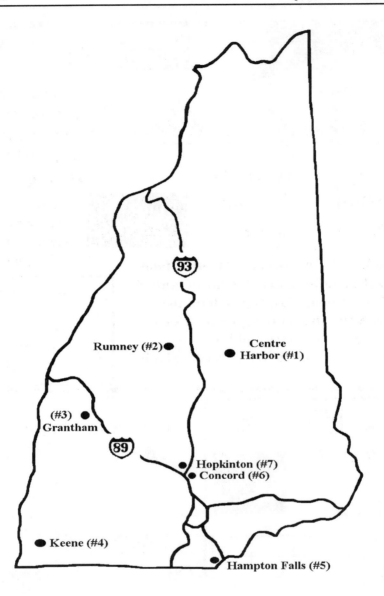

7 Featured Shops

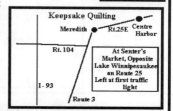

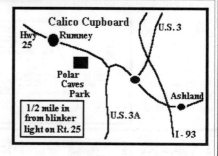

Grantham, NH #3

Sunshine Carousel

Tues - Sat 10 - 5

HCR 63   Box 2A
(603) 863-5754   03753
Owner: Elaine Pillsbury
Est: 1990   1200 sq.ft.

Quilting Supplies and classes. Large assortment of cotton fabrics, books, patterns, and notions. Also handmade gifts and crafts.

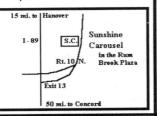

Keene, NH #4

The Moses House

Tues - Sat 10 - 4 or By Appointment

149 Emerald St.   03431
(603) 352-2312   Est: 1987
Owners: Fran & Russ Moline   1800 sq.ft.

The Best Quilting Fabrics, Books, Patterns, Supplies, Classes, Counted Cross Stitch PFAFF Dealer Featherweights Bought, Sold, & Repaired.

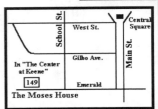

Hampton Falls, NH #5

The Silver Thimble Quilt Shop

Mon - Sat 9:30 - 5 Thur til 8 Sun 1- 5

Route 1 Shoppers Village   03844
(603) 926-3378   Opened: 1970
Owner: Patti Sanborn   3.000 sq.ft.

Oldest Quilt shop in New England! Over 1,000 bolts of 100% cotton Featuring Hoffman, Jinny Beyer, P&B, and more. Complete Quilt Shop!

Concord, NH #6

Golden Gese Quilt Shop

Tues - Fri 10 - 5 Sat 10 - 1

28 South Main   03301
(603) 228-5540   Est: 1987
Owner: Nancy Gesen   1200 sq.ft.

100% Cotton Fabric, Books, Patterns, Notions & Classes. Helpful Assistance.

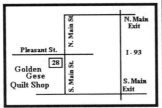

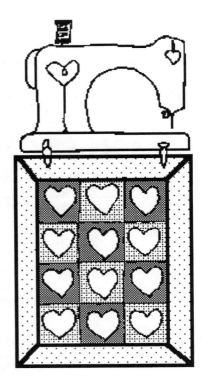

Hopkinton, NH   #7   *A Working Quilt Shop*

Country Quilter

369 COLLEGE HILL ROAD
HOPKINTON, NEW HAMPSHIRE 03229 • 603 / 746-5521

Tucked away on a scenic country road in a 200 year old barn is the Country Quilter – a unique working quilt shop offering a beautiful selection of quilts and quilt supplies, as well as wall hangings, pillows, and other handcrafted gifts.

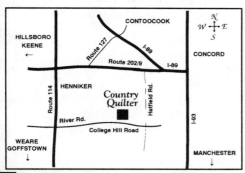

We carry over 1,500 bolts of 100% cotton fabrics (the largest inventory in the area) including Hoffman, Jinny Beyer, R.J.R., Gutcheon, Peter Pan, Momen House, and other hard to find brands.

We also carry notions...from batting (Buffalo Batting and Fairfield) to stencils, and a wide assortment of books and patterns.

"Sleeping Under a Quilt is Sleeping Under A Blanket of Love"

We welcome all visitors to our colorful shop, and we always enjoy taking the time to make you feel at home and unhurried. Our staff is comprised of expert quilters who welcome questions and tips from our customers and enjoy sharing what we have learned with our visitors.

DIRECTIONS:
Route I-89 North to Exit 5 (which is also Routes 202/9); continue west towards Henniker. Exit at Hatfield Road and follow the well-marked signs.

HOURS:
Open all year 'round. Mon.-Sat. 10.–5:30 Sun.12– 5:30.

Notes

New Hampshire Guilds:
Cheshire Quilter's Guild, P.O. Box 1481, Keene, 03431
Hannah Dustin Quilters Guild, P.O. Box 121, Hudson, 03051
Ladies of the Lakes Quilters' Guild, P.O. Box 552, Wolfeboro, 03894

Other Shops in New Hampshire:
Bedford	Martin's House of Cloth, Rt. 3
Bedford	The Patchworks, 133 Bedford Center Road
Dover	J.J.'s Fabrics & More, 559 Central Avenue
Nashua	Covered Bridge Quilting Shop, 449 Amherst

Philosophy of the Guide

I enjoy and appreciate my local quilt shops. I love quilting and find that it helps me get through much of every-day life.

I also love finding a quilt shop when I'm traveling. Traveling is stressful and a visit to a quilt shop can get things back into perspective. While traveling I have at times even gone out of my way to visit a shop.

Often this departure from the most direct route has led to other adventures and very enjoyable days (even for my husband).

My hope is that publishing this directory will make finding shops easier. Then we can all visit new shops, see what other people are up to, make new friends, and ensure a strong future for quilting.

SPICED WITH LOVE

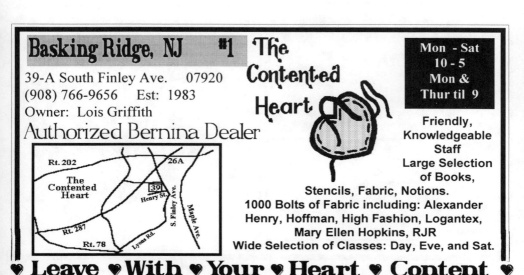
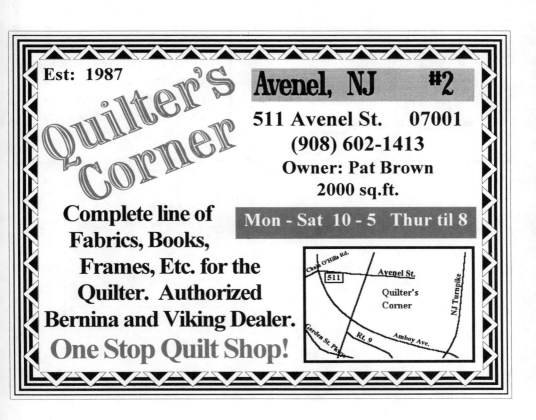

Warren, NJ #3

Prints Charming

Pheasant Run Plaza   07059
(908) 469-4700
Owner: Claudia Menendez
Est: 1981   1800 sq.ft.

**Mon - Fri
10 - 5
Thur til 9
Sat 10-4:30
Sun 11 - 4**

1500 Bolts of
Cottons from
every maker.
More than 400
patterns and books
in stock. All nec.
supplies. We're
Very Helpful!

Fair Haven, NJ #4

West End Fabrics

588 River Road   07704
(908) 747-4838   Est: 1989
Owner: Joy Bohanan   4200 sq.ft.

**Mon - Fri
9 - 5:30
Wed til 8
Sat 9 - 5**

**Known for beautiful fabrics,
innovative classes, friendly,
knowledgeable help, and
creative machine quilting.
Every Day is "show and
tell" at West End.**

Com-for-ter —
What you do
when she can't
Quilt anymore !

Allentown, NJ #5

Quilter's Barn

34 South Main St.   P.O. Box 295
(609) 259-2504   08501
Owner: Mary Boyer
           Est: 1975

**Mon - Sat
9:30 - 4
Thur til
7:30**

... all 100%
      cotton fabrics
... Books
... Patterns
... Notions,
... Batting
... classes
... personal service

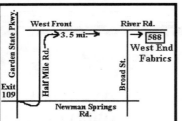

Manasquan, NJ   #6

Quilts n' Crafts

79 Main St.   08736
(908) 223-4429   Est. 1989
Owners: Jeanne Evans & Bobbie
1500 sq.ft.   Gallagher

**Mon - Sat
10 - 5
Mon &
Thurs til 7**

Everything a
Quilter needs and
just blocks from
the ocean. Great
Store—Great
walk around
town.

Toms River, NJ   #7

Crafty Fabrics

2479 Church Rd.   08753
(908) 255-8342
Owner: Diane McColley
Est: 1983   1200 sq.ft.

Tues - Sat   10 - 5

**Quilting Supplies
and Classes.
100% Cotton Fabrics,
Books, Patterns,
Batting & Notions.
Also Handmade
Pillows and Crafts**

Ocean City, NJ   #8

715 Asbury Ave.   08226
(609) 399-7166
Owner: Terry Calvi
Est: 1990   1900 sq.ft.

- **2000+ Bolts of 100% Cotton**
- **Classes**
- **Books**
- **Notions**
- **Craft Patterns**
- **Cross-Stitch**
- **Gifts.**

Summer
Mon - Fri
10 - 8
Sat 10 - 5
Sun 12 - 4
Winter
Mon - Sat
10 - 5
Sun 12 - 4

Calico 'N Cotton

Garden State Parkway
Exit 30 Rt. 52
34th St.

7th St.
8th St.
9th St.
Bay Ave.
West Ave.
Asbury Ave.
715
Atlantic Ocean

South Jersey's Most Complete Quilt Store

Manahawkin, NJ   #9

deb's Sew & Sew

**Mon - Sat
10 - 4:30**

449 E. Bay Ave.   08050
(609) 597-3276

Featuring 100% cottons by Jinny Beyer, Hoffman, South Sea Imports & more. Books, Patterns, Notions & Classes.

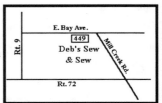

E. Bay Ave.
449
Deb's Sew & Sew
Rt. 9
Mill Creek Rd.
Rt. 72

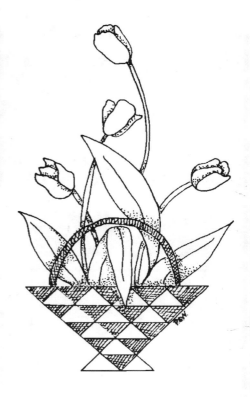

New Jersey Guilds:
Beach Plum Quilters, PO Box 204, Island Heights, 08732
Pieceful Shores Quilters Guild, 449 E. Bay Avenue, Manahawkin, 08050
South Shores Stitchers, PO Box 1103, Marmora, 08223
Jersey Shore Quilters, 415 Foreman Avenue, Point Pleasant, 08742
Molly Pitcher Stitchers, PO Box 467, Tennent, 07763
Woodbridge Heritage Quilters, PO Box 272, Woodbridge, 07095
Garden State Quilters, P.O. Box 424, Chatham, 07928
Love Apples, PO Box 89, Glendora, 08029
Turtle Creek Quilters, 27 W. church St., Jamesburg, 08831
Rebecca's Reel Quilters, PO Box 36, Middletown, 07748
Courthouse Quilters Guild, 121 Back Brook Rd., Ringoes, 08551
Berry Basket Quilters, 509 Paige Dr., Southampton, 08088
Beach Plum Quilters, PO Box 743, Toms River, 08753
Brownstone Quilters, P.O. Box 228, Warwick, 07463

Other Shops in New Jersey:

Bridgeton	The Strawberry Patch, 73 Landis Avenue
East Rutherford	Materially Yours, 200 Murrayhill Parkway
Haddonfield	The Little Shop, 143 Kings Highway E.
Lebanon	Budding Star, Rt. 22E, Lebanon Plaza
Medford	Country Collection, 109 Route 70
Midland Park	Bartson Fabrics, 240 Glen Ave.
Millington	Lou Souders Ctry Store, 1901 Longhill Road
Morris Plains	Aardvark & C, 748 Speedwell
Pitman	Norwyn's Fashion Fabric, 15 S. Broadway
Pleasantville	Lynda's Country Corner, 39 E. Verona Ave
Princeton	American Sewing Center, 301 N. Harrison St
Rio Grande	Olsen Sew & Vac Center, 121 Rt. 47 S.
Shrewsbury	Abigail's, 567 State Highway 35
Somers Point	Crafters Paradise Outlet, Somers Point Plaza
Somerville	Somerville Sewing Center, 45 West Main St
Trenton	Raymond's, 528 Route No. 33
Trenton	Raymond's, 930 Parkway Avenue
Vineland	The Pin Cushion, 36 Landis Avenue

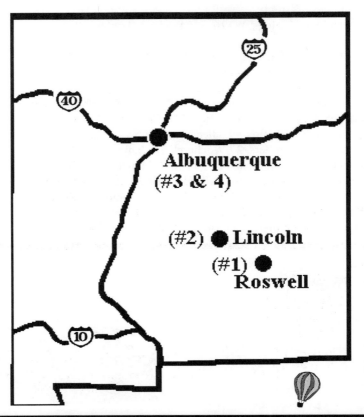

Albuquerque
(#3 & 4)

(#2) ● Lincoln
(#1) ●
Roswell

NEW MEXICO

4 Featured Shops

Roswell, NM   #1

Quilt Talk

223 N. Main St.   88201
(Inside Carousel of Fabrics)
(505) 623-0178   Est: 1994
Owner: J. Michelle Watts

Mon - Sat
9:30 - 5:30

100% cotton fabrics.
Books, patterns, notions, quilting classes & custom made quilts.

Lincoln, NM   #2

Lincolnworks

32 Main St.   P.O. Box 32
(505) 653-4693   88338
Owner: Becky Angell
Est: 1988   400 sq.ft.

Tues - Sat
10 - 4
Closed
Jan - June

100% Cottons, S.W. patterns, good conversation! Billy the Kid Country! !

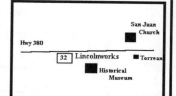

Albuquerque, NM   #3

I Have A Notion

3905 San Mateo N.E.   87110
(505) 883-1997
Est: 1986   3650 sq.ft.
Owners: Carolyn & Richard Norton

Mon - Fri
10 - 6
Sat 10 - 5
Sun 12 - 4

A real fabric store with heavy emphasis on quilting, stitchery, speciality yarns and unusual fabrics.

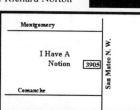

Albuquerque, NM   #4

The Quilt Works

11117 Menaul N.E.   87112
(505) 298-8210
Est: 1985   1750 sq.ft.
Owners: Shirley Brabson
& Margaret Prina

Mon - Fri
9 - 6
Sat 9 - 5
Sun 2 - 5

We have over 2400 bolts of cotton fabric. We're Friendly and Helpful !

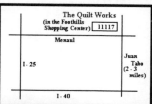

New Mexico Quilters' Association, P.O. Box 20562, Albuquerque, 87154
New Mexico Guilds:
Enchanted Quilter's Guild, 900 Catalina, Alamogordo, 88301
Los Alamos Piecemakers Quilters, P.O. Box 261, Los Alamos, 87544
Pecos Valley Quilters, 807 N. Missouri, Roswell, 88201
Northern New Mexico Quilters, P.O. Box 8350, Santa Fe, 87504

Other Shops in New Mexico:

Albuquerque	Ann Silva's, 3300 San Mateo E.
Farmington	The Sampler, 915 Farmington Avenue
Santa Fe	Quilts to Cover Your Fantasy, 201 Galisteo St.
Santa Fe	Quilts Ltd., 652 Canyon Rd.
Santa Fe	The Bedroom, 304 Catron St.
Santa Fe	Love Apples, 1519 Canyon Road
Tucumcari	Fabric Shop, 112 S. First

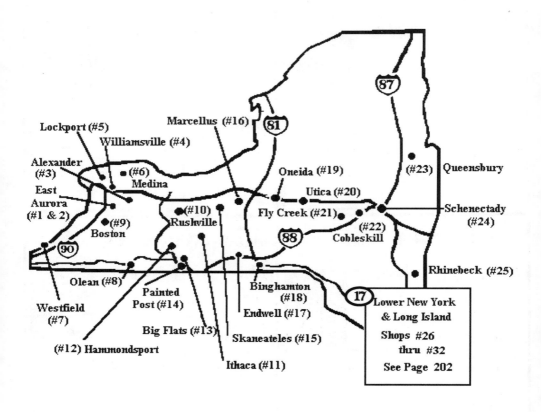

Lockport (#5)
Williamsville (#4)
Marcellus (#16)
Alexander (#3)
(#6) Medina
Oneida (#19)
(#23) Queensbury
East Aurora (#1 & 2)
(#10) Rushville
(#9) Boston
Utica (#20)
Fly Creek (#21)
Schenectady (#24)
(#22) Cobleskill
Rhinebeck (#25)
Olean (#8)
Westfield (#7)
Painted Post (#14)
Binghamton (#18)
Endwell (#17)
Big Flats (#13)
Skaneateles (#15)
(#12) Hammondsport
Ithaca (#11)

Lower New York & Long Island
Shops #26 thru #32
See Page 202

NEW YORK

32 Featured Shops

East Aurora, NY #1

Vidler's 5 & 10

680 - 694 Main Street   14052
(716) 652-0481
Owners: Bob & Ed Vidler
Est: 1930   13,000 sq. ft.

**Mon - Sat
8:30 - 6:00
Fri. til
9:00**

10,000 yards of calicos. Hundreds of Instruction books on quilting, sewing, crafts, knitting & needle crafts.
"It's a Fun Place to Shop"

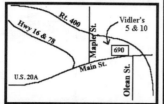

East Aurora, NY #2

Aurora Sewing Center

659 Main St. 14052
(716) 652-2811
Owners: Terry, Regis, & Barb
Est: 1978   3500 sq.ft.

**Mon - Fri
10 - 5
Thur til 9
Sat 10 - 4**

Over 1000 bolts of 100% cotton. Quilting Books, Supplies, Patterns, Classes. Sewing Machine / Serger Sales and Service.

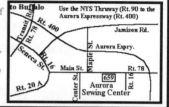

Rolling Hills ▟ Alexander, NY #3

QUILT ART
Quilter's Corner

3274 Broadway   14005
(716) 591-3606
Owners: Jennie Peck & Ann Kroll
1200 sq.ft. Est: 1988

**Mon - Fri 10 - 4
Tues til 9
Sat 12 - 4**

▟ **Your Complete Quilt Shop.**
Quilts, Fabric, Notions, Classes, 100%
Cottons, Books. We specialize in unique &
unusual fabrics from different parts of the
globe.   Plus a Gift Room.

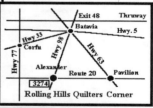

Williamsville, NY #4

Sew What

8226 Main Street   14221
(716) 632-8801   Est: 1990
Owner: Ann Shaw
1100 sq.ft.

**Mon & Wed
10 - 9
Thur - Sat
10 - 5**

Specializing in Quilting & Cross Stitch, we offer a large selection of unique and unusual fabrics, 100's of patterns & notions.
Come Browse!

Lockport, NY   #5

Pine Grove Workshop

5410 Stone Rd.   14094
(716) 433-5377
Owner: Judith Farnham
Est: 1982

**Mon - Sat
10 - 4:30**

**1500 Bolts 100% Cotton
Old and New Quilts
Hundreds of Books, Patterns, & Notions
Classes—Spring Seminar**

Medina, NY   #6

The Personal Touch

**Mon - Sat
9:30 - 5
Fri til 9**

435 Main Street   14103
(716) 798-4760
Owner: Nancy Berger
Est: 1981   2000 sq.ft.

Hundreds of
calicos, Books,
Quilting supplies.
QUILTS, classes.
A unique variety
of "juried" crafts
plus service with
a smile.

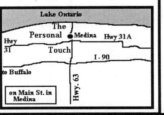

Westfield, NY   #7

Going to Pieces

**Mon - Fri
9:30 - 4:30
Sat 9:30 - 3**

106 East Main Street   14787
(716) 326-6494
Est: 1987
Owners: Gaye Mason & Judy Lyon

**We feature
unique gifts and
fabrics.**
We are located
5 minutes off of
I-90, with several
antique shops and
wineries.

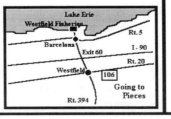

Olean, NY   #8

Calico Country

**Mon - Sat
10 - 5
Fri til 8**

803 West State Street   14760
(716) 372-5446
Owner: Betsy Leute
Est: 1983   1600 sq.ft.

Nine rooms full
of 1700 bolts of
100% cotton
fabric, books,
patterns, quilts,
gift items and
much more.

Rushville, NY #10

Quilting on a Country Lane

Mon - Sat 9 - 5

4594 Harvey Lane   14544
(716) 554-6507
Owner: Arlene Lee
Est: 1980

Quilt making supplies. Notions, Books, Fabric, Patterns, and Machine Quilting.

Ithaca, NY #11

Quilts 'n Things

**Mon - Wed 10 - 5:30
Thur 10 - 7
Fri & Sat 10 - 4**

980 Dryden Rd.   14850
(607) 277-6831   Est: 1986
Owners: Lorraine Sack, Judi Heath, Alanna Fontangalia, & Ramona Heck
1200 sq.ft.

A Shop for Quilters owned and operated by Quilters. 100% Cotton Fabrics, Notions, Books, Patterns. Lessons

Hammondsport, NY #12

Lake Country Gifts/Calicoes

Mon - Sat 10 - 5

67 Sheather St. Box 332
(607) 569-3530   14840
Owner: Margo Nelson   Est: 1988

Complete line of quilting supplies with 100% cotton fabric. Notions, Books. Handmade Quilts and unique country Gifts. Friendly, Helpful Service.

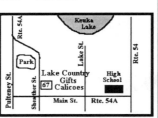

Big Flats, NY #13

The Village Sampler

**Mon - Sat 10 - 5
Thur 10 - 8:30**

2792 Canal St.   14814
(607) 562-7596
Owner: Carol A. Blakeslee
Est: 1986   2500 sq.ft.

Extraordinary Fabrics, Ideas, & Notions for the Quilter & Cross Stitcher. A Doll Crafter's Paradise. Gifts Too!

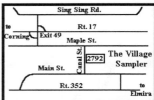

Painted Post, NY #14

The Country Store

**Mon - Sat 11 - 4:30
Thur til 8
Sun by Appt.**

449 South Hamilton   14870
(607) 962-1030   Est: 1982
Owner: John & Patricia Starzec
1500 sq.ft.

Fabric (over 1,000 bolts of Prints and Solids) 100% Cotton -- quilt classes, books and quilting supplies Unique gifts, & wallhangings. Our quilts are hand-quilted by Amish.

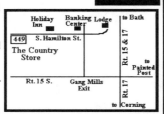

Skaneateles, NY #15

Patchwork Plus

Mon - Sat 10 - 4

36 Jordan Street   13152
(315) 685-6979
Owners: Carol Benson & Judi West
Est: 1987

1000 bolts of 100% cottons, books, notions, patterns; Plus friendly service in Skaneateles; Gateway to the Finger Lakes

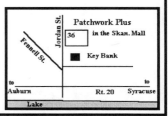

Marcellus, NY   #16

The Quilting Shoppe

2162 Lawrence Road   13108
(315) 673-1126   Opened: 1983   1800 sq.ft.
Owner: Elaine Lyon Fischer

100% Cotton   Fabrics

Mail Order
Visa/MC
Special Orders

Mon - Sat
9 - 5
Or By Appt.

100% Cotton
Fabrics
Over 1800 Bolts
Notions

Batting, Books, Hoops, Frames
Lessons
Quilted Jackets   Quilt Repairs   Quilt Washing
Quilts for Sale   Made to Order Quilts
Machine Quilting Service

Everything you need for Quilting
"What a Quilting Shop Should Be"

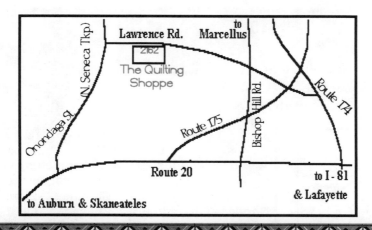

Endwell, NY #17

Sew Much More

2723 East Main St.   13760
(607) 748-8340
Owner: Nancy Valenta
Est: 1990   1750 sq.ft.

**Mon - Fri
9 - 5:30
Sat 9 - 1**

Over 1500 bolts of 100% cottons. Heirloom sewing, specialty threads, books and patterns galore. A delightful experience for your palette.

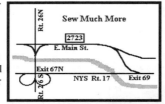

Binghamton, NY #18

Grandmother's Thimble

29 Kattelville Rd.   13901
(607) 648-9009
Owner: Anita Hurley
Est: 1988

**Mon - Fri
10 - 5
Thur til 8
Sat 10 - 4**

Totally devoted to Quilters!
700 bolts of 100% cotton fabric. Regional Bernina dealer. Full line of accessories.

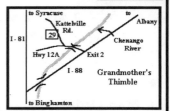

Oneida, NY #19

Cottons Etc.

228 Genesee Street   13421
(315) 363-6834   Est: 1980
Owner: Paula Schultz
1700 sq.ft.

**Mon - Sat
10 - 5
Thur til 8**

Our motto is "You Can Never Have Too Much Fabric!"
A Pot-pourri of Quilting & Fashion Fabrics, Notions, Books & Patterns

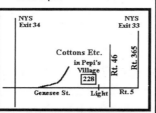

Utica, NY #20

**Mon - Fri
9:30 - 5:30
Sat 10 - 5**

2336 West Whitesboro St.   13502
(315) 735-5328 Est: 1991   2000 sq.ft.
Owners: Susan Kowalczyk & Sandra Jones

Tiger Lily Quilt Co.

**A shop with unusual fabrics for quilting & sewing.
Books, notions, patterns, gifts, classes and newsletter also.   Bernina Sub Dealer
Services Offered: Private Lessons, Quilt Basting, Specific classes for 4 or more.
Fabric always discounted 10%--no s&h added.**

Est: 1989

Fly Creek, NY   #21

Heartworks
Quilts and Country Wares

(607)
547-2501

July & Aug
Mon - Sat 11 - 5
Sept - June
Sat & Sun 11 - 5

Rte. 28   P.O. Box 148   13337
Owners: Margaret & Jim Wolff

A real country Quilt Shop.
Fine Cotton Fabrics, Quilts, Notions.
Custom orders, Quilt repair and hand
quilting for your quilt tops.

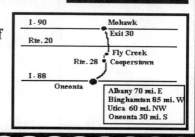

Cobleskill, NY   #22

The Yardstick

Burger King Plaza   12043
(518) 234-2179
Owner: Merilyn Ludwig
Est: 1975   2500 sq.ft.

Mon - Fri
9 - 9
Sat 9 - 6
Sun 11 - 5

Over 2000 bolts of
100% cotton fabrics,
books, notions,
patterns, classes,
Cross-Stitch, Yarn.
Friendly,
Knowledgeable
service.

Queensbury, NY   #23

The Quilting Bee

79 Lake George Rd.   (Rt. 9)
(518) 792-0845   12804
Owner: Joanne Loftus

Mon - Sat
10 - 5
Sun 12 - 5

Cotton fabrics
include designer's
calicos & solids,
books, patterns &
notions. Banner
flag supplies,
Antiques. Gifts
and Quilts.
Bernina Dealer.

Est: 1987   1500 sq.ft.

Schenectady, NY   #24

Country Cottons, Ltd.

Shaker Pine Mall   145 Vly Road
(518) 456-8885   12309
Owners: Dee Farina Albert &
             Cathy Gruyters-Riccio
Est: 1985

Mon - Sat
10 - 5
Wed & Fri
til 8

The latest in 100%
Cotton Fabrics &
Quilting supplies,
Classes, Books,
Patterns all
designed for the
enthusiastic
Quilter!

Rhinebeck, NY   #25

The Country Shop

3 Stone Church Road   12572
(914) 876-4674
Owner: Patricia Carl
Est: 1982

Tues - Sat
10 - 4:30

A full service
quilt shop with
hundreds of bolts
of wonderful
fabrics and lots of
ideas in a
friendly, homey
atmosphere.
BOOKS !

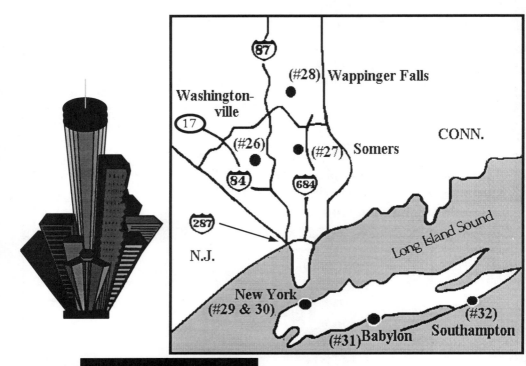

7 Featured Shops

LOWER NEW YORK & LONG ISLAND

Washingtonville, NY   #26

The Village Quilt

**Tues - Sat
10:30 -
4:30**

32 West Main Street   10992
(914) 496-5505
Owner: Audrey Perry
Est: 1982   900 sq.ft.

We offer very selective 100% cotton fabrics, complete quilting supplies and classes from beginner to advanced.

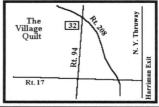

Somers, NY   #27

The Country Quilter

Route 100/202   10589
(914) 277-4820   Fax (914) 277-8604
Owner: Claire Oehler
Opened: 1990   1800 sq.ft.

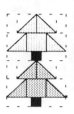

**Mon to Sat
9:30 - 5:30
Thurs 'til 9**

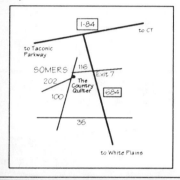

Quality Quilting Supplies

Over 2500 Bolts of 100% Cotton Fabrics
Over 600 Book Titles
Notions: Basic as well as Unusual
100s of Patterns
Cat's Meow Village Collectible Wooden Houses
Quilting Classes Year-Round
Lots of Samples on Display
Fast Mail Order Service
Come in and meet our Friendly, Helpful Staff!

Wappingers Falls, NY   #28

Quilt Basket

**Mon - Sat
10 - 4
Tues &
Thur til 6**

1136 Route 376   12590
(914) 227-7606   Est: 1989
Owners: Cathy & Allan Anderson
                        1200 sq.ft.
Quilt--doll--bear
fabrics, fur,
supplies, books
and patterns.
Come see our own
patterns, quilts
hangers & doll
stands.
Send SASE for
Catalog

New York, NY   #29

Lucy Anna Folk Art & Antique Quilts

Tues - Sat
Noon - 7
Sun
Noon - 6

502 Hudson Street   10014
(212) 645-9463
Owner: Karen Taber
Est: 1988   600 sq. ft.

Charming shop filled with handcrafted dolls, teddy bears & farm animals. Affordable quilts from 1880's thru the Depression.

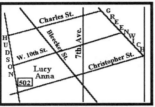

New York, NY   #30

Janos & Associates

110 East End Avenue
(212) 988-0407   10028
Owner: Barbara S. Janos
Est: 1976

By Appointment Only

Certified Appraisers
Quilt Appraisals our Specialty
Over 13 years experience
New York University Certified

Babylon, NY   #31

Needles & Art

Wed 10 - 8
Thur & Fri
10 - 5
Sat 10 - 3
Closed Saturdays
July & Aug

Montauk Hwy & Rt. 109   11702
Barbizon Bldg.   On Long Island
(516) 587-5300   Barbizon Bldg.
Owner: Doris Rullo   1200 sq.ft.
Est: 1985

Very bright and spacious with lots of natural light. 100% cotton fabric, books, notions, classes, and always friendly service.

Southampton, NY   #32

Tom's Quilts

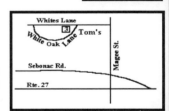
By Appointment Only

3 White Oak Lane   11968
(516) 726-6881
Owner: Tom Vonah
Est: 1987

Antique & new quilts. Quilt Tops, Crib Quilts. Peasonable Prices Send S.A.S.E. for Free Catalogue

New York Guilds:
Q.U.I.L.T., 79 Edgecomb St., Albany 12209
Clarence Log Cabin Quilters, 4895 Kraus Road, Clarence, 14031
Southtown Piecemakers Quilting , PO Box 340, East Aurora, 14052
Towpath Quilt Guild, PO Box 188, Fayetteville 13066
Wings Falls Quilter's Guild, Bay & Washington Sts., Glens Falls
Wiltwyck Quilter's Guild, PO Box 3731, Kingston 12401
Tumbstall Quilt Guild, Marcellus
Lake to Lake Quilt Guild, 4594 Harvey Road, Rushville, 14544
Kenan Quilters Guild, 433 Locust Street, Lockport 14094
East Long Island Quilters Guild, PO Box 1514, Southampton 11968
Empire Quilters, PO Box 6175, Grand Central Station, 10163-6019
Genesee Valley Quilt Club, PO Box 18321, Rochester 14618
Long Island Quilters' Society, Inc., PO Box 1660, Mineola 11501
Mohawk Valley Quilt Club, 31 Capardo Drive, Whitesboro 13492
Q.U.I.L.T.S., 1068 Maryland Avenue, Schenectady 12308
Smithtown Stitchers, Inc., PO Box 311, Smithtown 11787
Northern Star Quilters Guild, PO Box 232, Somers 10589

Other Shops in New York:

Albany	Knight's Designer Fabrics, 265 Osborne Road
Albion	The Golden Thimble, 121 E. Bank
Brentwood	Patches Fabric, 1853 Brentwood Road
Brockport	Findings and Fabrics, Inc., 80 Clinton Street
Bronx	Madison Quilt Shop, 2307 Grand Concourse
Brooklyn	Victoria's Quilts, 302 13th Street
Cadyville	Quilts N More, Route #1
Cazenovia	Cazenovia Quilt Shop, 3 Lincklaen Street
Cold Spring Harbor	Sentimental Stitches, 181 Main
Cooperstown	Material Things, 45 Main
Croghan	Fabric Hutch, Main Street
Dansville	Material Rewards, 128 Main Street
East Aurora	Countryside Gifts, 259 Main Street
East Hampton	Spring's Quilts and Crafts, 80 N. Main Street
East Rochester	Patricia's Fabric House, 333 West Commerical
Fairport	Pins & Needles, 282 Jefferson Ave
Floral Park	Patchwork Patch, 141 Tulip Ave.
Hampton Bays	Kalico Kitten, Montauk Hwy
Hicksville	Melani's Moods Ltd., 396 Woodbury Road
Horseheads	Mountain View Calico Shop, 703 S. Main
Ithaca	Quilts 'n Things, 980 Dryden Road
Kings Park	Friends & Neighbors Needlecraft Studio, 303 Kohr
Lakewood	Calico Cat, 172 W. Fairmount Avenue
Little Falls	Barbara's Fabric & Gift Shoppe, 624 E. Main Street
Madison	The Pin Cushion, Route 20
Mastic	Addie's Corner Shoppe, 1484 Montuk Highway
Middletown	We Quilt, Inc., 128 North Street
Newfane	Martha's Cupboard, 2714 Main
New York City	Park East Sewing Center, 1358 Third Avenue
New York City	Laura Fisher Antique Quilts & Americana, 1050 2nd. Ave.
New York City	Domino Patchwork, 327 Canal
New York City	Hirschl & Adler Folk, 21 East 70th Street
New York City	Quilters Passion Inc., 531 Amsterdam Avenue
New York City	Paron Fabrics, 60 W. 57th
New York City	American Antiques & Quilts, 799 Madison Avenue
New York City	Coeli Pearson Classic American Quilts, 11 Riverside Drive
New York City	Hands All Around, 986 Lexington Avenue
New York City	Quilts Plus, 86 Forsyth
New York City	Quiltessence, 979 Third Avenue
New York City	Victoria's Quilts, 427 E. 82nd. Street #4E
Oneonta	Stitching Post, 265 Main
Plainview	Melani's Moods Ltd., 14 Manetto Hill Mall
Port Jefferson	Stitchin Time, Inc., 326 Main Street
Poughkeepsie	Krakower Fabrics, 646 South Road
Queensbury	The Village Collection, R.D. #5 Lake George Road
Ravena	Log Cabin Fabrics, P.O. Box 252A Route #2
Rochester	Guild Crafters Studio, 274 Goodman Street N.
Rochester	Fabrics and Findings, Inc., 50 Anderson Avenue
Rockville Center	Bramson House, 5 Nassau
Roslyn	Arbor House, 22 Arbor Lane
Sea Cliff	Calico Square, Inc., 347 Glen Cove Avenue
Southampton	Duffy's Quilts & Things, 3 White Oak Lane
Stamford	The Yard Stick, 64 Main St.
Syracuse	AAAA Antiques, 101 E. Wells Avenue N
Warrensburg	I Love Fabric & Company, 50 River Street
Webster	Quilt Shop of Webster, 1575 State Road
West Oneonta	Country Fabrics, HCR Box 620

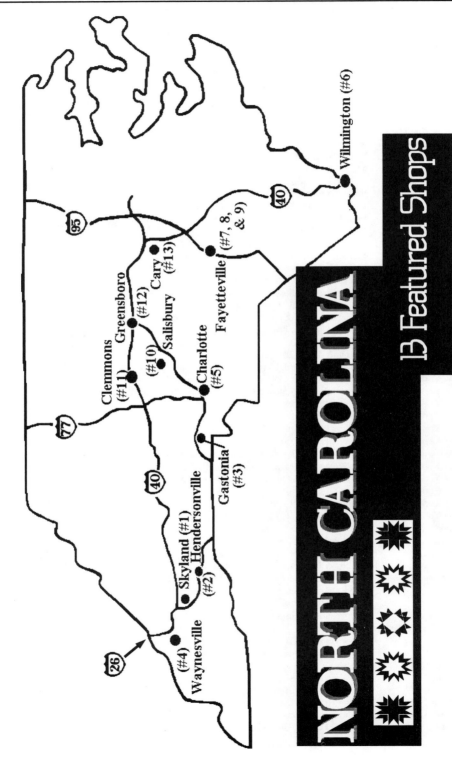

NORTH CAROLINA

13 Featured Shops

Wilmington (#6)

Cary (#13)

Greensboro (#12)

Salisbury

Clemmons (#11)

Charlotte (#5)

Fayetteville (#7, 8, & 9)

Gastonia (#3)

Skyland (#1)

Hendersonville (#2)

Waynesville (#4)

Skyland, NC #1

20 Rosscraggon Rd.
P.O. Box 819   28776
(704) 684-4802   Est: 1989
Owner: Julie Sherar

Great Lengths Fabrics

100% Cottons,
Books, Notions,
Classes.
Located in 100 Year
old Victorian
House.
Go to Great
Lengths to get
Great Fabrics.

Mon - Fri
10 - 5
Sat 11 - 4

Hendersonville, NC #2

Bonesteel's Hardware
& Quilt Corner

Mon - Fri
9 - 5:30
Sat 9 - 4

150 White Street   28739
(704) 692-0293
Owners: Pete & Georgia Bonesteel

Home of Georgia Bonesteel, Est: 1982
Hostess of the PBS series "Lap Quilting". Quilt Fabrics, Notions, Books and Patterns Avail.

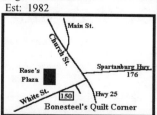

Thimble — A Quilter's
Shining armor,
in the night.

Gastonia, NC #3

Mary Jo's Cloth Store

Mon - Sat
9 - 5:45
Mon & Thur
til 8:45

401 Cox Rd.   Gaston Mall
(800) 627-9567   28054
Owner: Mary Jo Cloninger
Est: 1951   32,000 sq.ft.

"The Place" for investment sewers. Where variety is the greatest. Prices are the lowest and large quanities can be found.

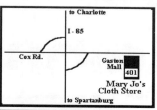

Mimi's Stitching Treasures

Waynesville area's best source for fabrics, laces and supplies for

Quilting
English Smocking &
Heirloom Sewing
Needle and Machine
Arts

Fabrics
Liberty of London	Hoffman
RJR	Alexander Henry
Spechler Vogel	Bear Threads

Gourmet Patterns
Children's Corner	Back Porch Press
Margaret Pierce	Becky B
Chery Williams	Debroah's Designs
Beaucoup	Little Memories

Threads
Mettler, Sulky, Madeira, Floche,
Silk Embroidery Ribbon

BOOKS !   BOOKS !   and
more BOOKS !

Sewing
Machines
Sales and
Service

Waynesville, NC   #4

Mimi's Stitching Treasures

502 Balsam Road
in "Hazelwood"   28738
(704) 452-3455   Est: 1987
Owner: Patricia Moore   1800 sq.ft.

Mon - Fri
10 - 5
Sat 10 - 2
Or By Appt.

See Our
Larger
Listing
This
Page

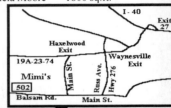

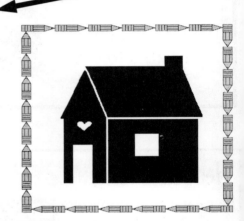

Charlotte, NC   #5

Quilter's Gallery

901 South Kings Dr. Suite # 135
(704) 376-2531   28204

Cotton Fabrics--
Traditional and
unusual prints,
Batiks, and
Homespuns.
Wide range of
books and
patterns. French
Heirloom Sewing
Supplies. Buttons
and trims.

Mon - Sat
10 - 4:30

Owner: Patti Cline & Cindy Page
Est: 1981   2000 sq.ft.

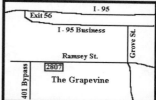
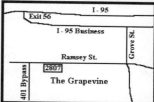
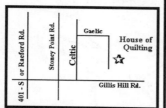

Fayetteville, NC   #9

Magnolia Station

Mon - Fri
8:30 - 3
Sat 10 - 3

119 Broadfoot Ave.
28305
(910) 486-5181
Est: 1993
Owners: Teri Coop Green & Dee Dalton

A unique collection of antique treasures, quilting supplies, and quality handmade items. Collectibles of all Kinds
"Sharing Things We Love"

Salisbury, NC   #10

Markey Fabric & Quilt Shop

Mon - Fri
9 - 6
Sat
9:30 - 5:30

126 Statesville Blvd.   28144
(704) 636-0252   Est: 1968
Owner: Beverly Rodgers

Featuring a Lg. selection of quilting fabrics & books.
Pfaff dealer.
Classes. Bridal and apparel fabrics.
Most Unique fabric shop for miles.

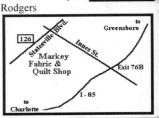

Clemmons, NC   #11

Fabric Village

Mon - Fri
10 - 5:30
Sat 10 - 4

2668 Lewisville-Clemmons RD.
P.O. Box 1605   27012
(910) 766-5273
Owner: Ann Roth   Est: 1992

We're new, but we're brimming with new fabrics, classes, and Quilting goodies!
Come See Us!

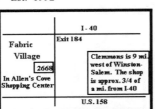

Come One and All !

Greensboro, NC #12

Fran's Quilt Shop

	Mon - Fri
	10 - 5
	Sat 10 - 4

519 State St.
27405
(910) 274-9805

Area's Largest
Selection of Quilting
Fabric, Books,
Notions, and gadgets.
Classes for
beginning,
intermediate &
advanced students

Cary, NC #13

Etc. Crafts

	Mon - Fri
	10 - 6
	Sat 10 - 5

226 E. Chatham St.   27511
(919) 467-7636
Owner: Jean Petersen

Large selection
of 100% Cotton
Quilting Fabrics.
Books and
Notions.

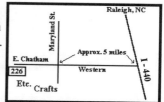

North Carolina Guilds:
Charlotte Quilter's Guild, PO Box 221035, Charlotte, 28222
Quilters by the Sea, PO Box, Wilmington, 28401
Forsyth Piecers & Quilters, P.O. Box 10666, Winston-Salem, 27108
Tarheel Quilters Guild, PO Box 36253, Fayetteville,28303
North Carolina Quilt Symposium, 200 Transylvania Avenue, Raleigh
Piedmont Quilters Guild, PO Box 10673, Greensboro, 27404
Durham-Orange Quilters' Guild, PO Box 51492, Durham, 27717-1492
Western North Carolina Quilters Guild, PO Box 3121, Hendersonville, 28793

Other Shops in North Carolina:

Asheville	Street Fair, 42 Battery Park Avenue
Aurora	Stitch N Sew, 109 E. Main Street
Bahama	Country Hearts Quilt & Gift Shop, 7603-B N. Roxboro Road
Black Mountain	N. E. Horton, 100 Sutton Avenue
Boone	Mayselle's Fabrics, 111 Boone Heights Shopping Center
Boone	The Log Haus, P.O. Box 272 Route #1
Burnsville	Needle Me This, 112 W. Main Street
Carrboro	NC Crafts Gallery, 212 West Main
Chapel Hill	Cotton Boll Creative Sewing Center, 91 S. Elliott Rd.
Chapel Hill	Countryside Antiques, P.O. Box 383 Route 9
Dunn	The Cutting Place, 510 E. Broad Street
Fayetteville	Sewing Center, 108 Owen Drive
Fayetteville	Village Fabrics, 2706 Bragg Blvd.
Fletcher	Carolina Fabric Outlet, 6024 Hendersonville Road
Franklin	Maco Crafts, 652 Georgia Highway
Goldston	Calico Quilt Antiques, Belview Avenue
Greensboro	Log Cabin Craftshop, 5435 Church Street
Greensboro	Fran's Quilt Shop, 521-A State Street
Greenville	Kay's Fabric & Fine Yarn, 608 E. Arlington Boulevard
Hendersonville	Mountain Memories, P.O. Box 273 Route #1
Hendersonville	Cloth of Gold, 1220 Spartanburg Hwy.
Hendersonville	The Fabric Center, Four Seasons Mall
Lake Lure	A Touch in Time Gift Shop, U.S. 74 Highway
State Road	Country Girl Fabrics, Klondike Road
Wilmington	Quilter's Bee, 2829 Vance St.
Winston	South Fork Cloth Shop, 3905 Country Club Road

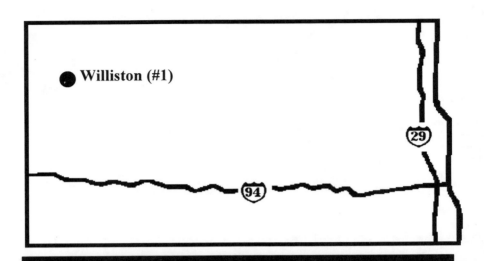

NORTH DAKOTA

1 Featured Shop

Williston, ND #1

QuiltMakins

**Mon - Sat
10 - 5:30**

16 East Broadway   58801
(701) 774-3315
Est: 1988   2200 sq. ft.
Owners: Dory Harstad & Tami Eide

100% Cottons,
Notions, Large
Selection of
books, classes,
and Friendly
Folk !

North Dakota Quilt Guilds:
Capital Quilters, Rt. 1 Box 342,
Bismark, 58501
Dakota Prairie Quilt Guild, PO Box
1723, Williston, 58801
Quilters' Guild of North Dakota, PO
Box 2662, Fargo, 58108

Other Shops in North Dakota:
Fargo   Quilter's Quarters, 604 Main Avenue
Jamestown   Stitches, 218 First Avenue S.
Minot   Carol's Etc., 22 S. Main

Willoughby (#35)
North Royalton (#34)
Toledo (#30)
Port Clinton (#31)
North Olmstead (#33)
Chesterland (#36)
Maumee (#29)
Brimfield (#37)
(#28) Bettsville
Youngstown (#42)
Amherst (#32)
(#24)
Wadsworth
Atwater
Canton (#43)
(#38)
Ashland (#27)
Kenton (#26)
Kidron (#23)
East (#41) Liverpool
Marion (#25)
Berlin (#22)
Delaware (#17)
Charm (#21)
Sugarcreek (#19 & 20)
Canfield (#39)
Spring - field (#13)
West Liberty (#16)
Plain City (#15)
Westerville (#18)
(#12) Brookville
Fairborn (#10)
Columbus (#11)
Caldwell (#40)
Kettering (#9)
Hilliard (#14)
Fairfield (#1)
Lebanon (#7)
Ross (#2)
Wilmington (#8)
Cincinnati (#3, 4, 5 & 6)

OHIO

43 Featured Shops

Fairfield, OH #1

Stitches 'n Such

Mon - Thur 10 - 8:30
Fri & Sat 10 - 4

702 Nilles Road   45014
(513) 829-2999   Est: 1980
Owners: Nancy Bolduc & Bev
3000 sq.ft.   Holdren

Over 2,000 bolts of 100% cotton fabrics. Large selection of books, patterns, & notions. Great models for inspiration. We are worth the trip!

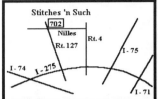

Scrapbag Quilt — A family album of favorite dresses and shirts.

Ross, OH #2

Undercover Quilt Shop

Mon - Thur 10 - 4:30
Fri & Sat 10 - 2

4267 Hamilton-Cleves Hwy
(513) 738-0261   Est: 1990
Owners: Dian Himes & Judy Huffman
1200 sq.ft.

Quilting Fabrics for traditional Quilters. Supplies Books, Patterns, Notions, Primitive Rug Supplies, Cushing Dyes, Stretch & Sew and silk ribbon.

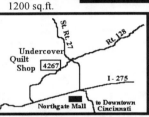

Cincinnati, OH #3

Creative Cottage

6934 Miami Ave.   45243
in "Madeira"   (513) 271-2028
Owner: Marie Tsacalis
Est: 1988   3300 sq.ft.
15 min. from downtown Cincinnati

QUILTING - Large selection of books, patterns, stencils & tools.
FABRIC - 1200+ bolts of exciting cotton.
CROSS STITCH - Over 4,000 books, 400+ cross stitch fabrics and accessories.
WALL STENCILING CLASSES AND WORKSHOPS

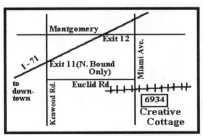

Mon - Sat 9:30 - 5:30
Wed & Thurs til 8:30
Sun 1 - 4

Cincinnati, OH #4

Ohio Star Quilt Shop

Mon - Fri 10 - 8
Sat 10 - 5
Sun 12 - 5

8315 Beechmont Ave.
45255
(513) 474-9355
Owners: Marianne &
Mark Schmitt
Est: 1993   1400 sq.ft.

Huge Selection of Quilting Supplies, Books, Classes and Notions. 1000 Bolts of Designer Fabric including RJR, Hoffman, Jinny Beyer, P&B

Cincinnati, OH #5

Sewing Basket

9536 Cincinnati-Columbus Road
(513) 779-2124   45241
Owners: Beth Bender & Madeline
Est: 1981   Goderre
2400 sq.ft.

Mon - Thur
10 - 8:30
Fri 10-5:30
Sat 10 - 5

Everything a Quilter wants plus counted cross stitch, yarn, paints, crafts and decorator fabrics.

Cincinnati, OH #6

Creations by Country Love

9384 Loveland-Madeira Rd.
(513) 984-1484   Est: 1986
Owner: Beverly Dickerson

Tues-Fri
10 - 6
Wed til 8
Sat 10 - 4

Quilting Fabric, Books, & Supplies. Classes. Custom Machine Quilting & Binding Service. Quilt Racks & Hangers. Baskets of all kinds.

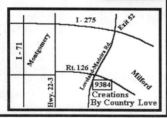

Lebanon, OH #7

The Village Sewing Shoppe

41 East Mulberry St.   45036
(513) 932-2552   Est: 1978
Owners: Glen & Nedra Whittington
3200 sq.ft.

Mon - Fri
9:30 - 5:30
Sat 9:30-5

Our shop has 3000 plus bolts of fabric; many patterns, books, sewing notions and supplies. Quality fabrics-- new ones arrive weekly.

Wilmington, OH #8

In Stitches

Mon - Thur
9 - 9
Fri & Sat
9 - 5

100 1/2 W. Main St.   45177
(513) 382-5559   Est: 1993
Owners: Joy Kersey, Susan &
                 Charlotte Henry

100% Cottons,
Patterns, Books,
Notions, Classes.
Viking & White
Sewing Machines
& Sergers
Unique Country
Gifts.

Kettering, OH #9

The Cotton Patch

Mon - Sat
10 - 4
Mon &
Thur til 8

1120 East Dorothy Lane
(513) 297-0090   45419
Owner: Susan Parr   Est: 1990
                            2000 sq.ft.

Dayton's only
quilting supply
shop. Fabric,
books, patterns,
notions, classes
and special orders.
Professional
Machine Quilting
available at low
rates.

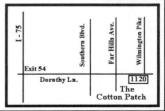

Fairborn, OH #10

Daisy Barrel, Inc.

Tues, Wed,
Fri, & Sat
10 - 4
Mon & Thur
10 - 8

19 West Main Street   45324
(513) 879-0111
Est: 1972   5,000 sq.ft.
Owners: Marjorie, Sandy, Judy,
                  Phyllis, & Gretchen

We specialize in
the best quality of
materials for the
quilter, cross-
stitcher, smocker
and stenciler. Our
experienced staff
will be glad to help

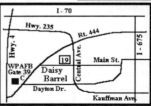

Helyn's Hoops

Owner: Gay
Dell

We manufacture /
wholesale the
"Hoop-de-deux" border
hoop and the "Cinch
Hoop", both invented by
the owner.

Columbus, OH #11

WE SHARE ONE SHOP
911 City Park Avenue   43206
(614) 443-9988

Mon - Sat   9 - 6
Additional Hrs by Appt.

Located in
German Village
Near Downtown
Columbus

Picking Up The Pieces

Owner: Pati
Shambaugh

Fabrics, books,
patterns, notions,
and supplies,
plus Pati's original
designs.

Brookville, OH   #12

Quilts N' Things

Mon, Tue, Thur, Fri 10 - 5
Sat 9:30 - 1:30

12322 Westbrook Rd.   45309
(513) 833-5188
Owner: Margaret Taylor
Est: 1984   2300 sq.ft.

Cotton Fabrics, Notions, Books, Stencils, Classes, Machine Quilting, Finished Quilts, Pillows, Wall Hangings, Aprons, & Bonnets

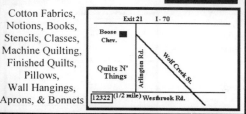

Hilliard, OH   #14

Stitchery Plus

Mon & Wed 10 - 6
Tue & Thur 10 - 8
Fri & Sat 10 - 5

3983 Main St.   43026
(614) 771-0657
Owner: Susan Mathewson
Est: 1981   5250 sq.ft.

Over 2000 bolts of 100% cotton fabrics. Quilting Supplies. Pfaff Sewing Machines. Counted Cross Stitch, Miniatures & Doll Houses.

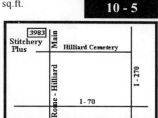

West Liberty, OH   #16

Oak Branch Quilt Shop

Tues- Sat 9 - 5:30

5093 St. Rt. 68 South   43357
(513) 465-9296   Est: 1989   400 sq.ft
Owner: Eleanor Kirkbride

100% cottons, Designer Fabrics, Panels, Books, Magazines, Notions, Q-Snap frames, Gift items, Greeting Cards, classes & workshops year 'round

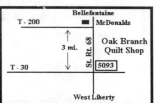

Springfield, OH   #13

Lettuce Quilt

Mon - Fri 10 - 5
Mon & Thur til 8
Sat 10 - 4

1037 Bechtle Ave.   45504
(513) 322-8100   Est: 1991
Owners: Sandra Deards &
2500 sq.ft.   Ruth Romaker

Thousands of quilt toys and fabrics to entice you.

A true Quilter's Toystore

Plain City, OH   #15

The Fabric Shoppe

Mon - Sat 9 - 5

9872 U.S. 42   43064
(614) 873-4123
Owner: Perry Yoder

Mgr. Mary Beachy

Specializing in: 100% Cottons, Fashion Fabrics, Lace Curtains by the yard. Prints & solids. Quilts; Custom Quilts and Quilting Supplies.

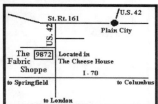
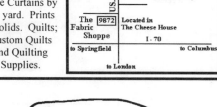

Delaware, OH #17

Yarn Barn

141 East Winter   43015
(614) 369-5537   Est: 1971
Owner: Pat Kirtland
1000 sq.ft.

Mon - Thur
11 - 7
Fri 11 - 8
Sat 10-5:30

Supplies for Quilting, Knitting, Crochet, Counted Cross-stitch, Crewel, Needlepoint, Tatting. Lotsa Books, Patterns, Buttons, Yarn, Etc.

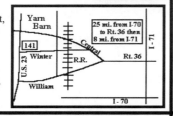

Westerville, OH #18

Calico Cupboard

24 N. State Street   43081
(614) 891-0938
Owner: Jane Seelig
Est: 1971   5000 sq.ft.

Mon - Fri
9:30 - 9
Sat 9:30-6
Sun 12 - 5

2000+ bolts of cotton fabrics, plus hundreds of patterns, books, notions and much more. Craft supplies & Gifts too! We're worth the trip

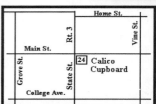

Sugarcreek, OH #19

Swiss Village Quilts and Crafts

113 S. Broadway   P.O. Box 514
(216) 852-4855   44681
Owners: Aden & Anna Hochstetler
Est: 1982   1250 sq.ft.   Free Brochure

Mon - Sat
9 - 5

Quality, local-made Quilts, Wallhangings and related items. Wooden toys Etc. Most items made locally by Amish Special orders gladly Accepted.

Sugarcreek, OH #20

Spector's Store

122 E. Main   44681
(216) 852-2113
Mgr: Mary Mullet

Mon - Sat
8:30 - 5
Fri til 8

Full Line of Fabric and notions. Quilt and Craft supplies. Excellent Values on Solid & Printed fabrics.

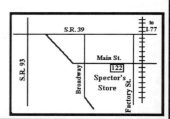

Charm, OH #21

Miller's Dry Goods

4500 S.R. 557   Est: 1965
Mail—Millersburg, OH 44654
Owners: The Miller Family

Mon - Sat
8 - 5

Beautiful selection of ready-made Quilts. Custom Quilting. Over 3000 bolts of fabric. Wall hangings, pillows, quillows, etc. Nice selection of quilt and pattern books.

Also — a whole barn full of quilts right beside us !

Berlin, OH #22

Gramma Fannie's Quilt Barn

**Mon - Fri
10 - 5
Sat 10 - 6**

4363 S.R. 39   at The Amish Farm
(216) 893-3232   44610
Owners: John Schrock & Joann
Est: 1991   Hershburger

Visit our unique shop specializing in our own line of patterns & kits, custom order quilts, top of the line quilt fabrics, books and stencils

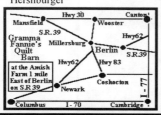

Kidron, OH #23

Hearthside Quilt Shoppe

**Mon - Sat
9:30 - 5
closed major
holidays**

13110 Emerson Rd.   Box 222
(216) 857-4004   44636
Owners: Clifford & Lena Lehman
est: 1990   Mgr. Cheryl Gerber
                           2400 sq.ft.

Amish and Swiss Mennonite Quilts, Wall Hangings made in our area. Large selection to choose from. Custom orders welcome! Catalog $2.00

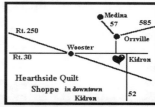

Wadsworth, OH #24

Sally's Shop

**Mon - Fri
10 - 5:30
Sat
9:30 - 3**

139 College Street   44281
(216) 334-1996
Owner: Sally Morrison
Est: 1975   2400 sq.ft.

Over 500 bolts of calicos + other fabrics -- patterns & books -- Also needlework -- yarns -- spinning & weaving fibers and equipment.

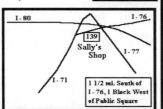

Marion, OH #25

Crafter's Joy

**Mon - Fri
11 - 7
Sat & Sun
11 - 4**

127 South Main St.   43302
(614) 382-4043   Est: 1991
              Owner: Joy
100% cotton   Watkins
quilting fabrics,
100's of quilting books and patterns plus all the "necessary notions". Also tole painting supplies, cross stitch supplies and handmade gifts.

Kenton, OH #26

Ye Olde Schoolhouse

**Sun 1 - 5
Mon 7 - 9
Tue, Wed,
Thur 12 - 9
Sat 12 - 5**

10389 C.R. 190   43326
(419) 675-1652
Owner: Dolores D. Phillips-
Est: 1978   Layman

Full Line Quilt Shop Notions & Novelties Books & Patterns Featuring Hoffman, RJR, Benartex, Kona Bay, Kauffman, Alexander Henry and more.

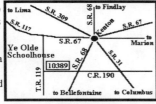

Ashland, OH #27

Country Charm Fabrics

**Mon - Fri
10 - 5
Sat 10 - 4**

1422 Township Road 593
(419) 281-2341   44805
Est: 1975   1200 sq.ft.
Owners: Cindy Doggett & Alice Finley

A Complete array of Quilting fabrics from the best mills in America. Notions, Quilt Frames, Classes, and all of the essentials for the Quilting Enthusiast.

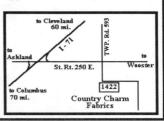

THE DOOR MOUSE

Est: 1979   3600 sq.ft.

Over 4000 bolts of cotton, patterns, and quilting supplies in a barn setting. Featuring quilts and many handcrafted memories, legends and heirlooms which capture the beauty and simplicity of rural life. Join our friendly staff for classes in the corn crib.

Mail Orders Welcome
Swatches available
Price based on quanity

5047 W. SR 12   44815
(419) 986-5667 3600 sq.ft.

**Mon - Thur 10 - 8
Fri & Sat 10 - 5
Last Sunday of
Month 12 - 5**

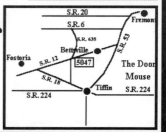

Bettsville, OH   #28

Owner: Mary Ann Sorg

Maumee, OH   #29

The Quilt Foundry

234 W. Wayne   43537   1000 sq.ft.
(419) 893-5703   Opened: 1981
Owners: Mary Beham, Margaret Okuley, Peg Sawyer, Gretchen Schultz

**Mon - Sat
10 - 4
Tues eve
7 - 9**

The Quilt Foundry offers friendly, personalized service in your search for wonderful fabric, quilting supplies, books and classes.

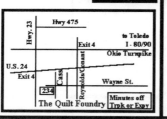

Toledo, OH   #30

Busy Bee Quilts

838 E. Broadway   43605-3010
(419) 691-2939   Est: 1991
Owner: Alice M. Horvath   1600 sq.ft.
Send LSASE for Machine Quilting Brochure

**Tue - Sat
9 - 4**

Our shop has 100% cotton fabrics, books, notions, lessons, etc. We do custom machine quilting. Mail orders accepted.

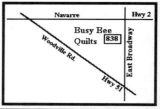

Port Clinton, OH   #31

Carol's Fabric Art

312 W. Third St.   43452
(419) 734-3650
Owner: Carol Swope
Est: 1984

**Tues - Sat 10 - 5
Tue & Thur eve
6:30 - 9**

Fabrics, Books, Patterns, Notions, Cross - Stitch Stencils.

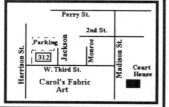

Amherst, OH #32

Quilts & Kreations

Mon - Sat
10 - 5
Mon &
Thur til 8

2272 Kresge Dr.   44001
(216) 282-8872
Owner: Sandie Whitaker
Est: 1980   1200 sq.ft.

Featuring
Patterns, Books,
Designer Fabrics,
Classes, Quilts &
Quilt Racks,
and Ready mades
for sale.

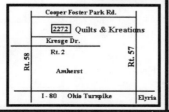

North Olmsted, OH #33

Hoops 'n' Hollers

Mon - Fri
10 - 9
Sat 10 - 6
Sun 1 - 5

24888 Lorain Road   44070
(216) 779-4700

Owner: Sandi
Luther

Quilting, Tole
Painting &
Stenciling
Supplies.
Antique and New
Quilts, Quilting
Service, Gifts,
Quarterly
Newsletter.
Authorized Bernina
Dealer. Classes.

School House — One place to learn piecing.

#34

LOG CABIN QUILTS

✳ We Do Machine Quilting
✳ Machine Basting
✳ Hand & Machine Binding

We have the Largest Selection
in Northeast Ohio of
90" wide 100% Cotton Fabrics

We Also Stock 108" & 120" Linings

40,000 Yards of 100% Cotton Fabric
AT or near WHOLESALE Prices

CALL PHYLLIS AT
(216) 237-7406

We Also Stock Polyester Batting on the Roll
We Stock Wool Batts for Comforters
15953 YORK RD. NORTH ROYALTON, OHIO 44133

New Location in 1995
910 Kimber Rd. Wooster Ohio   44691

CALL PHYLLIS AT
(216) 264-6690

Willoughby, OH #35

Erie Street Fabrics

Mon & Thur
10 - 8
Tues & Wed
10 -6
Fri & Sat
10 - 5

4134 Erie Street   44094
(216) 953-1340   Est: 1979
Owner: Mary Huey
3000 sq.ft.

Stocked with a unique assortment of cotton fabrics. Offering year-round classes in Quiltmaking, Smocking & Clothing. Authorized Bernina Dealer.

Rt. 2 Lakeland Frwy.
Erie Street Fabrics
4134
Rt. 91
Erie St.
Mentor Ave. (Rt. 20)
2 miles from Rt. 91 or Rt. 306
Rt. 306
I - 90

Chesterland, OH #36

Remembrances

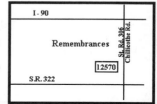

Mon - Sat
10 - 5

12570 Chillicothe Rd.   44026
(216) 729-1650
Owner: Cheryl Pedersen
Est: 1984   1200 sq.ft.

Cotton Fabrics, Notions, Books. Classes: quilting & dollmaking. Finished crafts also available.

I - 90
Remembrances
St. Rd. 306
Chillicothe Rd.
12570
S.R. 322

Brimfield, OH #37

Calico, Wicker & Thyme, Inc.

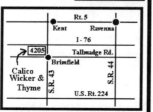

Mon - Fri
10 - 5:30
Thur til 8
Sat 10 - 4

4205 State Route 43   44240
(216) 678-3220   Est: 1980
Owner: Pat Knapp   2,000 sq.ft.

Area's most Complete Quilt Shoppe offering a large selection of 100% Cotton Fabrics, quilt books, patterns, notions and classes as well as FREE Inspiration and advice.

Rt. 5
Kent   Ravenna
I - 76
4205
Tallmadge Rd.
Brimfield
Calico Wicker & Thyme
S.R. 43
S.R. 44
U.S. Rt. 224

Youngstown, OH #38

Quilter's Quarters

8458 Market Street   44512
(216) 758-7072
Owner: Julie Maruskin
Est: 1989   900 sq.ft.

Mon - Fri
9 - 5
Sat 9 - 4

We carry quilting supplies, fabrics, tools, books and patterns. We teach hand and machine piecing, masterpiece quilting stitch, and applique.

Rt. 244
Mall
Quilter's Quarters
8458
Rt. 7
Western Reserve
Ohio Turnpike

Log Cabin and Pine
Tree —
For a Quilter,
found in the hope
chest; not in the
woods.

Canfield, OH   #39

Knitting Corners

Mon - Sat
10 - 5
Thur til 8

4254 Boardman-Canfield Road
(216) 533-5505   44406
Owners: June Bennehoof
4000 sq.ft.   & Linda Palmer

Complete
Needlework shop
featuring fabrics,
patterns & supplies
for quilting, cross
stitch, knitting,
needlepoint, crewel,
harganger, tatting &
battenberg lace.

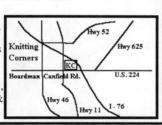

Caldwell, OH   #40

Townsquare Fabrics
& QUILT SHOP

507 Main Street
(614) 732-5351
res. (614) 732-4449
Owner:
Glendola Pryor
Est: 1985

Mon - Thur
9 - 5
Fri 9 - 8
Sat 9 - 2

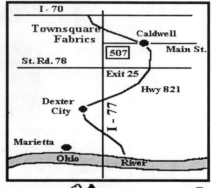

Cotton Fabric   Stencils
Quilting Supplies Batting
Patterns   Books
Q-Snap Quilting Frames
Daytime & Evening
Classes

East Liverpool, OH #41

Make Mine Country

13210 St. Rt. #7   44432
(216) 386-4609
Owner: Janet Householder
Est: 1987

**Tues - Sat
10 - 4**

Quilting fabrics,
supplies, books,
patterns, handmade
quilt items. Counted
Cross-stitch books,
Fabric,
Custom Framing.
Classes.

Atwater, OH #42

The J's Nest

791 Stroup Road   44201
(216) 947-2703
Owner: Martha McClay Strickler
Est: 1983   400 sq.ft.

**Tues - Sat
11:30 - 4:30
Or By
Appointment**

Approx. 600 bolts
of cottons,
notions, books,
stencils, lessons.
Will do machine
quilting.

Canton, OH #43

Schoolhouse Quilt Shoppe

2872 Whipple Ave.   44708
(216) 477-4767   Est: 1976
Owners: Judie & Bob Rolhernal

**Mon - Sat
9:30 - 5
Tues &
Thur til 8**

Lots of Fabric,
Quilts, &
Supplies **We
have a catalog of
fabrics and
original quilt
kits available.**
Send $2.00
Come Visit Us !

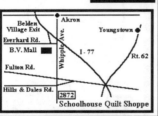

Area Guilds in Ohio:
The Cascade Quilters of Akron, 2270 Thurmont Rd., Akron, 44313
Old Uniontown Quilt Guild, Ashland
Townsquare Quilt Lovers, PO Box 207, Caldwell, 43724
Ohio Valley Quilters Guild, 7332 Zig Zag Lane, Cincinnati, 45242
Good Time Quilters, 129 W. Mound St., Circleville, 43113
Conneaut Quilters' Guild, 7194 Pitts Rd., Conneaut, 44030
The Quilt Foundry Guild, 234 W. Wayne St., Maumee, 43537
Buckeye Blossoms Quilt Guild, 11 McKinley St., Middletown, 45042
Maumee Bay Country Quilt Guild, Oregon
Ohio Star Quilters, 808 Jefferson St., Port Clinton, 43452
Clinton County Quilt Association, 2675 Melvin Road Sabina, 45169
Gathering of Quilters Guild, PO Box 631, Sylvania, 43560
Clinton County Quilt Assoc., Wilmington, 45177

Other Shops in Ohio:

Akron	A Piece in Time. 5590 Manchester Road
Akron	Darwin D. Bearley Antique Quilts, 98 Beck Avenue
Alliance	This & That Merchandise Outlet, 109 W. 23rd Street
Anna	Dishong Country Store, 2699 S. 25A
Barnesville	The Sewing Basket, 119 W. Main Street
Berlin	Helping Hands Quilt Shop, PO Box 183
Berlin	Plain & Fancy Fabrics, PO Box 74 German Village Shopping Center
Berlin	Country Craft Cupboard, Main Street
Brookville	Quilts N - Things, 12322 Westbrook Road
Canton	The Sewing Basket, 4804 Sherman Church Avenue S.W.
Chagrin Falls	O'Keefe's Stitchin' Time Shop, 25 S. Franklin Street
Chillicothe	Creations, 51 E. Water
Cincinnati	Village Crafters, 33 Eswin
Cleveland	Berlin Quilting, 3990 E. 71st Street
Columbiana	Heart of the Country, 14895 South Avenue
Columbus	The Quiltery, 2905 N. High
Columbus	Midwest Quilt Exchange, 495 S. Third Street
Columbus	Glass Thimble, 3434 N. High
Coshocton	Calico Harvest Dry Goods, 84 Pine Street
Coshocton	Heart of the Village, 432 N. Whitewoman Street
Coshocton	Tin Thimble, 432 N. Whitewoman Street
Creston	Quilt Country, 9581 Cleveland Road
Cuyahoga	Stitch, Piece, 'N Purl, 2018 State Road
Dalton	Village Collectables, 508 E. Main St.
Dayton	Sew-A-Lot, 518 Dayton Mall
Dayton	Sew Biz, 3098 Woodman Drive
Dayton	Stitching Post Sewing Center, 1946 E. Stroop Road
Dayton	Ann's Sew Biz, 3098 Woodman Drive
Dayton	The Golden Goose, 25 E. Franklin Street
East Palestine	Sew What, 239 N. Market
Findlay	The Ohio Farm House, 16056 U.S. Route 224 E.
Findlay	The Stitching Bear, 915 N. Main Street
Greenville	Extra Special Products, PO Box 777 5339 State Route 571 E.
Harrison	Betty Lou Quilting & Fabric Outlet, 110 Harrison Avenue
Hartville	Quilts Etc., 12380 Market Avenue North
Jackson	Country Notions, 110 Twin Oaks Drive
Lebanon	Oh Susannah, 16 S. Broadway
Lima	Country Side Stitch & Sew Shop, 1207 North McClure Road
Lisbon	Rita's Clocks & Amish Quilts, 40 N. Park Avenue
Loveland	Lady Bug Quilt Shoppe, 1464 Highway 28
Mansfield	Quilt Connection, 415 Park Avenue W.
Mansfield	Bev's Fabric Shop, 466 Melody Lane
Middlefield	Country Touch, 14277 Old State Rd.
Minerva	Calico Grandma's, 616 Valley Street
Mount Vernon	Jordan's Quilt Shop, 16 South Main Street
Mt. Eaton	Spector's Store, 1 W. Main St., P.O. Box 275
Navarre	Country Quilts, 6 Linter Court
Orrville	Grandma's House, 5598 Chippewa Rd.
Portsmouth	Clara's Sewing Center & Fabric Shop, 2227 6th
Richfield	Three Friends Antiques Company, P.O. Box 310, 3930 Broadview Road
Sandusky	Roll Country, 1107 E. Bogart Road
Shreve	Shreve Fabric & Craft Center, PO Box 504 102 S. Market Street
Shreve	Quilts -N- Things - Oak Furniture, PO Box 581 193 S. Market
Springboro	Sally's Quilts and Gifts, 250 S. Main Street
Stow	Stow Needlecraft, 3310 Kent Road
Streetsboro	Christine's Carpet & Quilt Shoppe, 8897 State Route 14
Troy	Robbins Nest, 1474 State Route 718
Walnut Creek	The Farmer's Wife, 4952 Walnut Street
Washington Court House	Bee in Stitches, 247 E. Court Street
Washington Court House	The Buckeye House, 825 Lincoln Drive
Waverly	Alice's Yarn & Stuff, 579 Blain Highway
Waverly	Stitch Shop, 305 N. Market
Wilmot	The Ohio Star Company, P.O. Box 176

Tulsa, OK   #1

The Quilters' Nook

5559 East 41st. Highland Plaza	**Mon - Fri**
(918) 627-6737 74135	**9:30 - 5:30**
Owners: Glen Jones & Anne	**Sat:**
Est: 1987 1700 sq.ft. Seereiter	**9:30 - 4:30**

<u>Fabric</u> - Always
100% Cottons.
<u>Notions</u> - To
  ease tasks.
<u>Patterns & Books</u>
  For inspiration
  & instruction.
  FRIENDLY
  SERVICE !

```
I - 244
The
Quilter's
Nook                    Yale  Sheridan
Take 41st &
Sheridan Exit   5559              41st St.
I - 44
                                  Broken
                                  Arrow
                                  Fwy (51)
```

Tulsa, OK   #2

Cotton Patch

8250 East 71st St.   74133
(918) 252-1995
Owners: Nancy & Mike Mullman
Est: 1977   1200 sq.ft.

**Mon - Fri
10 - 5:30
Tues til 7
Sat 10 - 5**

Large quilt
fabric
selection,
books,
notions, and
patterns.

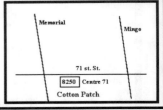

Oklahoma QUILTWORKS

9323 N. Pennsylvania 73120
(405) 842-4778
Barbara Stanfield & Carole Jo Evans
Est: 1988   2400 sq.ft.

| Notions
Patterns
Classes
Gifts | **Mon - Fri
10 - 5
Thur til 8
Sat 10 - 3** | 2500+ bolts of
Cotton Fabric
500+ Quilting
Book Titles |

Oklahoma City, OK   #3

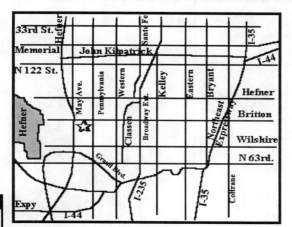

Come Visit us
in August of
Odd
Numbered
years for the
"Celebration
of Quilts"
Quilt Show

Enid, OK #4

The Quilting Parlor

118 North Independence   73701
(405) 234-3087
Owner: Patricia M. Russell
Est: 1981   3000 sq.ft.

**Mon - Sat
10 - 5**

2000 Bolts 100%
Cotton Fabrics,
Notions, Books,
Classes. Quilt
Camp - A
weekend retreat
of classes for the
quilter.

The Quilting Parlor	Randolph
118	
Down-Town Square	Broadway I-35
	412 (28 miles)

Lawton, OK #5

Hilltop Fabrics

8202 W. Lee   R.R. #4 P.O. Box 169
(405) 536-5776   73505
Owner: Rita Hill
Est: 1976   1500 sq.ft.

**Mon - Fri
9:30 - 5:30**

Home based quilt
shop. Lessons in
Lap Quilting.
Good selection of
calicos, solids
and notions.

(map) to Okla. City / I-44 N / 82nd. / 52nd. / 2nd. / Lawton Exit / Lee Blvd.W / 8202 / Hilltop Fabrics / 67th. / 23rd. / to Wichita Falls, TX

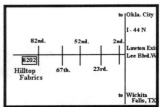

Washing —
Grandma's
Quilt in the
Bathtub but
no shirts in
the drawers.

Muskogee, OK #6

School House Quilt Shop

429 East Side Boulevard   74403
(918) 683-7825   Est: 1987
Owner: Mary Jane Youngblood
          2500 sq.ft.

**Mon & Fri
1 - 5
Tues, Wed,
& Sat 10 - 4**

100 % Cottons,
books, patterns,
notions, pillows
& Quilts, Quilt
Tops, Frames and
classes.
You all Come

	EastSide Blvd.
Freedonia	
Dayton St.	429 School House
Callahan St.	Quilt Shop
E. Broadway	
E. Okmulgee	

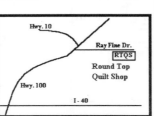

Gore, OK #7

Round Top Quilt Shop

Box 217   Ray Fine Dr.   74435
(918) 489-5652
Owner: Mardena Matthews
Est: 1985

**Tues - Sat
9 - 5**

Quilting Supplies
Fabric
Patterns, Books
Notions, Classes
Plus Finished
Quilts &
Wallhangings.

Hwy. 10	
	Ray Fine Dr.
	RTQS
	Round Top Quilt Shop
Hwy. 100	
	I-40

Notes

Oklahoma Quilters State Org., P.O. Box 5015, Bartlesville, 74005
Oklahoma Guilds:
Central Oklahoma Quilters Guild, P.O. Box 23916, O.K. City, 73123
Muskogee Area Quilting Guild, 405 Crabtree Rd., Muskogee, 74403
Pioneer Area Quilters' Guild, P.O. Box, 2726, Ponca City, 74604
Green Country Quilter's Guild, P.O. Box 35021, Tulsa, 74153

Other shops in Oklahoma:

Anadarko	Calico Patch Sewing Center, 105 W. Broadway St.
Bartlesville	Calico Moose, 502 S. Cherokee Avenue
Blair	Sam's Machine Quilting & Gifts, S.E. of City
Cheyenne	Granny's Quilt House, 201 E. Columbia
Chickasha	Off the Bolt, 323 Chickasha
Chouteau	The Quilt Shoppe, 101 S. Chouteau Avenue
Guthrie	The Pincushion, 124 W. Oklahoma Avenue
Henryetta	Quilt Barn, Box 296A Route 2
Norman	Patchwork Place, 914 W. Main
Oklahoma City	The Quilt Barn, 1335 SW 59th st.
Oklahoma City	Buckboard Antiques & Quilts, 1411 North May
Purcell	Sue Wilhite, 629 West Monroe St.
Shawnee	Sue's Sewing Shoppe, 2301 North Kickapoo
Tulsa	The Quilting B, 9433 E. 51st Street
Tulsa	Artistry & Old Lace, 3314 South Peoria

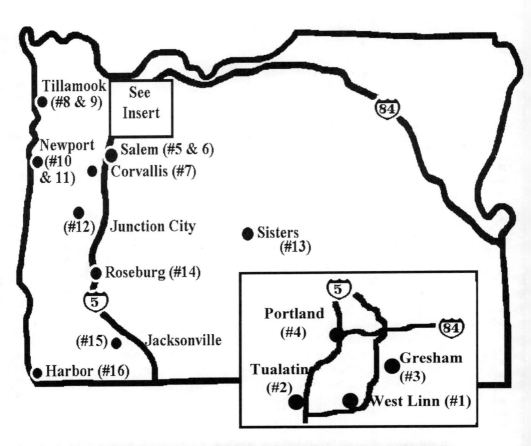

16 Featured Shops

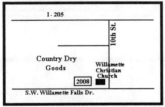
Crazy Quilt —
Often the refuge of
old family ties !

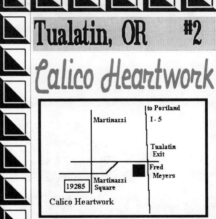

Gresham, OR #3

Oregon Country Fabrics, Inc.

Mon, Fri, & Sat 9:30 - 5
Tues - Thur 9:30 - 9

2025 E. Burnside   P.O. Box 2351
(503) 669-9739   97030
Owners: Vickie Peterson & Susan Miller   Est: 1991
1500 sq.ft.

Gresham's only quilting store. Over 1200 bolts of Hoffman, Jinny Beyer, P&B, plus many books, patterns & notions.

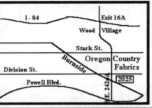

Portland, OR #4

Patchwork Peddlers

Thurs-Sat 10 - 4

2108-A N.E. 41st Ave. (basement)
(503) 287-5987   97212
Est: 1977   1200 sq.ft.
Owners: Mary Ann Cunningham & Corliss Marsh

Largest selection of quilt books in the Northwest; 1200 bolts of 100% cotton fabric

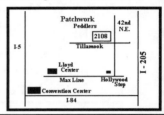

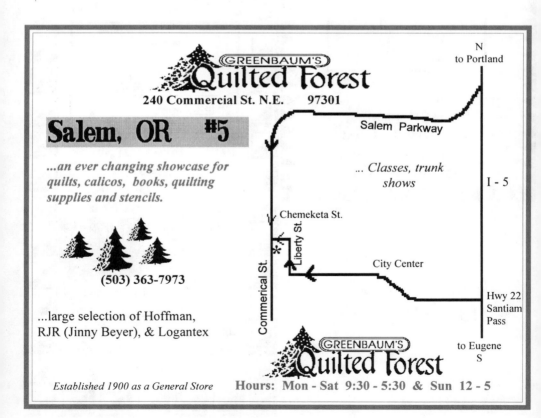

GREENBAUM'S Quilted Forest

240 Commercial St. N.E.   97301

Salem, OR #5

...an ever changing showcase for quilts, calicos, books, quilting supplies and stencils.

(503) 363-7973

...large selection of Hoffman, RJR (Jinny Beyer), & Logantex

... Classes, trunk shows

Established 1900 as a General Store   **Hours: Mon - Sat 9:30 - 5:30 & Sun 12 - 5**

Salem, OR   #6

Simply Friends

1313 Mill St. S.E.   97301
(In the Mission Mill Village)
(503) 363-9230   Est: 1993
Owners: Cindy Helsley & Bonnie McNeely

Tues - Sat
10 - 4:30

Located in an Historic Woolen Mill. A charming shop with 100% cottons, books, notions and over 200 doll and quilt patterns.

Corvallis, OR   #7

Quiltwork Patches

209 S.W. 2nd. Street   97333
(503) 752-4820
Owners: Brian & Jessy Yorgey
Est: 1979   650 sq.ft.

Mon - Sat
9:30 - 5

Over 1200 bolts of fine quality fabrics, plus a large selection of Quilter's tools and books.
Catalog $1.00

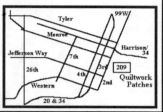

Tillamook, OR   #8

Latimer Quilt & Textile Center

2105 Wilson River Loop 97141
(503) 842-8622

Tues - Sat
10 - 4
Sun 12 - 4

A museum dedicated to the textile arts. We have classes for quilting, spinners, & weavers. Shows change every 2 months.

We are located north of Tillamook one block off 101 N by the Coronet Store and the Shilo Inn.

Tillamook, OR   #9

Jane's Fabric Patch

903 Pacific Ave.   97141
(503) 842-9392   Est: 1981
Owner: Jane Schoenborn

Mon - Sat
9 - 5:30
Summer -
Sundays &
Holidays
11 - 3

Coastal Retreat Multi-facetted Quilt shop. Large fabric selection, creative, knowledgeable and friendly ideas and assistance.

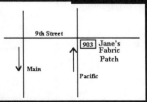

Newport, OR   #10

The Newport Quilt & Gift Co.

Mon - Sat 10 - 5

428 S.W. Coast Hwy.   97365
(503) 265-3492   Est: 1989
Owner: Julie Golimowski   2400 sq.ft.   Free Catalog

"The Most Complete Quilt shop on the Oregon Coast" Fabric, books, notions, gifts! Home of the Famous Lighthouse Quilt Blocks.

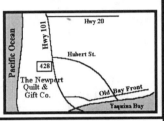

Newport, OR   #11

The Gingham Goose

Mon - Sat 10 - 6
Sun 11 - 4

1662 N. Coast Hwy   97365
(503) 265-8338   Est: 1976
Owners: Suzanne Huffman & Janice Harrison
                1096 sq.ft.   Brochure $2.00

Quality hand crafted gifts, dolls & decor with a country flair. Over 600 bolts quilting fabric and 250 quilting & craft patterns. Home of Internationally known "The Gingham Goose" pattern line.

Junction City, OR   #12

Country Corner Quilting

Tues - Fri 10 - 5
Sat 10 - 4

189 W. 6th Ave.   97448
(503) 998-2289

Complete line of Fabric, Notions, Books, & Patterns. Machine Quilting, Custom & Ready to buy Quilts & Crafts. Classes

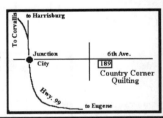

#13

Mon - Sat 10 - 5
Sun 11 - 5

(503) 549-6061
Owner: Jean Wells
Est: 1975
Fabric Finders Fabric Club $15 a year.

A fantasy of cotton fabrics for quilting, doll and santa patterns, quilt books, and ideas galore. Sisters Outdoor Quilt Show, 2nd Sat. in July

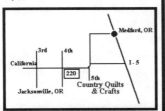

Area Guilds:
Mary's River Quilt Guild, PO Box 1317, Philomath 97370
Northwest Quilters, PO Box 3405, Portland 97208 (503) 222-1991
Mountain States Quilters Guild, 404 Pavillian, Grants Pass 97526
Junction City Quilt Guild, 1225 W. 10th Street, Junction City 97448
Coast Quilters, 2360 Longwood Drive, Reedsport, 97467
Umpqua Valley Quilt Guild, 1624 W. Harvard Ave., Roseburg, 97470
East of the Cascade Quilters, PO Box 280, Sisters, 97759
Mid Valley Quilt Guild, PO Box 621, Salem, 97308-0621
Tillamook County Quilters, 6735 Tillamook Ave., Bay City 97107

Other shops in Oregon:

Beaverton	Mill End Retail Store, 12155 SW Broadway
Bend	Mountain Country Mercantile, 1568 Newport Ave.
Corvallis	Sewing Plus/Country Calico, 6120 S.W. Ctry. Club Dr.
Corvallis	Briar Rose Quilt Shop
Eugene	The Quilt Patch, 23 E. 28th
Eugene	Factory Fabrics, 2165 West 7th
Florence	Laurel Street Fabrics, 208 Laurel St.
Florence	Nan Sal Fabrics, 1749 Hwy 101
Jacksonville	Calico Junction Fabric Boutique, 115 West California
Lakeview	EM Calico Country, 7 N.E. Street
Port Orford	Country Carousel Fabrics, 1634 Oregon, PO Box 1043
Portland	Geri Miner, 524 N.W. 23rd
Portland	Mill End Retail Store, 9701 SE McLoughlin Blvd.
Portland	Amish Quilt Shop, 5331 S.W. Macadem
Portland	Itchins to Stitch, 15715 S. W. 116th Avenue
Portland	Scarborough Fair, 4442 N. E. 131 Pl.
Reedsport	Quilt Connections, 850 Broadway Avenue
Salem	Thread Bear Studio, 1313 Mill S. E.
Scappoose	Country Cloth & Craft, 52547 Columbia River Hwy.
Springfield	Jean Marie's Fabrics, 637 Main

Quilt Show —
A gathering
with love on
all the walls.

Sunbonnet Sue —
A Young Girl that
seams to show up at
every quilt show.

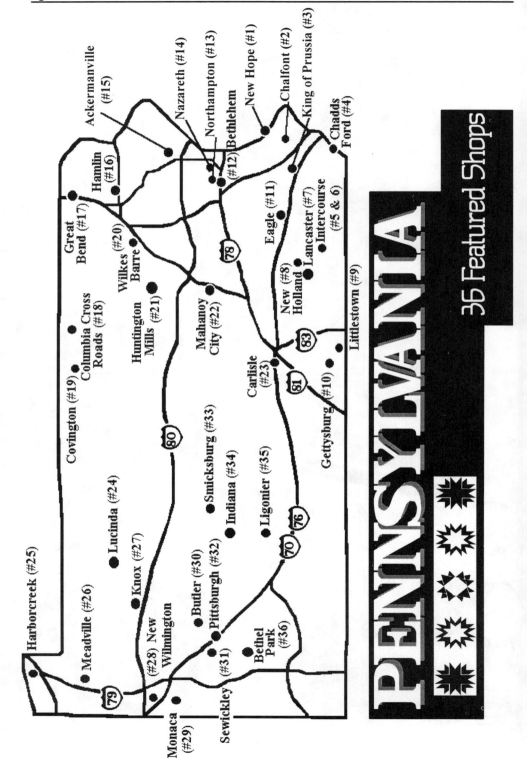

PENNSYLVANIA

35 Featured Shops

New Hope, PA   #1

Grandmother's Flower Garden

10 E. Randolph
    18938
(215) 862-0955
Owners: Sibby &
George Hillman
Est: 1989

Featuring over 250 antique and vintage quilts, and always a large selection of antique and vintage tops. Antique quilts laundered and restored, dated and appraised. The owners present programs to groups on trends and developments in American quilts from 1840 to 1940, and also mount antique quilt shows and sales as fundraisers for organizations.
Specializing in reproduction fabrics, with genuine vintage fabrics always available, and offering other cotton fabrics, books, patterns, frames, supplies and lessons.

Open 7 Days a Week 10 - 5

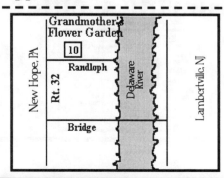

Chalfont, PA #2

THE COUNTRY QUILT SHOP

3303 Limekiln Pike
(intersection of County
Line Rd. & Rt. 152)
(215) 822-3522
Owner: Cyndi Hershey
Est: 1987 1500 sq.ft.

An assortment of over 2200
bolts of the finest 100%
cotton fabrics–
RJR, P&B, Hoffman, Horton,
Marcus Bros., Alex. Henry, etc.
BOOKS, PATTERNS,
TOOLS, & NOTIONS
Classes for all levels
Experienced quilters eager to help
with any project.
Located in a charming 18th
century house.
Stop in and experience the
excitement.

Tues - Sat   10 - 5
Wed & Thur til 9   Sun 1 - 5

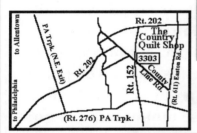

Steve's King of Prussia Sewing Center

The area's best
selection of quilting
fabrics, books, and
supplies—including
Bernina, BabyLock,
and Singer sewing machines,
sergers, and accessories.

**Mon - Fri
10 - 9
Sat 10 - 5
Sun 12 - 5**

King of Prussia, PA #3

(610) 768-9453
**156 West Dekalb Pike, Valley Forge
Shopping Center, Rt. 202**

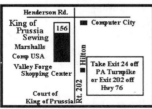

Chadds Ford, PA #4

A Patch of Country

22 Olde Ridge Village   19317
(610) 459-8993   Est: 1983
Owner: Karen Reed
                2,200 sq.ft.

Mon - Sat
10 - 5
Thurs &
Fri til 8
Sun 12 - 5

Quality Cottons, Notions, 250+ Book Titles, Patterns. Mail Order and Special Order Service. Year-round classes with full student support.

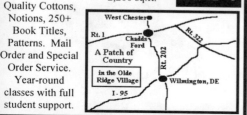

Intercourse, PA #5

The Country Market at Intercourse

3504 Old Philadelphia Pike 17534
(717) 768-8058   3200 sq.ft.
Owner: Dorothy Freyer Est: 1992
Send SASE for list of Pellon Patterns

April - Nov
Mon - Sat
9 - 5
Dec - March
Mon - Sat
10 - 5

Come Meet the Amish with their Quilts--
Hand made Pellon quilt patterns - pillows - crib quilts - wallhangings - Crafts Furniture

Intercourse, PA #6

The Old Country Store

3510 Old Philadelphia Pike 17534
(717) 768-7101

Mem. Day - Oct 30
Mon - Sat 9 - 8
Nov - May   Mon - Sat
Thur&Fri til 8   9 - 5

A quilter's paradise. Large selection of fabrics, notions, local crafts and more! Also a Quilt Museum featuring stunning antique quilts.

Lancaster, PA #7

Patchwork Dollhouse

8 Meadow Lane   17601
(717) 569-4447
Owner: Brenda Watson
Est: 1980   1500 sq.ft.

Mon - Sat
10 - 4
Wed & Fri
til 8

Classes, Fabric for Quilting and Smocking, Books, Patterns, Notions. Bernina machines and accessories. French machine sewing.

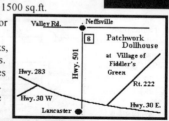

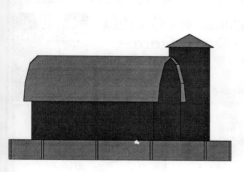

New Holland, PA #8

Witmer Quilt Shop

**Mon - Sat 8 - 6
Mon & Fri Til 8**

1070 West Main Street　17557
(717) 656-9526
Owner: Emma Witmer
Est: 1961　2 Rooms　420 sq.ft.

Over 100 new quilts on 2 beds and shelves. About 50 antique. No supplies. I make all my quilts a little different! Free Brochure!

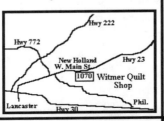

Littlestown, PA #9

The Quilt Patch

**Mon - Sat 9:30 - 5
Sun April - Dec 1 - 5**

1897 Hanover Pike　17340
(717) 359-4121　Est: 1979
Owners: Lew & Kitty Hillard
1300 Calicoes　8000 sq.ft.
Hoffman, Homespuns, Waverlys, etc. etc. etc
Supplies, Quilts, Fine Gifts, Collectibles (i.e. Dept. 56 Tom Clark), Curtains, Heritage Lace. Art Gallery

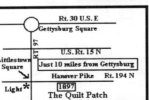

Gettysburg, PA #10

Needle & Thread

**Mon - Thur 9:30 - 6
Fri 9:30 - 8
Sat 9:30 - 5**

2215 Fairfield Rd.　17325
(717) 334-4011
Owner: Darlene Grube
Est: 1985　7000 sq.ft.

FULL LINE FABRIC STORE 10,000 bolts to Choose from—Pendleton, wools, silks, cottons.
Books & Patterns

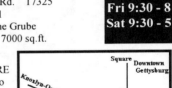
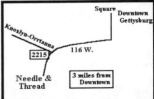

Eagle, PA #11

Tudor Rose Quilt Shop

**Mon - Sat 10 - 5
Wed til 8
Sun 12 - 4**

Route 100 at Byers Rd.
(610) 458-5255　19480
Owner: Jane Russell
Opened: 1990　1200 sq.ft.

All Fabrics 100% cotton.
Everything a quilter needs plus friendly smiles, expert help.

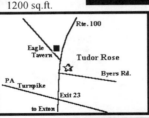

Bethlehem, PA #12

Schlosser Quality Quilt Frames

**Mon 10 - 1
Tues & Wed 10 - 5
Thur 10 - 8
Fri 10 - 6
Sat 10 - 4**

25 Club Avenue　18018
(610) 758-8488　Est: 1989
Owner: Wilma Schlosser

Fabric--Notions
Books--Patterns
Frames for both quilter and needleworkers. Antique Quilts. Singer Featherweights. Notions for Cross Stitchers.

Northampton, PA #13

Dave Iron's Antiques

Open Daily

223 Covered Bridge Road
(215) 262-9335   18067
Owners: Dave & Sue Irons
Est: 1970   1200 sq.ft.

Over 125 Old
Quilts & Tops
of varied Price
Range.

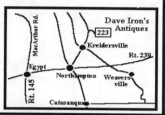

Nazareth, PA #14

The Quiltery

**Tues- Fri
10 - 5
Sat 10 - 2**

1 Hall Square   18064
(215) 759-9699
Owner: Beverly Repsher
Est: 1982

**A Complete
Quilt Shop.**
100% Cotton
Fabric -- books,
notions, patterns,
and classes.
Special quilt orders
made. And always
friendly service.

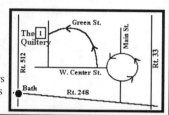

Ackermanville, PA #15

The Village Barn

**Mon - Thur
9:30 - 5:30
Fri 9:30-8
Sat 9:30-4**

1547 Mill Road   18013
(610) 588-3127   Est: 1975
Owners: Ditta Van Gemen &
1000 sq.ft.   Marijke Philipsen
Complete Quilt
Shop. 1000 Bolts
100% Cotton
Fabrics, Books,
Notions, Classes.
Machine Quilting
Service. Helpful
Staff. Lg.selection
of Country Gifts.

Hamlin, PA #16

Ye Olde Sewing Emporium

**Tues - Sat
10 - 5
Summer
May Vary**

Rt. 191, St. John's Centre   Box 190
(717) 689-3480   18427
Owner: Sandra Cinfo   Opened: 1991

A Unique Shop
Specializing in
Fabrics, Notions,
Books, Classes,
Ribbons, and
Gifts for Quilters,
Sewers and
Needlecrafters.

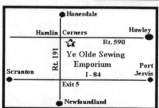

Great Bend, PA #17

Quilt 'n Stitch

**Tues - Fri
10 - 4
Sat 11 - 4**

200 Main Street (Rt. 11)
(717) 879-5255   18821
Owner: Carol A. Darrow
Est: 1989   800 sq.ft.

Quality 100%
Cottons, Quilting
Supplies, Books
& Classes.
Counted Cross
Stitch.
Small Town
Friendly Personal
Service.

Columbia Cross Roads, PA #18

The Strawberry Patch Calico Shop

Mon - Sat
Summer
9 - 4
Winter
9 - 5

RD 3　　Box 44　　16914
(717) 549-6111　Est: 1981
Owner: Jeanne Wilber　3200 sq.ft.

Extraordinary selection of fabric, Quilting Supplies. Home of RCW Publishing. Quilters gathering place. The Quilt Shop with Love.

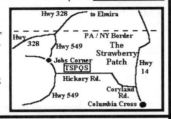

Covington, PA #19

The Farm House
A Country Quilt Shop

R.R. #1　Box 58　16917
(717) 549-2136　Est: 1992
Owner: Shirley Welch
"Making quilts is an American Tradition"

Mon - Sat
10 - 4

A place for time-worn, traditional quilting. Learn my great-grandmother's technique for making over 500 quilts called "crow footing".

Wilkes Barre, PA #20

The Quilt Racque

Tues - Sat
10 - 5
Summer
Sats 10 - 3

183 N. Main St.　(Shavertown)
(717) 675-0914　18708
Owner: Marianne S. Williams

Antique Quilts　Est: 1988　560 sq.ft.
1880 - 1930's
All Sizes
New Handmade
Quilts, Vintage Lace
& Linens,
Pillowcases, Doll
Beds, Thimbles,
Sewing Collectibles
Quilters Jewelry

Huntington Mills, PA #21

Create-A-Patch

Wed - Sat
10 - 5
Class
nights til 9

Rt. #239　P.O. Box 2A　18622
(717) 864-2736　eve. 864-3630
Owners: Judy & Rich Mikilitus
　　　　Est: 1990
　　　　2400 sq.ft.

One Stop shopping for all your Quilting Needs. We offer Workshops & private lessons. Mail orders acpt. We aim to please. Cert. "Quilt in a Day" instructor.

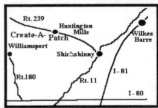

Mahanoy City, PA #22

Linda's Country Quilt Shoppe

Mon - Fri
10 - 5
Sat 10 - 1

30 W. Centre St.　17948
(717) 773-2317　Est: 1992
Owner: Linda Truskowsky

Complete Line of Quilting Supplies. Over 1000 fabrics to choose from. Handmade Gift Ideas - and Quilts.

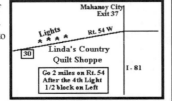

Carlisle, PA #23

Calico Corners

Tues- Fri
9 - 4
Or By Appt.
July Hrs.
Vary
Please Call

341 Barnstable Road　17013
(717) 249-8644
Owner: Janet Shultzabarger
Est: 1984

Personal attention to quilters needs. 100% cottons, notions, books, classes. Very reasonable prices and service with a smile.

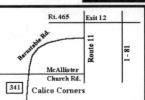

Country Bear Creations

Lucinda, PA   #24

34 Maple Drive   16235   (814) 226-8893
Owners: Keith & Sharon Kennedy
Opened: 1988   1200 sq.ft.

Mail Orders Welcome
MC   Visa   Discover

Mon - Sat   9:30 - 5:30

Bed &
Breakfast
with Quilter
Vacations

Quilt Kits
100% Cotton Fabrics
90", 108", & 120" Backing
Stencils, Books, Patterns, Tools, Supplies
& Classes

Custom Made
Shelves,
Quilting Frames,
& Quilt Racks

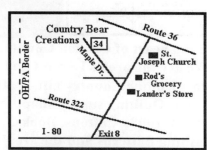

Harborcreek, PA   #25

Calico Patch Quilt Shoppe

3229 Davison Road   16421
(814) 898-2978   Est: 1984
Owners: Jim & Millie Ward
1400 sq.ft.

**Mon - Fri
10 - 5
Thur til 8
Sat 10 - 4**

Largest Quilt Shop in tri-state area with country prices; home of original "No Punch Thru" leather Thimble.

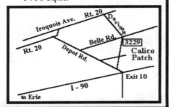

Meadville, PA   #26

The Quilt Square

246 Chestnut St.   16335
(814) 333-4383   Est: 1981
Owner: Gail McClure
2000 sq.ft.

**Mon - Fri
10 - 5
Sat 10 - 3
June - Aug
Closed Mon**

RJR, Hoffman, South Seas and many more designer fabrics. Latest books and patterns. A staff who loves to see what you've done, so bring it in.

Knox, PA   #27

Est: 1987

Countryside Crafts & Countryside Quilts

**Owners:
Jolinda Tharan (Crafts)
& Sally Byers (Quilts)
P.O. Box 255   RD # 2   16232
Exit 7 from I - 80**

(814) 797-2434

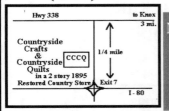

**Mon - Sat
10 - 4:30
Sun
1 - 4:30**

In the heart of Clarion County. We are the area's Largest and Most Unique Country gift, craft and Quilting supply shop. With 100% Cottons, Books, Quilting Patterns and the area's largest supply of craft patterns.

New Wilmington, PA   #28

The Quilting Bee

126 South Market St.   16142
(412) 946-8566   Est: 1981
Owners: Linda & Gail Miller
800 sq.ft.

**Tues - Sat
10 - 4:30**

750 Bolts Cotton/Designer fabrics. Quilts finished or custom made. Complete line of patterns, books, notions, classes and great service.

Monaca, PA #29

The Quilt Basket

**Mon - Sat
10 - 4**

1116 Pennsylvania   15061
(412) 775-7774
Owner: M. Maxine Holmes
Est: 1984

The Quilt Basket
is a complete quilt
shop offering lots
of classes & all the
supplies: i.e.
fabrics, patterns,
books, and
notions.

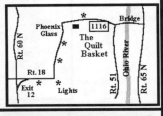

Butler, PA #30

Patches Pretties N Lace

**Mon - Fri
10 - 5
Tue & Thur
til 8
Sat 10 - 3**

235 A New Castle Rd.   16001
(412) 287-2901   Est: 1989
Owner: Pat Ulrich   1200 sq.ft.
    100% Cottons   Elna Dealer
    including
    Homespuns.
    Books, Patterns,
    Classes.
    Hinterberg Frames
    & Hoops on
    Display.
    Exclusive Amish
    Stencils

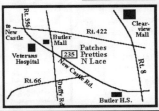

Sewickley, PA #31

TAPAS

**Tues - Sat
9:30 - 5**

441 1/2 Walnut St.   15143
(412) 741-9575
Owner: Janet Daugherty
Est: 1991   220 sq.ft.

Ready made
Quilts
Custom Quilts
Quilt Repair
Quilted
Clothing

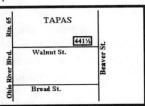

Pittsburgh, PA #32

Piecing It Together

**Mon - Sat
10 - 5
Thur til 8**

3458 Babcock Blvd.   15237
(412) 364-2440   Est: 1986
Owners: Sally Saylor & Patricia
1200 sq.ft.   Altmyer

Complete line of
quilting supplies,
100% cotton
fabrics, books,
notions, patterns,
and classes. Lots
of samples.
Personal, friendly.

Smicksburg, PA   #33

Yoder's Quilt Shop

Sept - May
Mon - Sat
9 - 5
June - Aug
Mon - Sat
9 - 7

RD #1 Box 267   Hwy 954 N
(412) 397-9645   16256
Owners: Sue & Jay Hurtt
Est: 1988

A large assortment of
Amish-made quilts,
wallhangings, fabric,
notions, patterns, and
quilting supplies.
Over 1000 bolts of
fabric at an everyday
discount.

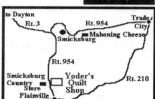

Indiana, PA   #34

Harriet's Quilt Shop

Mon - Sat
10 - 5

271 Philadelphia St.   15701
(412) 465-4990
Owner: Harriet Yatsko
Est: 1980   3000 sq.ft.

A nice selection
of cotton fabrics,
stencils, books,
patterns, thimbles
and notions.
Classes: Basic
hand sewn
sampler to quick
machine piecing

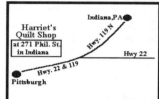

Ligonier, PA   #35

Ligonier Quilt Shop

Mon - Sat
10 - 5

R.R. #1 Ligonier Mini-Mall
(412) 238-6359   15658
Owner: Susan Blank
Est: 1979   1000 sq.ft.

Handmade Quilts
Extensive line of
Quilting supplies
Fabrics, Books,
Stencils, Patterns.
Classes.
Helpful, Friendly
service.
We ship orders.

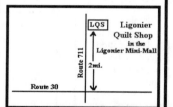

Bethel Park, PA   #36

Quilters Corner

Mon - Sat
10 - 5
Thur til 9

5304 Park Ave.   15102
(412) 833-8449   1500 sq.ft.
Owners: Vivian Dibrell &
Est: 1989   Mary Beth Hartnett

Offering a complete collection of
exquisite cotton fabrics, books, patterns,
notions, and classes in quiltmaking and
dollmaking.

Pennsylvania Guilds:
Beaver Valley Piecemakers, 302 Windy Ghoul Estates, Beaver, 15009
Centre Pieces, P.O. Box 657, Boalsburg, 16827
LeTort Quilters, PO Box 260, Carlisle, 17013
Brandywine Valley Quilters, P.O. Box 953, Concordville, 19331
Hands All Around Erie Quilt Guild, 1420 Lord Rd., Fairview, 16415
Gone to Pieces, 200 Main Street, Great Bend, 18821
North East Crazy Quilters Guild, Harborcreek
Hands all Around Erie Quilt Guild, Harborcreek
Log House Quilt Guild, PO Box 5351, Johnstown, 15904
Red Rose Quilter's Guild, P.O. Box 944, Lancaster, 17603
Laurel Mountain Quilters, Ligonier Town Hall, Ligonier, 15658
Ligonier Quilters, Ligonier Town Hall, Ligonier, 15658
Keystone Quilters, 5540 Beverly Pl., Pittsburgh, 15206
Loyal Hannahs Quilt Guild, 512 Chestnut St., Saltsburg, 15681
Pennsylvania Quilters Association, 825 N. Webster Ave., Scranton, 18510

Other Shops in Pennsylvania:

Allentown	Fisher Textiles, 4111 Mauch Chun Road
Altoona	R Quilt Shop, 1800 Pleasant Valley Blvd.
Bart	Village Dry Goods, 1098 Georgetown Road , Box 10
Bethlehem	Paul's Fabrics, 22 S. Commerce Way #15
Bird in Hand	Grandma's Quilt & Pillow Shop, Plain & Fancy Farm
Bird in Hand	Fisher's Hand Made Quilts, 2713-A Old Philadelphia Pike
Camp Hill	Country Patchwork, 1603 Carlisle Road
Clarks-Summit	Carriage Barn Antiques, 1550 Fairview Road
Corry	Take a Stitch Fabric Shop, 109 N. Center Street
Coudersport	George's Fabric Center, RD #3 Box 73
Doylestown	Sew Smart Fabrics, 53 W. State Street
East Earl	Cedar Lane Dry Goods, 322 Sheep Hill Road
Effort	Country Quilterie, Route 115 N.
Emmaus	Julie's Sewing Basket, 379 Chestnut
Factoryville	Patchwork Shop Antique Quilts, P.O. Box 3360 Route #3
Gipsy	Village Variety Store, 33 Main Street
Girard	Crafts & Occasions, 9141 Ridge Road
Glenside	Granny's Sewing Den, 243 Keswick Avenue
Goodville	H. W. Oberhiltzer & Son Store, 1585 Main Street
Gordonville	Twin Maples Quilt Nook, 172 S. New Holland Road
Grove City	Calico Loft, 311 S. Center Street
Harrisburg	Quilt Emporium, 5922 Linglestown Road
Haverton	Quilting Cottage, 1910 Darby Road
Intercourse	Nancy's Corner, 3503 Old Philadelphia Pike
Kutztown	Country Junction, Route 222
Lahaska	Quilts Incredible, P.O. Box 492
Lahaska	Hentown Country Store, Peddler's Village
Lancaster	Strawberry Patch, 112 Willow Valley Square
Lancaster	Rag Shop Fabric & Craft, 2734 Columbia Avenue
Lancaster	Eighteen Thirty House, 1830 Ursinus Avenue
Mahanoy City	Chesko Fabrics, 301 E. Centre
Malvern	Gathering Memories, 30th & 401 Great Valley Shpg Center
Media	The Hen House. 300 W. Baltimore Pike
Menden Hall	The Quilt Rack, P.O. Box 327
Milan	Laurel Hill Calico Shop, Route 1
Newville	Authentic Amish Quilts & Collectibles, 1602 Walnut
Philadelphia	Cottontales, 186 E. Evergreen Avenue
Pittston	Edelstein's Fabrics, R.R. 141 South Main
Sayre	Mary's General Store, 927 W. Lockhart
Sayre	The Stitching Post, 206 Desmond
Scottsdale	Scottsdale Fabric & Quilt Shop, 103 Pittsburgh
Scranton	Scranton Fabric Center, 1779 N. Keyser Avenue
Shippack	Village Quilts, 4088 Shippack Pike
Soudertown	The Souder Store, 357 Main Street
Washington	Ginger's Fabrics, 891 Henderson Avenue
Washington Crossing	Bittersweet, 1116 Taylorsville Road
West Point	Country Stitching, 21 Garfield Avenue
Williamsport	Country Stitchery, 919 Lycoming Creek Road
Willow Grove	Yours, Mine & Ours Sewing, 219 Easton Road
Yardley	Gallo Rose, 70 N. Main Street

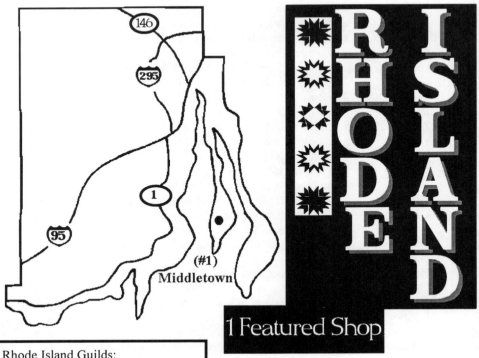

1 Featured Shop

Rhode Island Guilds:
Narragansett Bay Quilters, Box 614,
    East Greenville, 02818
Quilters by the Sea, PO Box 708,
    Portsmouth, 02871

Middletown, RI   #1

Quilt Artisan

**Mon - Fri
10 - 5
Sat 10 - 4**

747 Aquidneck Avenue   02842
(401) 846-2127 or (800) 736-4364
Owners: Linda Hilliard & Irene King
Est: 1984   2500 sq.ft.

Large selection of
cotton fabrics.
Hoffman,
Henry's etc.
Books, Sterling
Thimbles, Classes
& Workshops
Quilts & Gifts

Other Shops in Rhode Island:
Chepachet   Country Hang-up, Inc.
            401 Putnam Pike
Cranston   Cranston Mercantile
            1390 Cranston Street
East Greenwich   "Wood ""N Needles,
        Ltd.", 5865 Post Road
Pawtucket   Lorraine Fabrics
            593 Mineral Spring Avenue
Westerly   The Pincushion
            14 Broad St.

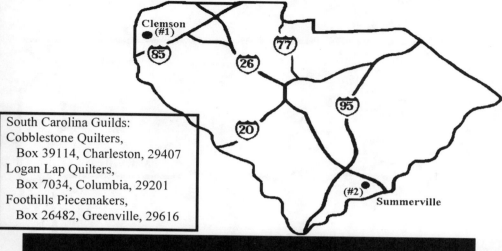

Clemson (#1)

South Carolina Guilds:
Cobblestone Quilters,
    Box 39114, Charleston, 29407
Logan Lap Quilters,
    Box 7034, Columbia, 29201
Foothills Piecemakers,
    Box 26482, Greenville, 29616

(#2) Summerville

SOUTH CAROLINA

2 Featured Shops

Clemson, SC   #1

Heirlooms & Comforts

405 College Avenue Suite 120
(803) 654-9507   29631
Owner: Sara Ballentine
Est: 1984   1300 sq.ft.

**Mon - Fri
9:30 - 5:30
Sat
9:30 - 4**

Upstate's most
complete quilt
shop--fabrics,
tools, books,
patterns, notions,
classes--in a
friendly
atmosphere.

Hwy 123
Hwy. 133
Hwy. 76
Keowee Tr.
College Ave.
Heirlooms &
Comforts
to
I-85
405
in the Shops of
College Place

Summerville, SC   #2

People, Places, & Quilts

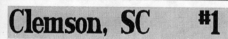

129 West Richardson Ave.
In Cauthen's old Hardware Store
(803) 871-8872   29483
Owner: Diane F. Wilson Est: 1990

**Mon - Sat
10 - 5
Sun by
Appt. Call
871-4000**

Fabric & Quilting
        Supplies.
Antiques, Folk
Art, and Quilts
OF COURSE !
Everything one of
a kind and hand
made in the U.S.A.

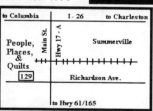

to Columbia   I - 26   to Charleston
Main St.
Hwy 17 - A
People,
Places,
&
Quilts   Summerville
129
Richardson Ave.
to Hwy 61/165

Other Shops in South Carolina:

Aiken	Sewing Gallery, 1384 Whiskey Rd.
Charleston	Cottage Quilters, 975 Savannah Highway
Columbia	The Quilt Cottage, 2213 Augusta Road W.
Easley	The Quilt Gallery, 141 Patchwork Row
Greenville	Jasmine Heirlooms, 101 Ashford Avenue
Greenville	Classic Keepsakes, 626 Congaree Road
St. George	Quilt House, 59 Eighth, W. Bilton Boulevard

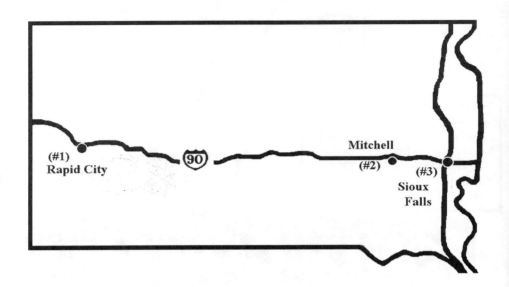

Downtown

Rapid City, SD   #1

on the road to Mt. Rushmore

*Specializing in
necessities & niceties for quilters.
100% cotton fabrics
books —— notions —— gifts —— lessons*

Pioneer Quilts

801 Columbus   57701
(605) 342-6227   Est: 1985
Owner: Kate Bradley

Mon - Fri
9 - 5
Sat 9 - 4

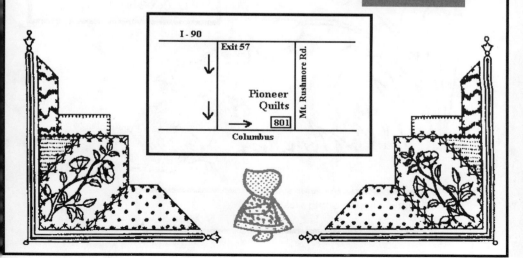

I - 90
Exit 57
Mt. Rushmore Rd.
Pioneer
Quilts
801
Columbus

Mitchell, SD   #2

314 North Main Street

Mon 9 - 8
Tues - Sat
9 - 5:30

(605) 996-0947   Est: 1987
Owners: Kay Miller & Carma Popp   1200 sq.ft.

100% cottons, Books, and Patterns. Classes. Fashion Fabrics. Friendly, helpful staff. Authorized Pfaff Dealer **PFAFF**

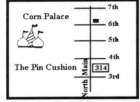

Corn Palace
7th
6th
5th
4th
The Pin Cushion | 314
3rd
North Main

Sioux Falls, SD   #3

Heirloom Creations

Mon - Fri
9:30- 5:30
Saturday
9:30 - 4

2131 S. Minnesota   57105
(605) 332-4435
Owner: Cleo Snuggerud
Est: 1989   2000 sq.ft.

Over 1500 bolts of 100% cottons. Top Quality fabrics and notions. Everything to delight the quilter's palette.

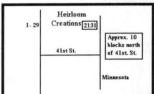

I- 29
Heirloom Creations 2131
41st St.
Approx. 10 blocks north of 41st. St.
Minnesota

South Dakota Guilds:
South Dakota Quilters' Guild,
HCR 88, Box 6A, Clearfield
Heartland Quilters Guild,
Box 195, Mitchell
Black Hills Quilters Guild,
P.O. Box 2495, Rapid City

Other Shop in South Dakota:
Winner   The Sewing B, 225 S. Main St.

Quilting Forever

Housework Whenever

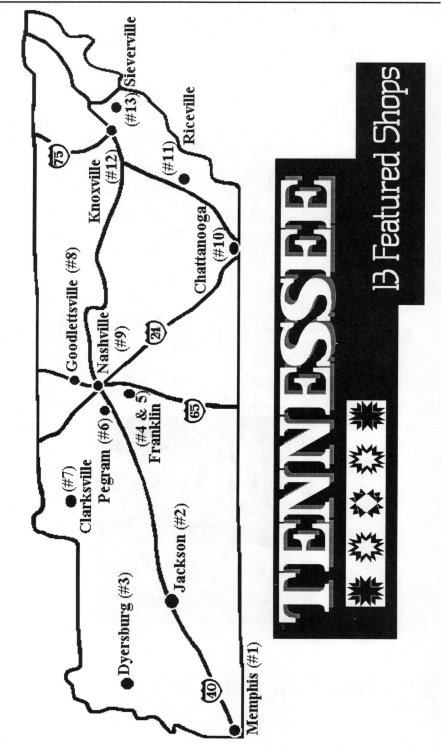

TENNESSEE

13 Featured Shops

Sieverville (#13)

Riceville

Knoxville (#12)

(#11)

Chattanooga (#10)

Goodlettsville (#8)

Nashville (#9)

Franklin (#4 & 5)

Pegram (#6)

Clarksville (#7)

Jackson (#2)

Dyersburg (#3)

Memphis (#1)

75

75

24

65

40

Memphis, TN   #1

Quilts & Crafts

Fabrics, books, quilt & craft patterns, notions and cross-stitch supplies.   Classes.
Over 1,000 bolts of cotton
Over 1,500 patterns
Crafters' Gallery
featuring local crafts.

1/2 mi. on right | 2830 Quilts & Crafts
Jackson Ave.
Exit 8
I - 40
to Little Rock, AR
240 Loop around Memphis
I - 40 to Nashville
I - 55
to Jackson, MS

Mon - Sat 9:30 - 4:30

2830 Austin Peay #9   38128
(901) 373-4004
Owner: Marie May
Est: 1991   2,000 sq.ft.

Jackson, TN   #2

Sew Many Ideas

31B Wiley Parker Road   38305
(901) 668-7819   Est: 1990
Owners: Jeanne Bird McClain &
Betty Bird

Tues - Fri 10 - 5
Sat 10 - 2

1100 sq.ft.

Authorized Bernina Dealer. 100% cotton fabric by Hoffman, J. Beyer, M.E. Hopkins, + many more. 100's of Books, Notions, Q-snap frames, craft patterns, Classes

I - 40
Carriage House
Sew Many Ideas | 31B
Wiley Parker Rd.
Hwy. 45 Highland

Dyersburg, TN   #3

Sew Many Ideas

219 S. Mill Avenue   38024
(901) 286-4721   Est: 1988
Owners: Jeanne Bird McClain &
Betty Bird

Mon - Fri 10 - 5
Sat 10 - 3

4000 sq.ft.

Authorized Bernina Dealer. 100% cotton fabric by Hoffman, Jinny Beyer, M.E. Hopkins, P&B + many more. Notions, Books, Q-snap frames, craft patterns.

to 78
Court St.
Market St. | Court Square | Main St.
Sew Many Ideas | 219 | Mill Ave. | Cedar St.
to 51

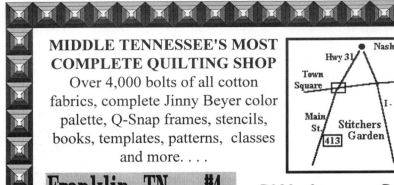

Pegram, TN #6

Harpeth Clock & Quilt Company

Mon - Sat
9 - 5

462 Hwy 70   P.O. Box 40
(615) 646-0938 or (800) 238-4284
Owners: Richard & Margaret Murray
Est: 1978   4500 sq.ft.

Quilting supplies & Instructions. Large assortment of cotton fabrics, books, patterns, notions and Handmade Quilts. Plus Clocks.

Harpeth Clock & Quilt Company
462   U.S. Hwy. 70
Memphis   McCory Lane   I - 40
Exit 192   Nashville
4 mi. from I - 40
20 min. west of Nashville

Clarksville, TN #7

Country Quilting

Mon - Fri
10 - 5
Sat 10 - 4

1953 Madison St.   37043
(In the Tradewinds South
Shopping Center)
(615) 551-3650

Smocking & Heirloom Sewing Fabrics, Notions, Gifts, Books, Patterns, Classes, Workshops, Seminars. Pfaff & Bernina Dealer

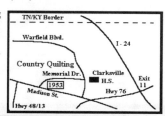

TN/KY Border
Warfield Blvd.   I - 24
Country Quilting
Memorial Dr.   Clarksville H.S.   Exit 11
1953
Madison St.   Hwy 76
Hwy 48/13

Goodlettsville, TN #8

Quilter's Attic

Mon - Fri
9 - 4
Sat 9 - 2

760 Old Dickerson Pike   37072
(615) 859-5603
Owner: Jenny Moss
Est: 1987   1200 sq.ft.

Everything imaginable for the Quilter. Fabric, books, patterns, notions in a country setting adjoining an 1804 Country Home.

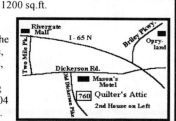

Rivergate Mall
I - 65 N   Briley Pkwy.
Two Mile Pk.   Opryland
Dickerson Rd.
Mason's Motel
760   Quilter's Attic
2nd House on Left

Nashville, TN #9

Sharon Spigel Fine Antique Quilts

Owner: Sharon Spigel
(615) 373-4759
Est: 1990

By Appointment Only

Fine Antique Quilts from the nineteenth and early twentieth centuries. Some vintage textiles and linens. Call us for an appointment and directions.

Chattanooga, TN #10

Crazy Quilt Sewing Center

Mon - Fri
10 - 6
Sat 10 - 4

2260 Gunbarrel Rd.   37421
(615) 894-2522

100% Cottons, Patterns, Notions, Books, Classes. Authorized Viking & White Dealer. Quality service. **A Great Place to Shop.**

E. Shallowford Rd.
Exit 5   K-Mart
Hamilton Place Mall   Foodmax
I - 75   Gunbarrel Rd.
2260   Crazy Quilt
I - 24   Lowe's

Riceville, TN #11

Lena Beth Carmichael Antique Quilts

309 County Road 70   37370
(615) 462-2892
Est: 1988

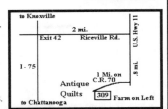

By Chance or Appt.

1940's and older Quilts, tops, blocks. Inventory of 75 - 125. The quality ranges from cutters to museum pieces. Also offer lectures, & appraisal services.

Quilt Craft

Opened: 1985
1350 sq.ft.
Large Selection of 100% Cotton Fabrics including Homespuns and reproduction fabrics. Also Quilting Books, Supplies and Classes.

**Tues - Sat
10 - 5**

Knoxville, TN #12

**We're Adjacent to Each Other
2315 Kimberlin Heights Dr.
(615) 573-0769   37920
Owner: Eva Earle Kent**

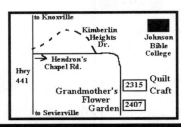

Grandmothers' Flower Garden

Quilt and related Art Shows.
1900 sq.ft. Classroom and meeting space in restored farm house at 2407 Kimberlin Hgts Dr. Our# (615) 577-6312 Call for events Schedule

---

Sevierville, TN #13

Five G's

1060 Alpine Drive   37862
(615) 453-3994   Opened: 1972
Owners: R.C. & Helen Hayden
5600 sq.ft.

7 Days each Week 9 - 6

Come visit our complete Quilt Shop. Fabric, books, kits, patterns, quilt frames and wearables. Also a large display of Quilts for sale.

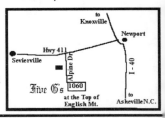

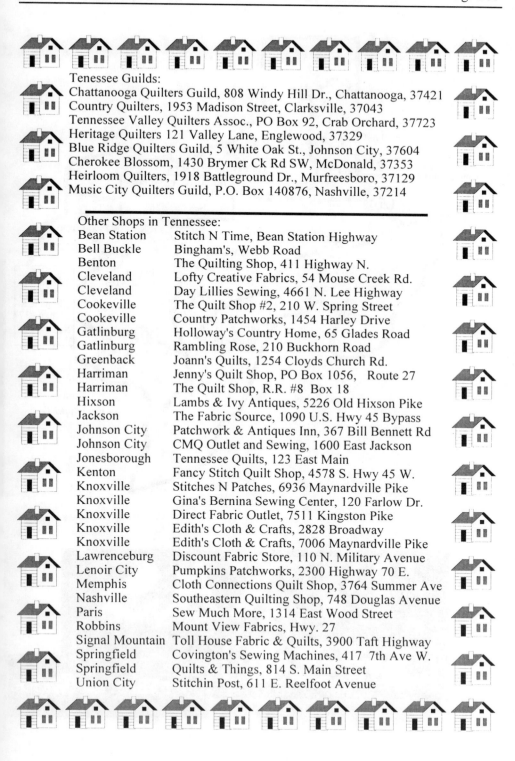

Tenessee Guilds:
Chattanooga Quilters Guild, 808 Windy Hill Dr., Chattanooga, 37421
Country Quilters, 1953 Madison Street, Clarksville, 37043
Tennessee Valley Quilters Assoc., PO Box 92, Crab Orchard, 37723
Heritage Quilters 121 Valley Lane, Englewood, 37329
Blue Ridge Quilters Guild, 5 White Oak St., Johnson City, 37604
Cherokee Blossom, 1430 Brymer Ck Rd SW, McDonald, 37353
Heirloom Quilters, 1918 Battleground Dr., Murfreesboro, 37129
Music City Quilters Guild, P.O. Box 140876, Nashville, 37214

Other Shops in Tennessee:

Bean Station	Stitch N Time, Bean Station Highway
Bell Buckle	Bingham's, Webb Road
Benton	The Quilting Shop, 411 Highway N.
Cleveland	Lofty Creative Fabrics, 54 Mouse Creek Rd.
Cleveland	Day Lillies Sewing, 4661 N. Lee Highway
Cookeville	The Quilt Shop #2, 210 W. Spring Street
Cookeville	Country Patchworks, 1454 Harley Drive
Gatlinburg	Holloway's Country Home, 65 Glades Road
Gatlinburg	Rambling Rose, 210 Buckhorn Road
Greenback	Joann's Quilts, 1254 Cloyds Church Rd.
Harriman	Jenny's Quilt Shop, PO Box 1056,　Route 27
Harriman	The Quilt Shop, R.R. #8　Box 18
Hixson	Lambs & Ivy Antiques, 5226 Old Hixson Pike
Jackson	The Fabric Source, 1090 U.S. Hwy 45 Bypass
Johnson City	Patchwork & Antiques Inn, 367 Bill Bennett Rd
Johnson City	CMQ Outlet and Sewing, 1600 East Jackson
Jonesborough	Tennessee Quilts, 123 East Main
Kenton	Fancy Stitch Quilt Shop, 4578 S. Hwy 45 W.
Knoxville	Stitches N Patches, 6936 Maynardville Pike
Knoxville	Gina's Bernina Sewing Center, 120 Farlow Dr.
Knoxville	Direct Fabric Outlet, 7511 Kingston Pike
Knoxville	Edith's Cloth & Crafts, 2828 Broadway
Knoxville	Edith's Cloth & Crafts, 7006 Maynardville Pike
Lawrenceburg	Discount Fabric Store, 110 N. Military Avenue
Lenoir City	Pumpkins Patchworks, 2300 Highway 70 E.
Memphis	Cloth Connections Quilt Shop, 3764 Summer Ave
Nashville	Southeastern Quilting Shop, 748 Douglas Avenue
Paris	Sew Much More, 1314 East Wood Street
Robbins	Mount View Fabrics, Hwy. 27
Signal Mountain	Toll House Fabric & Quilts, 3900 Taft Highway
Springfield	Covington's Sewing Machines, 417　7th Ave W.
Springfield	Quilts & Things, 814 S. Main Street
Union City	Stitchin Post, 611 E. Reelfoot Avenue

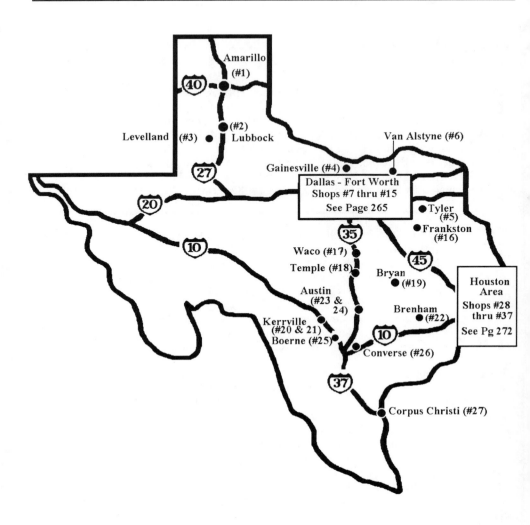

37 Featured Shops

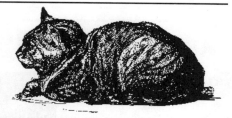

Amarillo, TX   #1

R & R Quilts and More

Mon - Fri
9:30 - 5:30
Sat 10 - 5

2817 Civic Circle   79109
(806) 359-6235   Est: 1993
Owners: Millie Riggs & DeAnna
2200 sq.ft.   Randall

Friendliest shop in
Texas.
We offer a large
selection of 100%
cotton fabrics,
classes, supplies,
and books.

I - 40
R & R Quilts
Wolflin
S. Georgia
2817
Civic Circle
Blackburn

Lubbock, TX   #2

The Quilt Shop

Mon - Sat
10 - 5

4525 50th. Street   79414
(In the Sunshine Sq. Shopping Center)
(806) 793-2485
Owner: Sharon Newman   Certified Appraiser
Est 1979

We have 1500
bolts of cotton,
books, supplies &
classes.
Appraisals by
appointment.

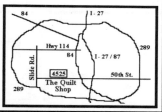

84   I - 27
Hwy 114   289
84   I - 27 / 87
Slide Rd.
4525   50th St.
289   The Quilt
Shop

Levelland, TX   #3

717 Houston St. 79336
(806) 894-6267

Owner:
Traci Cowan

Cover Ups

Mon - Fri
9:30 - 5:30
Sat 9:30 - 4

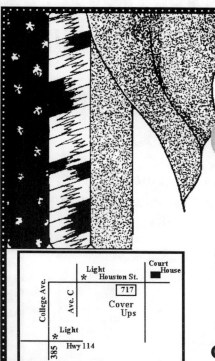

Light
Court
House
Houston St.
College Ave.
Ave. C
717
Cover
Ups
Light
385
Hwy 114

Offering both Quilting fabric and fashion fabric.
Large selection of Quilting books, patterns and notions.
Classes Available for all levels

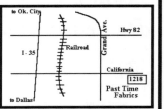
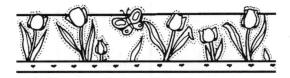

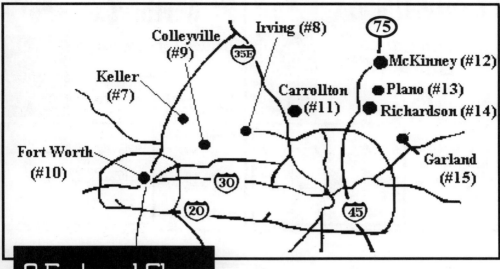

9 Featured Shops

FORT WORTH DALLAS AREA

Keller, TX   #7

Grandma's Quilts

111 W. Vine St 76248
(817) 431-1348
Owner: Helen L.
Madden
Est: 1991

100% Cotton
Fabrics for
Quilters. Notions,
Patterns, Books,
Etc. Etc.

**Tue - Fri
10 - 6
Sat 9 - 3**

Irving, TX   #8

Quilting Etc.

1111 W. Airport Frwy.   75062
(214) 570-4458
Owner: T J Tamny
Est: 1992   2300 sq.ft.

**Mon - Fri
10 - 6
Sat 10 - 5**

Fabric,
Patterns,
Notions,
Gifts, Classes.
5 miles from
DFW Airport!

Colleyville, TX #9

The Calico Cupboard

Mon - Fri
10 - 5
Thurs til 8
Sat 10 - 4

6409 Colleyville Blvd.   76034
(817) 481-7105   Est: 1984
Owner: Sandy Barker
2000 sq.ft.

The largest &
best selection
of 100% cotton
fabric in the
Metroplex.

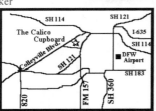

Ft. Worth, TX #10

Quilter's Emporium

Tues - Fri
10 - 5:30
Sat 10 - 3
Sun and eves
during Classes

3526 W. Vickery Blvd.   76107
(817) 377-3993   Est: 1993
Owners: Pam Durham & Robin
5000 sq.ft.   Tyler

Complete line of
quilting supplies
& fabric;
Antique furniture;
Vintage jewelry;
Clothing;
Gifts

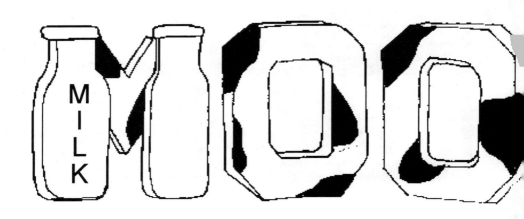

Carrollton, TX #11

The Old Craft Store

Mon - Sat
10 - 5
Thurs til 7

1110 W. Main Street   75006
(214) 242-9111
Owner: Melba Hamrick
Est: 1971   3000 sq.ft.

100% Cottons,
full-service quilt
shop. Patterns,
notions - nestled
among antiques
& old-fashioned
U.S. Post Office.

McKinney, TX   #12

Sharon's

QUILT DEPOT

3000 Plus
BOLTS
of
FABRIC

Est: 1989   6800 sq.ft.
215 East Louisiana Street   75069

(214) 548-2762

**Owners: Sharon Blevins &
Jane Mitchell**

"A Quilter's Quilt
Store"

Monday
9:30 - 9
Tues - Sat
9:30 - 5

30 Minutes North of Dallas on Highway 75

Plano, TX #13

Country Calicos

Mon 10 - 8
Tues - Sat
10 - 5

801 E. 18th St.   75074   (214) 423-2499
Owner: Betty Woods Opened: 1989   1000 sq.ft.

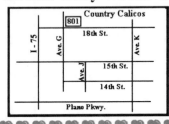

Country Calicos
801
I - 75   Ave. G   18th St.   Ave. K
Ave. J   15th St.
14th St.
Plano Pkwy.

Quilting books, notions, and fabrics.
Hand made hammered and mountain
dulcimers and recordings. Wide
selection of classes on quilting and
other fabric related crafts.

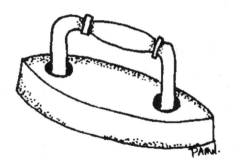

Richardson, TX #14

Quilt Craft

19 Richardson Heights Village
(214) 437-2250   75080
Owners: Catherine & Judy Bracken
Est: 1993   1900 sq.ft.

Mon - Sat
10 - 6

Fabrics, Notions,
Lots of Books,
Quilting Supplies
PLUS Needlepoint,
Cross Stitch,
Rug Hooking &
other Crafts.
Numerous Classes

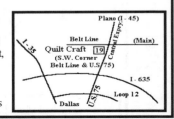

Plano (I - 45)
I - 35   Belt Line   Central Expwy.   (Main)
Quilt Craft 19
(S.W. Corner
Belt Line & U.S. 75)
I - 635
U.S. 75   Loop 12
Dallas

Garland, TX #15

Suzy's

Mon - Fri
10 - 5
Sat 10 - 3

111 North 6th   75040
(214) 272-8180
Owner: Suzanne Cook
Est: 1989   4200 sq.ft.

A Complete
Quilt Shop
Country Clothing
Gifts &
Accessories
Candles, Classes

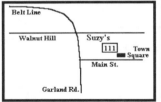

Belt Line
Walnut Hill   Suzy's
111   Town
Square
Main St.
Garland Rd.

Frankston, TX #16

Artistic Needle

Wed - Sat 10 - 4

612 Hwy. 155 N   75763
(903) 876-4345
Owner: Judy Dwyer

Est: 1990   1500 sq.ft.

100% Cotton Fabrics as well as current books, patterns, and notions. The only Full service specialty Quilt Shop in East Texas !

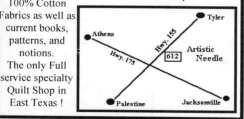

Waco, TX #17

The County Fair Quiltpatch

Mon - Sat 10 - 5:30

1401 Lake Air Dr.   76710
(817) 776-5710
Owner: Lee Fadal
Est: 1979   1700 sq.ft.

Great Selection of 100% Cotton Fabrics, Books, and Notions. Friendly Knowledgeable Service.

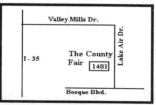

Temple, TX #18

Cotton Patch Quilt Shop

**Mon - Fri 10 - 5:30
Sat 10 - 2**

902 South 3rd.   76504
(817) 771-2301
Owner: Peggy Leonard
Est: 1985   1000 sq.ft.

100% Cottons, Patterns, Books, Notions, and Smocking Supplies.

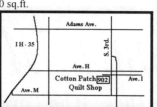

Bryan, TX #19

Pruitt's Quilt Shop

3803 C S. Texas Ave.   77802
(409) 846-1711
Owner: Glenn Pruitt
Est: 1991

Large selection of vibrant colored cottons, quilting books, patterns, & supplies. Silk ribbon by the yard.

Mon - Sat 10 - 6

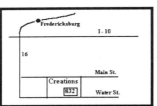
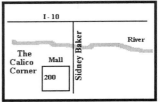

Austin, TX #23

Gem Fabric

**Mon, Tues,
Thur 10 - 8
Wed, Fri,
Sat 10 - 6
Sun 12 - 5**

13776 Hwy. 183 N. #108
(512) 258-8061   78750
Owners: Dorothy & Reynolds
Est: 1968   Bixler

Beautiful Fabrics,
Books,
Patterns,
Helpful Tools,
Lots of Classes,
Authorized Dealer:
New Home &
Viking

Austin, TX #24

The Quilt Store, Inc.

**Mon - Fri
10 - 5
Sat 10 - 4**

3309-A Hancock Drive   78731
(512) 453-1145
Owner: Laurie Evans
Est: 1984   1500 sq.ft.

A large selection
of domestic and
imported cotton
fabrics, books,
notions, patterns,
and much more.

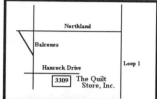

Boerne, TX #25

Sew Special

**Mon - Sat
9 - 5
Sun 12 - 5**

112 South Main Street   78006
(210) 249-8038
Owners: Three Quilting Nuts !
Est: 1987   1800 sq.ft.

"The Best Little
Quilt Shop by a
Country Smile"
Cottons, books,
patterns, notions,
classes, & Help !

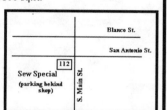

Converse, TX #26

General Store /
Quilt Studio

**Tues - Fri
1 - 5
Sat 10 - 3**

305 S. Seguin   78109
(210) 659-7278
Owners: Rosalie & Les Bourland
Est: 1985   2094 sq.ft.

400 Bolts 100%
Cotton Fabric,
Books, Patterns,
Quilt Frames,
Batting
and other
supplies.
Quilt
Classes.

Corpus Christi, TX #27

The Quilt Bee

**Mon - Fri
9 - 5
Sat 9 - 3**

Your Complete Quilting Shop

**5410 Everhart   78411   Est: 1990
(512) 992-4515   1200 sq.ft.
Owners: Marcia Anderson,
Sue Howe, June Spencer,
& Lynette Gonzalez**

**The Newest Patterns, Notions,
and Fabric. The Quilt Bee has the
largest book supply in South
Texas. Classes - Quilts, Quilted
Clothing, Dolls and Techniques**

MAKE A QUILT...TAKE TIME FOR THINGS THAT MATTER

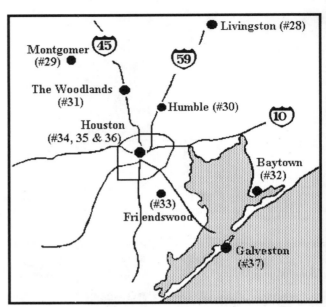

HOUSTON AREA

10 Featured Shops

Livingston, TX #28

Quilts 'n Things

Mon - Fri
9:30 - 5:30
Sat 9:30 - 2

505 N. Drew   77351
(409) 327-7179
Owner: Frances McDonald

**Complete
Quilting
Headquarters.**
Fabric, Notions,
Patterns, Books,
Classes.

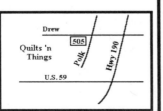

Montgomery, TX #29

Treasured Quilts

**Please Call
for an
Appointment**

Rt. #3 Box 18   77356
(409) 539-3525
Owner: Marie Tacker
Est: 1984

Quilts,
Wallhangings,
to your
specifications.

Special orders
welcome. I work out
of my home—please
call for directions.

Humble, TX #30

It's A Stitch

9725 FM 1960 Bypass 77338
(713) 446-4999
Owners: Judy & John Curtis
Est: 1992 1875 sq.ft.

**Mon - Fri
10 - 5:30
Sat 10 - 5**

—Large selection of
quilting fabrics
—Patterns, books,
notions
—Classes
—Bernina and
Bernette sewing
machines &
sergers

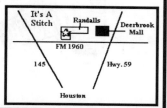

The Woodlands, TX #31

Plain & Fancy

418 Sawdust Rd. 77380
(713) 367-1021
Owner: Sandra Contestabile

**Mon 10 - 9
Tue - Fri
10 - 6
Sat 10 - 4**

Largest Selection
of Fabric in
Houston

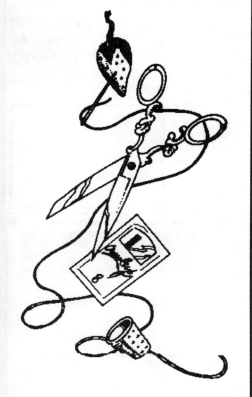

Baytown, TX #32

Designer Fabric & Quilt Shop

1100 W. Lobit 77520
(713) 420-2694 Est: 1991
Owners: Irene Fulcher & Katrinka Roden
2000 sq.ft.

**Mon - Fri
9 - 5
Sat 9 - 4**

One of Harris
County's Largest
Quilt Shops.
Notions, Books,
Machine Quilting
Hand Quilting,
Lessons, etc.

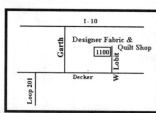

Friendswood, TX #33

Quakertown Quilts

607 S. Friendswood Dr. 77546
(713) 996-1756
Owner: Pat Bishop
Est: 1988 3000 sq.ft.

**Mon - Fri
10 - 5
Tue & Thur
til 7
Sat 10 - 4**

Complete Quilt
Shop.
1400+ bolts of
cotton fabric.
Books, Patterns,
Notions &
Gift Items

Houston, TX #34

Great Expectations

14520 Memorial Drive Suite #54
(713) 496-1366   77079
Owner: Karey Bresenhan
Est: 1974

**Mon - Fri 10 - 6
Sat 10 - 5**

Largest selection
of Quilts in the
City. Large
selection of
Fabric, Books,
Notions &
Patterns.
Quilting Classes.

```
                    I - 10
      Ashford                          Kirkwood
              Great Expectations
               14520      Memorial

      Dairy
                    West Leimer
```

Houston, TX #35

Accessory After the Fact

Mon - Sat 10:30 - 5:30

5516 FM 1960 West   77069
(713) 440-8871   Est: 1985
Owner: Marcia Schanzmeyer   2400 sq.ft.

Shop loaded with
Fabrics, patterns,
books, notions.
Also a wonderful
gift and home
accessory
section....

```
      Accessory
      After the Fact
         5516  FM 1960 W.

   Champion Forest Dr.
         Veteran's Memorial
              Kuykendahl
                              I - 45
```

Houston, TX #36

Quilt Quarters

1410 B Blalock   77055
(713) 468-5886
Est: 1986   1800 sq.ft.
Owners: Grace Campbell &
        Kay Tanner

**Mon 10 - 9
Tues - Sat 10 - 4**

Friendly, helpful,
All cotton fabrics
large book,
stencil selection,
Restoration &
repair.
Located off I - 10

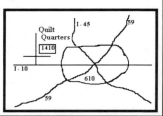

Galveston, TX #37

Quilts by the Bay

**Mon - Sat 10 - 5:30
Thur til 9**

5923 Stewart Rd.   77551
(409) 740-9296
Owner: Patricia Stephenson
Est: 1991   2500 sq.ft.

Charming shop
by Galveston Bay with top quality
fabrics, classes, notions, &
unique gifts for every occasion.

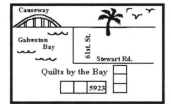

Area Guilds:
Quilters Guild of Dallas, 15775 N. Hillcrest, Dallas 75248
Quilters Guild of Plano, PO Box 260216, Plano 75026
Allen's Quilters Guild   contact: Marcia Baker (214) 517-7556
Denton Quilt Guild   contact: Billie Ingram (817) 382-3806
McKinney Quilter's Guild   contact: Peggy Tomlinson (214) 548-2762
Quilting, Et Cetera   contact: Dee (214) 548-2762
Quilter's Guild of Arlington   contact: (817) 429-4940
Cotton Patch Quilt Guild   contact: Debbie Hagar (903) 883-4230
Red River Quilter Guild, Rt. 1, Box 504, Nocona, 76255
Wildflower Quilt Guild, 902 S. 3rd., Temple (817) 771-2301
High Plains Quilters Guild, 2433 I-40 West, Amarillo 79109
Greater San Antonio QG, PO Box 65124, San Antonio 78265
Bay Area Quilt Guild , 1094 Scarsdale Box M237, Houston, 77089
Lampasas Quilt Guild, 303 South Western, Lampasas, 76550
Homespun Quilters Guild, 5009 Lake Highlands Drive , Waco,   76710

Other shops in Texas:	
Abilene	Country Pleasures, 727 Hickory St.
Amarillo	Quilting Bee, 8742 River Road
Arlington	Berry Patch Fabrics, 4714 Little Road
Arlington	Quilted Hearts & Co., 1205 South Bowen Rd.
Austin	Quilts 'N Things, 4406 Burnet Rd.
Austin	Country Sewing & Quilting, 10209-A FM 812
Baytown	The Rocking Chair Quilt Store, 47 Ward Street
Beaumont	The Piecemaker, 3677 Calder
Caldwell	My Spare Time, Rt. 3 Box 264
Corpus Christi	The Fabric Store, 4938 S. Staples
Corpus Christi	Bay Tree Creations, 4642 Kostoryz
Dallas	Not Just Quilts, 11535 Jupiter Rd.
Denison	Mom's Quilts, 14316 S. Armstrong Avenue
Denton	Margie's Fabrics Unlimited, 118 N. Locust
Eldorado	Pat's Sew 'N Sew, 111 S.W. Main
Fort Worth	Cherrie's Quilt Shop, 4320 Wichita St.
Fort Worth	Berry Patch Fabrics, 4995 S. Hulen
Fredericksburg	Jabberwocky, 203 East Main
Garland	Bell's Bernina Sewing Center, 3884 S. Shiloh Rd.
Georgetown	Handcrafts Unlimited, 104 W. 8th
Houston	Hidden Treasures, 5116 Lawndale St.
Houston	Sew Contempo Fabric Shop, 18123 Egret Bay
Houston Galleria	'N Calicos Too, 10115 Hammerly
Jefferson	Quilter's Corner, RR #1 Box 1354
Lancaster	Bell's Bernina Sewing Center, 125 Historic Town Sq.
Lewisville	The Pepper Tree
Lockney	The Old Blue Quilt Box, West of City
Marble Falls	Blue Bonnet Designs, 21B S. Highway 281
Memphis	Greene Dry Goods Company, 109 S. Sixth Street
Midland	The Needle Nook, 3211 W. Wadley Ave.
Pasadena	The Fabric Hut, 2232 Strawberry
Pittsburg	Quilts & More, Hwy 11 East
Plano	The Fabric Affair, 810 N. Central Expy. Suite 114
Plano	Plano Sewing Center, 2129 B W. Parker Rd.
Richardson	The Fabric Affair, 339 Dal-Rich Village
Rosenburg	Needle Ark, 1220 6th
San Angelo	The Cutting Corner, 4112 Sunset Drive
San Antonio	Page's Sewing Machines, 5860 Rigsby Ave.
San Antonio	Las Colchas, 110 Ogden Street
San Antonio	Grandma's Quilt Attic, 13883 Higgins Rd.
Spearman	Jo's This n' That, 216 Main
Spring	Creatively Sew, 26407 Preston
Spring	Juliene's, 26303 Preston #B
Sulphur Spring	Misczellaneous, 631 N. Davis
Sunrise Beach	Patches, 103 Sunrise Drive
Tulia	Joyce's Quilting Shop, 25 N. Armstrong Avenue
Victoria	Stitches N More, 2007 N. Navarro Street

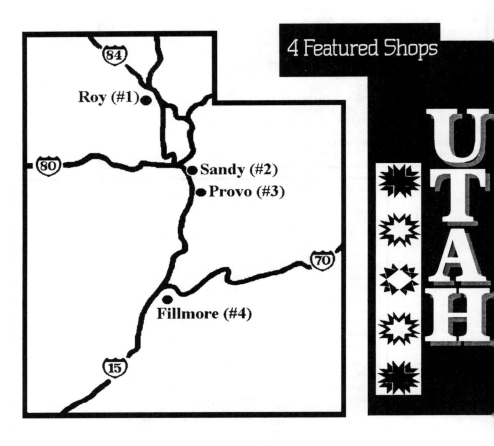

4 Featured Shops

Roy (#1)

Sandy (#2)

Provo (#3)

Fillmore (#4)

UTAH

Roy, UT   #1

Marlene's Quilts

Everyday
9 - 9
**Please
Call First**

3118 West 5200 South   84067
(801) 825-0547
Owner: Marlene Larsen
Est: 1982

Stock Approx.
100 quilts - also
do special orders
- I work out of
my house so
calling first is
helpful.

3100 West   3118
                   Marlene's
                   Quilts   5200
                             South
          5600 South

Roy Exit

Utah Quilt Guild, P.O. Box 17032,
   Salt Lake City, 84117
Utah Guilds:
Ogden Quilt Guild, 340 N.
   Washington Blvd, Ogden, 84404
Roy Pioneer Quilters,
   4232 S. 2275 West, Poy, 84067
Dixie Quilt Guild, P.O. Box 507,
   St. George, 84771

Sandy, UT #2

Quilt, Quilt, Quilt

**Mon - Sat
10 - 5
Mon & Thur
til 9**

11 East Main   84070
(801) 255-2666

Owner:
Dorthey Chase
Est: 1988
3000 sq.ft.

I - 15 | 9000 E. | State St.
Quilt Etc.
[11]
(8720 S.) Main St.

♦ **Over 6500
Bolts of
Fabric**
♦ **Notions**
♦ **Books**
♦ **Patterns**
♦ **Classes**

Provo, UT #3

The Stitching Corner

**Mon - Sat
10 - 6**

480 N. Freedom Blvd.   84601
(801) 374-1200
Owner: Scott Blackham
Est: 1990   3500 sq.ft.

Pfaff authorized
dealer;
3000+ bolts of cotton;
classes daily;
quilting notions,
patterns, threads.
Knowledgeable
Quilters.

500 North
The [480]
Stitching | Corner
400 North
Freedom Blvd. | 100 West | University Ave.
Center St.

Fillmore, UT #4

Territorial Statehouse State Park

**Daily
9 - 5**

P.O. Box 657   84631
(801) 743-5316
Est: 1930

First capitol
building of
Utah. Pioneer
Quilts on
display. Quilt
show annually.

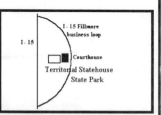

I - 15 Fillmore
business loop
I - 15
Courthouse
Territorial Statehouse
State Park

Other Shops in Utah: LaVerkin, Zion Handicraft, P.O. Box 270
Logan   Grandma's Quilts, 93 E. 100 S.
Ogden   Gardiner's Sewing, 1508 Washington Blvd.
Salt Lake City   The Grace Co.-Quilting Frames, 801 W 1850 S ,
Salt Lake City   Gentler Times Quilt Shop, 4880 S. Highland Circle
Salt Lake City   Mormon Handicraft, 105 North Main
West Jordan   Village Quilt Shop, 1095 W 7800 S
West Salt Lake City   Quilters Patch, 2370 S. 3600 W.

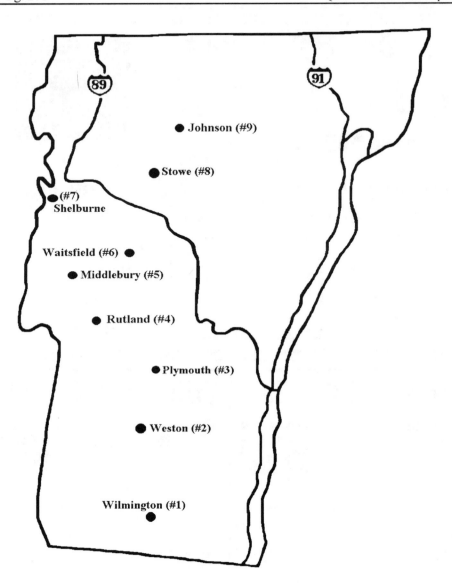

9 Featured Shops

Wilmington, VT #1

Norton House

1836 Country Store Village Box 579
(802) 464-7213   05363
Owner: Suzanne Wells Wurzberger
                          Est: 1967
                          1600 sq.ft.

7 Days a Week 9 - 5

A Quilter's Paradise !
Enormous collection of
100% Cotton including
designer Hoffman
Fabrics. Books-
Pattern-Notions-
Needlework-Candles-
Gifts-Sale Tables

	Route 100	
W. Main St.		Route 9
1836 Norton House		

Weston, VT #2

Weston House

Route 100   P.O. Box 82
(802) 824-3636   05161
Owners: Joanne & Richard Eggert
                          Est: 1978
                          1500 sq.ft.

June - Oct 7 days 10-5 Nov - May Fri - Mon 10 - 5

Quilting Supplies,
books and
patterns. Huge
selection of yard
goods--including
Roberta Horton's
"LINES" fabrics.
Finished Quilts,
wallhangings,
pillows too!

Village Green · Mobil Station · Post Office · Weston House · to Rutland, Ludlow · to Chester · West River · to Londonderry

Plymouth, VT #3

Calvin Coolidge Birthplace

Plymouth Notch Historic District
(802) 672-3773   Est: 1956
P.O. Box 247   05056
                          10 Museums
                          Buildings

Daily Late May – mid Oct 9:30 - 5:30

Several late 19th
Century Quilts on
Permanent
exhibition.
Including one
pieced by Calvin
Coolidge when he
was 10 years old.
(Tumbling Blocks)

Hwy 107 · Hwy 12 · Hwy 100 · West Bridgewater · Woodstock · U.S. 4 · Plymouth Union · Calvin Coolidge Birthplace

Rutland, VT #4

Country Quilt & Fabric

R.R. #3 (Rt. 4 E.)   Box 7352
(802) 773-3470   05701
Owners: Pat & Lynne Benard
                          Est: 1982   1400 sq.ft.

Mon - Sat 9:30 - 5 Sun 12 - 5

3000+ bolts of
100% cotton
fabrics --
Hoffman, South
Seas, P&B, RJR,
plus notions,
Books & Patterns
Custom Orders
too

Rt.4 Business · Rt. 7 · Rt.4 W. · Rutland Mall · Rt. 4 E. · Hogge Penny · Country Quilt & Fabric · 2.6 miles From Rt.7

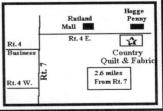
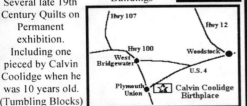

Middlebury, VT #5

Charlotte's Collections

Mon - Sat 10 - 5

Star Mill at Park Street   05753
(802) 388-3895

Owner: Charlotte Fisk   Est: 1989

Full service Quilt Shop. Hoffman our Specialty. Metrosene Threads. In-Stock Quilts & Custom Orders. All natural Knitting Yarns & Supplies.

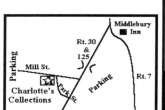

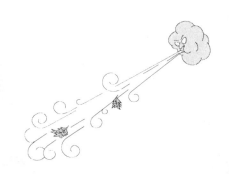

Shelburne, VT #7

Quiltsmith

Mon - Sat 10 - 5 Sun 12 - 4

Tenneybrook Sq.   2011 Shelburne Rd.
(802) 985-3688   05482
Est: 1981   2400 sq.ft.
Owners: Judy, Joyce, Jeanne, Lorraine, & Corine

Everything for the Quilter:
Fabric, Books & Notions. Also cross-stitch, knitting & needlepoint supplies. Vermont's largest collection of decorative stencils.

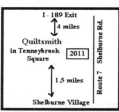

Waitsfield, VT #6

Cabin Fever Quilts

Mon & Wed - Sat 10 - 5

The Old Church   Route 100
P.O. Box 443   05673
(802) 496-2287   Est: 1976
Owner: Vee Lowell

1200 Sq.ft.

Cabin Fever Quilts offers Amish/Mennonite hand quilted quilts plus custom made tied comforters. Fabric, Quilting Supplies & much more!

Johnson, VT #9

Sterling Quiltworks, Ltd.

Tues - Fri 9:30 - 5 Sat 10 - 3

Rt. 15   1.2 mi. W of Johnson
At the Corner of Foote Brook Rd.
(802) 635-2775   05656
Owner: Frances Butler Est: 1989

100% cotton fabrics, notions, books, patterns. Large & small quilts. Gifts. Expert instruction in the fine art of quilting.

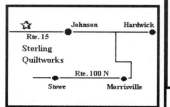

Stowe, VT #8

Prints & Patches

Mon - Sat 10 - 5

P.O. Box 1205   Main St. 05672
(802) 253-8643   or (800) 800-8643
Owner: Mary Johnson
Est: 1979   1400 sq.ft.

Come on into our Retail shop in Stowe, where we create our own Vermont quilts. Antique & Hand quilted quilts also.

Vermont Guilds:

Oxbee Quilter's Guild, P.O. Box 148, Bradford, 05033
Heart of the Land Quilter's Guild, R.R. #1 Box 263, Hartland, 05048
Maple Leaf Quilter's Guild, Box 7400, Mendon, 05701
Champlain Valley Quilt Guild, 2011 Tenneybrook Square, Shelburne, 05482

Other Shops in Vermont:

Bennington	Simply Stitches, 423 Main
Jeffersonville	Smugglers Creations Quilt Shop, Route 108
Johnson	Broadwoven Fabric Mill, R.R. # 2 #1035
Manchester	Valerie's Quilt Shop, Route 7A
Newfane	Newfane Country Store, P.O. Box 56 Route 30
North Clarendon	Quilt Barn of Vermont, 286 East Street
Shelburne	Hearthside Quilts/Peter Coleman, P.O. Box 429
Stowe	Yankee Lady Quilts, 3017 Stowe Hollow Road
Williamsville	Carriage House Comforters, P.O. Box 111
Winooski	Yankee Pride, Champlain Mill

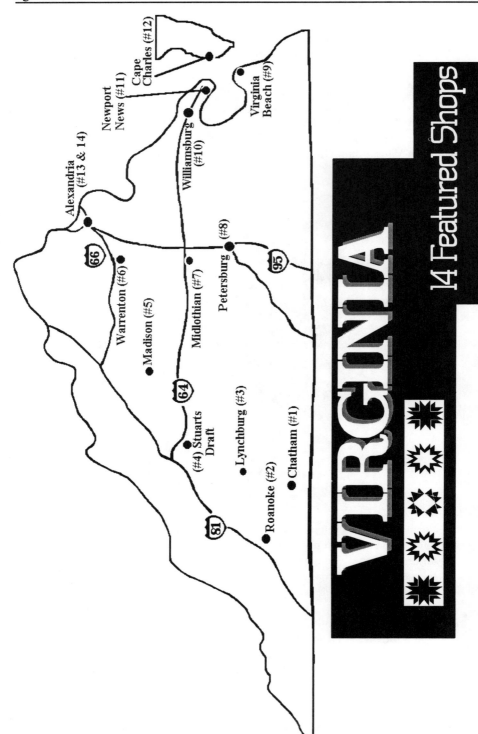

Chatham, VA   #1

Apple Tree Quilts

Rt. #2 P.O. Box 107B
(804) 432-0615   24531
Owner: Eileen S. Gore
Est: 1988   900 sq.ft.

**Tues - Fri
9:30 - 5:30
Sat
9:30 - 4**

Serving the Quilter's Every Need, with 100% Cotton Prints & Solids, Quilting Notions, Quilt Classes and Bernina Sewing Machines.

Rt. 703   Rt. 29

ATQ Apple Tree Quilts

Roanoke, VA   #2

Touch of Country

I - 81
Peters Creek Rd.
Rt. 11
Williamson Rd.
I - 581
Touch of Country
Hershberger Rd.
5524
Orange Ave.
Rt. 460
Roanoke
Vinton

Tues - Sat   10 - 5

Custom Machine Quilting for customers our speciality.

Quilts   45" Fabrics 90"   Notions   Batting   Crafts

**5524 Williamson Rd.   (Lamplighter Mall)   24012
Owner: Lula Parker   (703) 563-4755**

Lynchburg, VA   #3

Quilted Expressions

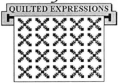

QUILTED EXPRESSIONS

3226 Old Forest Rd.   24501
(804) 385-6765

Mon. - Fri.:   9:30 - 5:30
Sat.:   9:30 - 4:00

Owner: Roberta Whitt
Opened: 1992

More than **1200 bolts** of Top Quality 100% Cotton Fabrics. Full line of Sewing Notions, Quilting Supplies, and Books. Instructional Classes for Quilting, Sewing and Craft Projects.

Traveling Clubs/Groups welcomed - Please call ahead for us to prepare a special event for you.

Speak/demonstrate products for many types of Clubs/Groups.

We have an active **Pfaff Club** and handle **all Pfaff** Sergers/Sewing Machines, featuring **Pfaff's electronic 6250** the **"Quilters' Dream Machine"**

Mail Order inquiries invited.

Authorized Pfaff Dealer
** Sales and Service **

Stuarts Draft, VA   #4

The Candy Shop & Fern's Fabrics

Mon - Sat 10 - 5

10 Highland Drive   24477
(703) 337-0298
Owners: Dan & Barbara Yoder

Est: 1983   1000 sq.ft.

Unique country store, owned & operated by Amish-Mennonite family. Beautiful quilts, fabrics, patterns, books & more. Custom orders welcome!

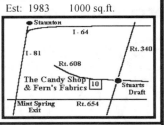

Madison, VA   #5

Little Shop of Madison

320 S. Main St.   P.O. Box 452
(703) 948-4147   22727
Owner: Thelma Shirley
Est: 1978   3000 sq.ft.

Tues - Sat 10 - 4

Hundreds of Fabrics and All other Quilters' Indulgences.

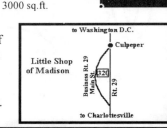

Sugar & Spice
and everything
nice . . . that's
what Quilters
are made of !

Warrenton, VA #6

Quilter's Confectionery

79 W. Lee Hwy.   22186
(703) 347-3631
Owner: Karen S. Walker
Est: 1993   1200 sq.ft.

**Mon - Sat
9:30 - 5**

"Candy" Shop for
Quilters. No Fat
No Cholesterol
No Calories!
Only the Good Stuff
Quilts are made of.
Latest Quality
Merchandise.

[Map: to I-66, Quilter's Confectionery, Bus. 29, Lee Hwy, 29, Light, Blackwell Rd., 79]

Midlothian, VA #7

**Mon - Fri
10 - 6
Sat 10 - 5
Class eves.
7 - 9**

**13196 Midlothian Pike
(804) 379-7727
Owners: Jean Crouch & Laura Goode
Est: 1990   2400 sq.ft.**

1200 Bolts of Fabric:
Hoffman, RJR, Roberta Horton, Marcus, Etc.
Great selection of books, notions, templates,
smocking supplies, classes and patterns.

[Map: I-64, Richmond, Sew Special, Inc. 195, 6 miles west in the Village Marketplace, 13196, Midlothian Pike, Powhite, 95]

Petersburg, VA #8

Lolly's Quilt Shop

246 North Sycamore   23803
(804) 732-5848
Owner: Carolyn Hatcher
Est: 1991   1500 sq.ft.

**Mon - Sat
10 - 5**

Quilting Supplies,
Fabric, Notions,
Q-Snap Frames.
Hinterberg
Frames. Plus
Quilting Books.

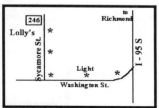

Virginia Beach, VA #9

What's Your Stitch 'N Stuff. Inc.

5350 Kempsriver Dr. #104
(804) 523-2711   23464
Owners: Holly Erdei-Zuber &
Irene Erdei

**Mon - Sat
10 - 5
Thur til 8
Sun 12 - 4**

100% Cotton Fabrics
and Thread. Books,
Patterns, Notions,
Beads, Silk Ribbon,
Novelty Items.
PLUS ALWAYS
FRIENDLY
SERVICE!

Williamsburg, VA #10

Needlecraft Corner

7 Days a Week 9 - 5

7521 Richmond Rd.   23188
(804) 564-3354   Est: 1977
Owner: Sherry & John Barnett

Over 3,000 bolts of 100% Cotton Fabrics. Home of "Granny Nanny's Quilting Gadgets" Miniature Patchwork Stamps, Impressions and patterns.

Map: to Richmond, I-64, Hwy. 607, U.S. 60, Exit 231A "Norge", Pottery Factory, Hwy 646, Needlecraft Corner in The Candle Factory

Newport News, VA #11

Nancy's Calico Patch

Mon - Sat 10 - 5

21 Hidenwood Shopping Center 23606
(804) 930-0819 or 877-9414
Owner: Nancy Gloss   Est: 1987

We have fabrics, books, patterns, supplies, & classes for Quilting, Smocking, & Heirloom sewing plus Elna sewing machine sales & Service.

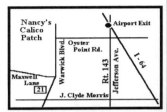

Map: Nancy's Calico Patch, Airport Exit, Warwick Blvd., Oyster Point Rd., Maxwell Lane, 21, Rt. 143, Jefferson Ave., I-64, J. Clyde Morris

Cape Charles, VA #12

Quilts & More

Mon - Sat 9 - 5

315 Mason Avenue   23310
(804) 331- 3642
Owner: Henrietta Morris
Est: 1990   600 sq.ft.

Quilts, other handmade items by owner. Quilting, X-stitch craft supplies. Fabrics of all kinds, patterns, notions and more.

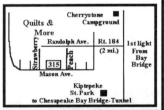

Map: Cherrystone Campground, Quilts & More, Strawberry, Randolph Ave., Rt. 184, 1st light From Bay Bridge (2 mi.), 315, Peach, Mason Ave., Kiptepeke St. Park, to Chesapeake Bay Bridge-Tunnel

Alexandria, VA #13

Quilt N Stuff

Mon - Sat 10 - 5 Wed til 8

1630 King Street   22314
(703) 836-0070   Est: 1986
Owner: Madeline Shepperson
     1740 sq.ft.

Bright, friendly shop with excellent selection of cotton fabrics, books and supplies. Specialities: African, Indonesian, Guatemalan and Japanese Cottons.

Map: King St., U.S. 15, King St. Metro, Diagonal Rd., Daingerfield Rd., 1630, Quilt-n-Stuff, Telegraph Rd., (Rt. 236) Duke St., Washington St., Old Town Alexandria, U.S. 1 North, Exit 2B, Exit 1B, Beltway I-95, Wilson Bridge

Alexandria, VA #14

Rocky Road to Kansas

Mon - Sat 10:30 - 5 Sun 1 - 5

215 South Union Street
(703) 683-0116   22314
Owner: Dixie Kaufman
Est: 1980   560 sq.ft.

Large Selection of Antique/Vintage quilts. Quality new Quilts and many quilt related items. Other American Crafts.

Map: Visitors Center, Torpedo Factory, King St., Fairfax St., Lee St., Art Center, Union St., Prince St., Rocky Road to Kansas, 215, Duke St., Potomac River, In "The Carriage House" second floor

Virginia Guilds:
White Oak Mountain Quilters, Dry Fork
Virginia Star Quilters Guild, P.O. Box 1034, Fredericksburg, 22402
Shenandoah Valley Quilters Guild, P.O. Box 913, Harrisonburg, 22801
Madison County Quilters Guild, PO Box 452, Madison, 22727
Richmond Quilter's Guild, Richmond
Star Quilters Guild, P.O. Box 5276, Roanoke, 24012
Tidewater Quilters Guild, P.O. Box 62635, Virginia Beach, 23462
Colonial Piecemakers, 201 Yorkview Rd. Yorktown, 23692

Other shops in Virginia:

Bedford	Style & Stitches, 202 Washington Street
Boones Mill	Boone's Country Store, Route 116
Bristol	The Quilt Shop, 2000 Euclid Avenue
Burke	Glass & Calico, 6030-K Burke Commons Rd.
Charlottesville	Les Fabriques, 2156 Barracks Road
Charlottesville	Quilts Unlimited, 1023 Emmet Street N.
Charlottesville	Stitches, 406 E. Main
Charlottesville	Early Times Workshop, 1821 Seminole Trail
Chesapeake	Quilts & Other Warm Things, 1369 S. Military Hwy.
Chester	The Busy Bea, 11934 Centre Street
Dayton	Clothes Line, Hwy. 42 South, P.O. Box 70
Fairfax	The Quilt Patch, 3932 Old Lee Highway
Fredericksburg	Quilts 'N' Treasures, 721 Caroline St.
Fredericksburg	Crafts N' Stitchery, 2020 Plank Road
Grafton	Heritage Hut, 6429 George Washington Mem. Hwy.
Hot Springs	Quilts Unlimited, Cottage Row
Manassas	Quilt Arts, 8565 Sudley Road
McLean	Apple Pie - Country Design, 1382 Chain Bridge Rd.
Occoquan	The Country Shop, 302 Mill Street
Powhatan	Julia's Quilt Shop, Flatrock Village Shopping
Reston	Appalachian Spring, 11877 Market Street
Richmond	Country Charm, 5714 Grove Avenue
Roanoke	Needle Fever, 5220 Williamson Road N.W.
Stafford	The Quilt Block, 2852 Jefferson Davis Hwy. #113
Vienna	Le-Petite-Coquillage, 109 Park Street N.E.
Vinton	The Cotton Gin, 905 Hardy Road
Virginia Beach	Quilt Works, 3101 Virginia Beach Blvd. #106
Williamsburg	Quilts Unlimited, 440A Duke of Gloucester Street
Winchester	Quilt Shop at Millwood Crossing, 381 Millwood Ave.
Wytheville	Sew What Fabrics, 155 W. Main Street

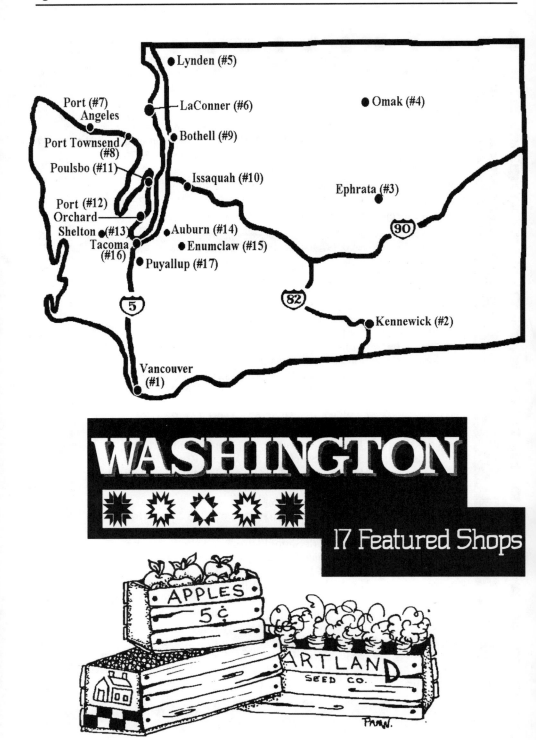

Lynden (#5)

Omak (#4)

Port (#7)
Angeles

LaConner (#6)

Port Townsend
(#8)

Bothell (#9)

Poulsbo (#11)

Issaquah (#10)

Ephrata (#3)

Port (#12)
Orchard

Auburn (#14)

Shelton (#13)

Enumclaw (#15)

Tacoma
(#16)

Puyallup (#17)

90

82

Kennewick (#2)

5

Vancouver
(#1)

WASHINGTON

17 Featured Shops

APPLES
5¢

ARTLAND
SEED CO.

#1

Connie's Calicos Too

6100 NE 131st Ave. ♥ Vancouver, Wa. 98682
(206)254~6150
Mon. 9:30~8pm ♥ Tues.~Sat. 9:30~5pm
owner ~ Connie Speed ♥ opened 1985

Quilters and crafters alike will lose themselves in Connie's unique shop. You will always find hundreds of dolls, quilts and wreaths on display; and of course, it's always Christmas with all the trimmings to surely put a smile on your face.

We also offer classes and all the fabric (over 1200 bolts of choice cotton calicos), books, patterns and notions to make your special project complete.

You owe it to yourself to visit Connie's Calicos Too ~ the crafter's candy store!

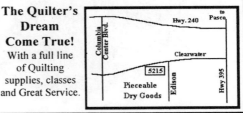

Kennewick, WA   #2

Pieceable Dry Goods

5215 W. Clearwater
(509) 735-6080   Est: 1991
Owners: Terry Guizzo &
1800 sq.ft.   Barbara Ward

Mon - Fri
10 - 5:30
Sat 10 - 5

The Quilter's Dream Come True!

With a full line of Quilting supplies, classes and Great Service.

Ephrata, WA #3

Dry Creek Gallery

Mon - Fri 9:30 - 5
Sat 10 - 4

(ADBA) Calico Country
245 Basin St. N.W.   P.O. Box 536
(509) 754-5664   98823

Owner: Dianne Recknagel
Est: 1983

Dry Creek Gallery is located in a new Victorian style building. Specializing in Quilts for Sale, Complete line of Quilting Fabrics & Supplies.
It adjoins an Expresso shop with a gazebo for outside seating.

Omak, WA #4

Needlelyn Time

Mon - Sat 9 - 6
Sun 12 - 4

9 North Main   98841
(509) 826-1198
Owner: Lyn Hruska
Est: 1986   3000 sq.ft.

Fabrics, Notions, Quilting Supplies. Sewing Machines and Cross-Stitch Supplies. Also Classes.

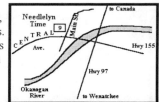

Lynden, WA #5

Fabric Cottage

Mon - Sat 9 - 5:30

510 Front St.   98264
(206) 354-5566   Est: 1979
Owner: Grace Mulder   2500 sq.ft.

Lynden's greatest selection for the enthusiastic quilter and crafter. Wonderful samples to inspire you. A friendly staff to help you.

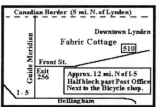

LaConner, WA #6

Creighton's Quilts

Open Daily Tues by Chance

2 Locations: 705 B S. 1st St.
503 E. Morris St.
(in the Morris St. Antique Mall)
(206) 466-5504   Est: 1988
Owner: Ann Bodle-Nash   Free Newsletter

Antique and New Amish quilts for sale: also quilting books, notions, countrywares, folk art, & braided rugs. Qualified Quilt Appraiser.

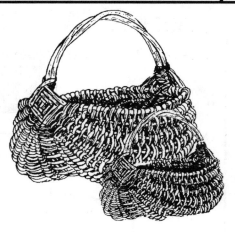

Quilt Quarters

Port Angeles, WA   #7

123 West First
98362
(206) 452-6899
Est: 1992 1400 sq.ft.
Owners: Donna Ball
Kris Cornell &
Lauretta Ehling

100% Cotton Fabrics

Momen House, Hoffman,
Kona Solids, Jinny Beyer,
Gutcheon, South Seas,
P&B, Dutch Java Batiks,
Kaufman and new fabrics
all the time.

Victoria Ferry
Railroad Ave.
Parking | Front St.   101W
Oak | Laurel | Lincoln
123
First St.
Quilt Quarters

**Gateway to: Victoria, B. C. via Coho Ferry
Olympic National Park**

Quilting Supplies

Excellent Selections
of Notions, Stencils,
Patterns, and Books
for serious quilters.

**Mon - Sat 10 - 5
Thurs 10 - 8:30**

Specialities

We carry a large selection
of Folkwear Patterns
used for authentic
clothing designs. We are
also proud of our
excellent selection of
classes serving the
beginning to advanced
quilter.

Port Townsend, WA #8

1010 Water St.   98368
(206) 385-4254
Est: 1993
2100 sq.ft.
Owners:
Laurel Watson
& Sylvia Schulte

Best Selection of Books.
Large Selection of 100% cotton fabrics.
Complete line of notions, patterns & classes. Gifts for the Quilter.

Mon - Sat 10 - 5:30
Sun 10 - 5

Bothell, WA #9

Keepsake Cottage Fabrics

23732 Bothell-Everett Hwy.   98021
(206) 486-3483   Est: 1985
Owners: Delberta Murray & Julie Stewart
1000 sq.ft.

Mon - Sat
10 - 6
Thurs til 8
Sun 11 - 5

Quilting Fabrics, patterns and notions. In the heart of Bothell's Country Village. Also cross-stitch and English Smocking.

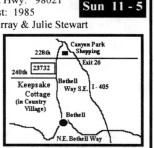

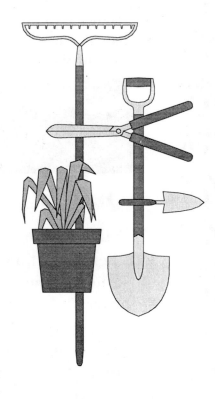

Issaquah, WA #10

The Loft

709 N.W. Gilman Blvd.   98027
(206) 392-5877
Owner: Marybeth Mills

Mon - Sat
10 - 6
Sun 12 - 5

Est: 1972

Complete Quilt
Shop.
Experienced and
personable help.
Great selection of
samples for
inspiration.
Fabric, Books,
Patterns, Classes
galore !!

I-90

N.W. Gilman Blvd.

709
The Loft

Front St.

Poulsbo, WA #11

Heirloom Quilts

Mon - Sat
10 - 5:30

18954 - C Front St.   P.O. Box 1957
(206) 697-2222   98370
Owners: 5 Quilters
Est: 1981   2000 sq.ft.

Quilting fabrics
& Supplies,
Smocking &
Cross-stitch
supplies. Plus
Classes.

On Front Street
in Downtown
Historic Poulsbo

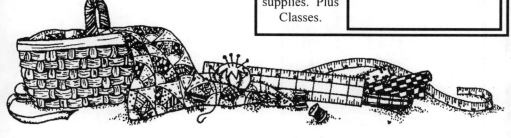

Grandmother's
Flower Garden —
Flowers that
need love,
but no watering !

Port Orchard, WA #12

Quilts & Creative Sewing

Mon - Sat
10 - 5:30
Thurs til 8
Sun 11 - 4

591 Bethel Avenue   98366
(206) 895-3076   Est: 1992
Owner: Fran Reiter   1785 sq.ft.

Quilting Fabric,
Books, &
Supplies. Over
200 solids. We
also offer soft
craft patterns and
supplies.

Quilts &   591
Creative
Sewing

Tremont St.
1.6 mi.

Bethel

16

Clifton Rd.

Lund
Rd.

Lund
Ave.

Shelton, WA   #13

CJ's
Labor of Love
Quilt Shop

(206) 426-0065

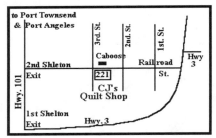

221 W. Railroad Suite 'C'
98584
Owners: Joan Kowalsky &
Candice Makos

Mon - Fri   10 - 5
Sat   10 - 4

A full line Quilt Shop.
Notions, Patterns &
Frames for every taste.
Wide Selection of
Hoffman, Gutcheon &
Kona Bay Fabrics.

Auburn, WA   #14

CALICO CAT and
other Fine Fabrics

218 E. Main   98002
(206) 939-0885   1300 sq.ft.
Owner: Mary Stanton   Est: 1992
Free Newsletter

Over 2000 fine
cotton fabrics.
Extensive book
collection.
Notions, Patterns,
Classes. Accept
Visa, MC, Disc
Mail Order Avail.

Mon - Fri
10 - 8
Sat 10 - 5
Sun 12- 5

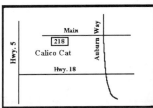

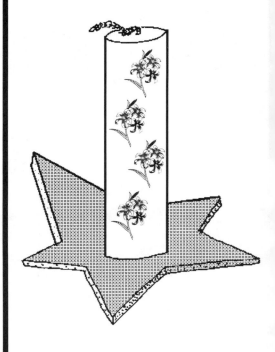

Enumclaw, WA #15

Country Quilts & Crafts

**Mon - Fri
9 - 5
Sat 10 - 3**

1240 Griffin Ave. 98022
(206) 825-8551
Owner: Mary Hampton

Country Quilts offers the finest of cotton calicos, notions, quilting supplies, and <u>LOTS</u> of Classes.

to Seattle
Auburn
Enumclaw Hwy.
Wells St.
Country Quilts 1240
Blue Building
Griffin St.

Tacoma, WA #16

Quilts Northwest

**Mon - Sat
10 - 5
Wed til 8
Sun 12 - 4**

7017 27th. Street West
(206) 564-0059   98466
Owners: Dee Jensen
                & Cathy Mitchell

Best Quilt Shop in Tacoma. Fabric, Books, Patterns, Notions and Classes.
Come See Us!

To Find Us: From I - 5 take the Bremerton/Gig Harbor exit (Hwy 16). Exit at Jackson Ave. Turn left and go 1 1/2 miles to 27th St. West. Turn left on 27th and go two blocks. We're located in the Weathervane Square.

Sewing Room —
Where work is
play, escape
from cares of the
day !

1206 E. Main
(206) 845-1532
2000 sq.ft.
Owner:
Evie Griffin

Puyallup, WA #17

The Quilt Barn

- ♥ Fine 100% Cotton Quilting Fabrics
- ♥ Complete Quilting Supplies & Notions
- ♥ Lots of Patterns & Books
- ♥ Knowledgeable Staff
- ♥ Day & Evening Classes
- ♥ Open 7 days a week
- ♥ Free Mailer
- ♥ "Special Friends" Monthly Show

I - 5
Puyallup River
161
167
E. Main
1206
Meridian
5th St.
15th St.
Pioneer
The Quilt Barn
512
S. Hill Mall

Serving
Quilters for
over 13 years!

**Mon - Sat
10 - 5
Thur til 9
Sun 12 - 5**

Area Guilds:
Northwest Quilting Connection, 906 35th St., Anacortes, 98221
Quilt Guild, The Fabric Cottage, Lynden, 98264
Quilters Anonymous, PO Box 322, Lynnwood, 98046
Port Orchard Quilters Guild, PO Box 842, Port Orchard 98366
Kitsap Quilters, PO Box 824, Poulsbo, 98370
Comforters, 9424 125th Ct. E, Puyallup, 98373
Puyallup Valley Quilters, PO Box 1421, Puyallup, 98371
Tri City Quilters, PO Box 215, Richland, 99352
Pacific Northwest Quilters, PO Box 22073, Seattle, 98122
Contemporary Quilt Assoc., 1134 N. 81st St., Seattle, 98103
Sunbonnet Sue Quilt Club, PO Box 211, Sequim, 98382
Clark County Quilters, PO Box 5857, Vancouver, 98668

Other shops in Washington:

Battle Ground	Country Manor Fabric & Crafts, 7812 NE 179th
Blaine	Country Cottage, 9872 Harvey Road #A
Chehalis	Sisters, 476 N. Market Blvd.
Clinton	Island Fabrics, P.O. Box 737
Edmonds	The Calico Basket, 410 Main
Everett	Quilt with EASE, 3122 Broadway
Everson	The Quilt Garden, 8310 Gillies Rd.
Kent	Quilter's Delight, 302 W. Harrison
Leavenworth	Dee's Country Accents, 220 9th St.
Lynden	Calico Country, 527 Front Street
Mt. Vernon	Calico Creations, 400 S. First Street
Newport	The Pin Cushion, 306 S. Washington Avenue
Ocean Shores	I Love 2 Quilt, 899 Point Brown Ave. NW
Port Orchard	Christina's Heritage, 802 Bay St.
Richland	Quiltmania, 248 Williams Blvd.
Seattle	In the Beginning, 8201 Lake City Way NE
Seattle	Nancy's Sewing Basket, 2221 Queen Anne N.
Seattle	Comfort by Akiko, 1510 11th Ave.
Seattle	Claire Murry Quilts, 517 Olive Way
Sequim	The Pine Cupboard, 609 W. Washington #1129
Sequim	The Pine Cupboard, 127 W. Washington
Spokane	Quilting Bee, S. 405 Dishman-Mica Rd. (Moving)
Stanwood	The Quilt Shop
Tacoma	Gutcheon Patchworks, 917 Pacific Ave. #305
Yakima	Valerie's Quilts & More, 4001 Summitview #25

QUILT POX

Very Contagious

Symptoms wrinkles up nose when a quilt is referred to as a 'blanket', constant need for the warmth provided by a handmade quilt. Seems to wander around in a daze not hearing others when considering the next project. Always seems to be carrying something in a pillow case. Often heard mumbling: "fat quarter", "1/4 inch seam allowance", or "where did I get this material?". Has been known to attack people mistreating quilts.

The Only Hope

Make as much time for quilting as possible.

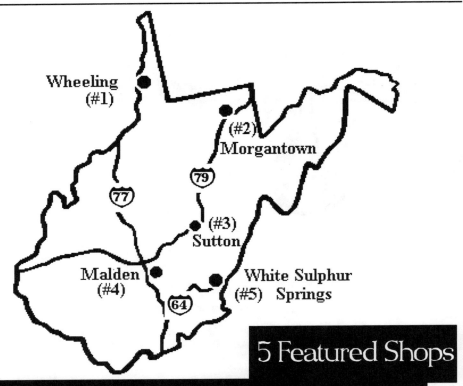

5 Featured Shops

WEST VIRGINIA

Wheeling, WV   #1

Janet's Quiltery

**Mon - Fri
10 - 4:30
Sat 10 - 2**

113 Edgington Lane   26003
(304) 242-2790
Owner: Janet Andrews
Est: 1989   800 sq.ft.

Cotton fabrics,
quilt books,
templates for
quilting, 1000
cross-stitch
books, cross-
stitch fabric,
classes, &
personal service.

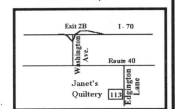

Morgantown, WV   #2

The Sew Inn. Ltd.

**Mon 10 - 8
Tues - Fri
10 - 6
Sat 9:30-5**

595 Willey St.   26505
(304) 296-6802
Owner: Virginia Showers
Est: 1973   1500 sq.ft.

Wonderful collection of
quilting cottons, books,
notions & classes.
Bridal & Special occasion
fabrics. Knowledgeable &
Friendly service.
Authorized Viking
Dealer.

**Easy Access from
I - 79 or I - 68.
Located on Rt. 119
one block out of
the downtown area**

Sutton, WV #3

The Quilt Supply Shop

701 N. 3rd. St.   26601
(304) 765-5176   Est: 1983
Owner: Ann Hickman

**Mon - Thur
9 - 5
Sat by Appt.**

Tiny shop filled with 100% cotton fabric. You will find all notions, patterns, and quilting tools 20% off all the time!

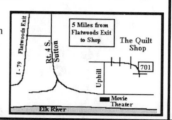

Malden, WV #4

Cabin Creek Quilts

4208 Malden Drive   25306
(304) 925-9499
Quilting Co-op. Dir.: James Thibeault
Est: 1971

**Mon - Sat
10 - 4
Sun 1 - 4**

Quilting supplies, fabrics, Quilts, Wall Hangings, Folk Dolls, Place Mats in old historical "Hale House". Small Group Retreats Offered.

Take Exit 96 off I-77/64 two miles east of State Capitol building. Go 1/2 mile on Rt. 60E Turn off at Malden Exit. Old pink Hale House 500 feet off exit on left

---

White Sulphur Springs, WV #5

Morningstar Quilts

The Greenbrier
The Creative Arts Colony
(304) 536-4003
Owner: Jane Morningstar

**April - Dec
Mon - Sat
10 - 5
Sun 10 - 3
By Appt.
Jan-March**

This tiny shop overflows with new and antique Quilts, Jewelry, Quilted Clothing, Pillows, Quilted Animals, Soft Sculpture and handcrafted Gifts.

Est: 1991

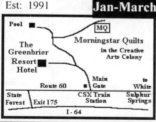

Other Shops in West Virginia:

Clarksburg	Clarksburg Sewing Center, Route 2
Farmington	Cotton Patch, Route 250 N.
Huntington	Marks Antiques, 617 Fourteenth Street W.
Kingwood	Eleanor's Quilt & Fabric Shop, Route 7 E.
Lewisburg	Quilts Unlimited, 203 E. Washington Street
Sophia	Quilt Fabrics and Craft Corner, Main Street
St. Albans	Village Sampler, 71 Ole Main Plaza
St. Mary's	Zepora's Quilt Shop, 116 Lafayette Street
Williamstown	The Beehive, 103 West 9th Street
Winfield	Fern's Fabric and Quilt Shoppe, Rural Route 34

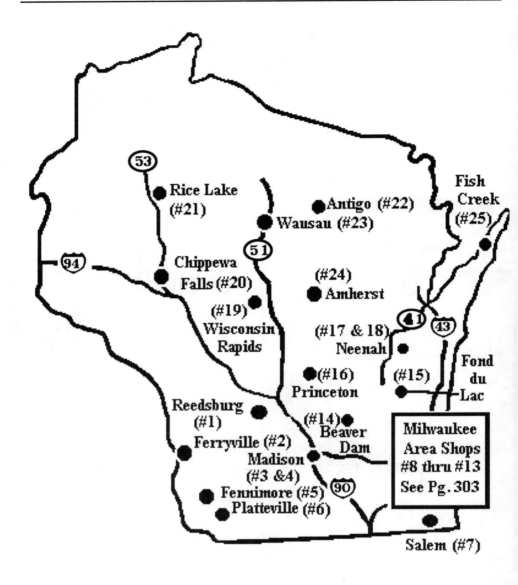

Fish
Creek
(#25)

53
Rice Lake
(#21)

Antigo (#22)
Wausau (#23)

51

94

Chippewa
Falls (#20)

(#24)
Amherst

41   43

(#19)
Wisconsin
Rapids

(#17 & 18)
Neenah

Fond
du
Lac

(#16)
Princeton

(#15)

Reedsburg
(#1)

(#14)
Beaver
Dam

Milwaukee
Area Shops
#8 thru #13
See Pg. 303

Ferryville (#2)
Madison
(#3 &4)

90

Fennimore (#5)
Platteville (#6)

Salem (#7)

WISCONSIN

25 Featured Shops

Reedsburg, WI #1

Quintessential Quilts

940 East Main   53959   (608) 524-8435
Owner: Terry Antholz   Est: 1989   4800 sq.ft.

Large selection of fabric, books,
patterns, & quilting supplies.
All your quilting
needs located under
one roof!
Continuous schedule
of classes.
Mail orders and newsletter
available upon request.
WISCONSIN'S BEST KEPT
QUILTING SECRET!

Mon - Sat   9 - 5   Fri til 7
Sun (May thru Dec) 12 - 4.

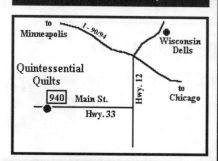

Ferryville, WI #2

Olde Tyme
Quilt Shoppe

Mon - Fri
10 - 5
Weekends by
chance or
call first.

R.R. #2   Rush Creek Rd.   Box 215
(608) 648-2081   54628
Owner: Virginia Johnson   900 sq.ft.
Est: 1986

Custom made
Quilts--Hand dyed
fabric, notions.
Hand or machine
quilting. 100%
cotton thread
1200 yard spools
Virginia's original
quilts. Classes also

Madison, WI #3

Quilter's Workshop

6101 Odana Road   53719
(608) 271-4693
Owner: Joan Pariza
Est: 1990   2400 sq.ft.

**Mon - Fri
9:30 - 5:30
Thur til
8:30
Sat 9:30 - 5**

Madison's only shop devoted to Quilters -- over 2000 bolts -- all 100% cotton -- includes latest in Hoffman, Jinny Beyer -- Patterns, Books, Notions ...

Mineral Point Rd.
Gammon Rd.
Grand Canyon Dr.
Whitney Way
Odana Rd.
Quilter's 6101 Workshop
Beltline - Hwy 12

Madison, WI #4

The Stitcher's Crossing

6816 Odana Road   53719
(608) 833-8040   Est: 1980
Owners: Elaine Boehlke & Kit
2200 sq.ft.   Thomsen

**Mon - Fri
9:30 - 5:30
Thur til
8:30
Sat 9:30-4**

Unique shop for all your quilting and cross stitch needs. All of our wonderful models and displays will inspire you.

Gammon Rd.
The Stitcher's Crossing
6816
Odana Rd.
I - 90
Rt. 12 & 18

Fennimore, WI #5

Yard & Yard Shop

960 Lincoln Ave.   53809
(608) 822-6014
Owner: Doris Monroe
Est: 1974

**Mon - Fri
9 - 5
Sat 9 - 3**

Quilt Supplies, Classes, Fashion Fabric Patterns New Home Sewing Machines — Sales and Service.

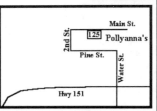

to Boscobel (Hwy 61N)
U.S. Hwy 18   4th St.
Yard & Yard Shop 960
Lincoln Ave.
12th St.   U.S. Hwy 18
(Hwy 61S)
to Lancaster   to Madison

Platteville, WI #6

Pollyanna's

125 East Main   53818
(608) 348-9276   Est: 1990
Owners: Sue Wagner &
2100 sq.ft.   Betty Kerkenbush

**Mon - Fri
9 - 5
Thur til 8
Sat 10 - 4**

Large selection of 100% Cotton Fabrics, Quilt Books, Doll Patterns. Yarns & yarn books. For sale: Quilts, dolls, knit & crocheted items

Main St.
2nd St.
125 Pollyanna's
Pine St.
Water St.
Hwy 151

Salem, WI #7

COLONIAL FABRICS LTD

24417   75th Street   53168
(414) 843-3682
Est: 1991   1200 sq.ft.

**Tues-Thur
10 - 6
Fri 10 - 8
Sat 10 - 5
Sun & Mon
by appt**

Specialized Quilting & Patchwork shop. Visit us for "Homespun" service for all your quilting needs.

North
Hwy. 83
U.S. 45
I - 94
Hwy. 50
75th. St.
24417
Colonial Fabrics
Salem   Bristol
WI - IL Border

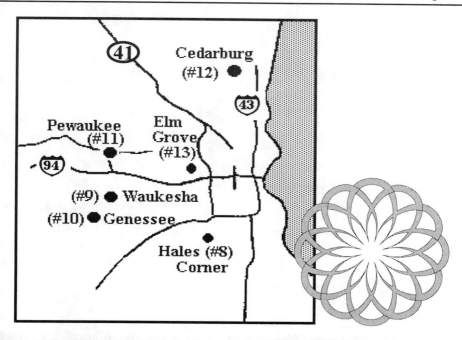

MILWAUKEE AREA
6 Featured Shops

Hales Corners, WI   #8

Hearthside Quilters Nook

10731 W. Forest Home Ave.
(414) 425-2474   53130
Owners: Carol Baker & Jan
Est: 1979   2800 sq.ft.   Krueger

**Mon - Sat
9 - 5
Mon & Thur
til 9
Sun 12 - 4**

Beautiful Fabric
Selection, Books,
Patterns, Notions,
Smocking & Heirloom
Sewing Supplies.
Christmas year Round.
"Where Friendly
service is a Tradition!"

Waukesha, WI   #9

Genesee Woolen Mill

S. 40 W. 28178 Hwy.59
(414) 521-2121   53188
Owners: Kay Menning & Sarah
Est: 1989   Pietenpol
2600 sq.ft.

**Mon, Tues,
Thurs, Fri
10 - 4**

Wool Carding
Mill. Shop
feature wool batts,
cotton fabric,
wool related
items. Hand-Tied
Comforters.
Call for Tours

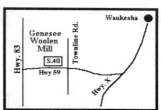

Genesee Depot, WI   #10

American Quilting Co.

S. 42 W. 31230 Hwy 83
(414) 968-3400   53127
Owners: Carol & Les Knutsen
Est: 1992   2400 sq.ft.

**Mon - Fri
10 - 5
Thur til 8
Sat 10 - 4**

Biggest and best selection of quilting fabrics and supplies in Southeast Wisconsin.
Classes Available.
Authorized Pfaff Sales & Service

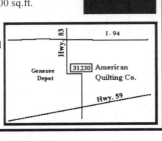

Pewaukee, WI   #11

Pamella's Place

2010 Silvernail Road   53072
(414) 544-5415
Owner: Pamella Gray
Est: 1987   3350 sq.ft.

**Mon - Thur
9:30 - 8:30
Fri
9:30-5:30
Sat 9:30 - 5**

Featuring over 4,000 bolts of fabric, books and patterns (quilting, sewing doll and craft) and Bernina sewing machines.

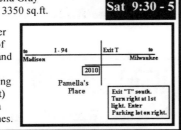

to Madison — I-94 — Exit T — to Milwaukee

2010

Pamella's Place

Exit "T" south.
Turn right at 1st light. Enter Parking lot on right.

Cedarburg, WI   #12

Cedarburg Woolen Mill

W 62 N 580 Washington Ave.
(800) WIS-WOOL   53012
Owner: Kay Walters   Est: 1981   6000 sq.ft.
Tours: 1860 Machinery Visit Historic Cedarburg

**Mon - Fri 9 - 6
Thur til 8
Sat 9-5   Sun 12-5**

Custom Wool Carding, Wool Batts, 100% Cotton Fabric, Notions, Books, Patterns.
Spin/Weave/Knit Feather/Down Supplies. Free Catalog

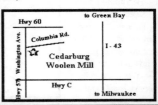

Hwy 60   to Green Bay
Columbia Rd.
Washington Ave.   I-43
Cedarburg Woolen Mill
Hwy 57   Hwy C
to Milwaukee

Elm Grove, WI #13

Books Patterns Notions

Patched Works, Inc.

In a Western Suburb of Milwaukee
13330 Watertown Plank Rd.
(414) 786-1523   53122
Owner: Trudie Hughes
Est: 1978   6000 sq.ft.

**Mon - Fri
9 - 5
Wed til 8
Sat 9 - 4**

5000 bolts
of Cotton Fabric
Hundreds of Books &
Patterns for the
Quiltmaker

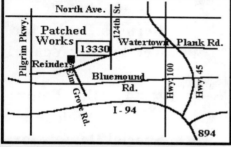

**Owned by a
Master
Fabricaholic**

Beaver Dam, WI #14

Nancy's Notions, Ltd.

**Mon - Fri
9 - 5
Sat 9 - 4**

333 Beichl Ave.   53916
(414) 887-7321   Est: 1985
Owners: Nancy & Richard Zieman
3000 sq.ft.   Free Catalog

Large selection of
brand name 100%
cottons, sewing
and quilting
notions, patterns,
and supplies.
Home of "Sewing
With Nancy".

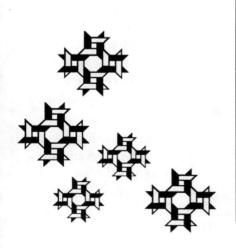

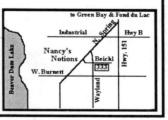

Fond du Lac, WI   #15

Fond du Lac Quilting

15 North Main Street   54935
(414) 921-3816 or (800) 594-9064
Owner: Peggy Eckerstorfer

Monday thru Thursday
9:30 to 5:00
Friday - 9:30 to 7:00
Saturday - 9:30 to 4:00

Fond du Lac Quilting
is one of Wisconsin's
Largest Quilt Shops ! !
The best selection of
Quilting Fabrics,
Books, and Patterns in
the state !
Bernina Dealer for
over Twenty Years !

Bus Tours
Welcome
Special Demo's for
tour groups

We are the Host of two of the largest quilting events in the mid-west:
Quilter's Escape & Summer School for Quilters

Quilter's Escape Summer School
July 22nd, 23rd, & 24th, 1994
Featuring National Instructors:

- ♥ Patricia Campbell - Hand Applique
- ♥ Kathy Sorenson - Fabric Dyeing
- ♥ Debra Wagner - Machine Piecing & Applique
- ♥ Wendy Gilbert - Machine Piecing
- ♥ Bill & Jackie - Amish Basket Weaving
- ♥ Margaret Pieceson - Paper Piecing (Hand)
- ♥ Pat Cox - Stained Glass
- ♥ Mackie - Beginner Quilting
- ♥ Flavin Glover - Log Cabin and Wearable Art

Quilter's Escape
February
3rd, 4th & 5th, 1995
National Teachers to
be announced

Our Quilting Events
consist of Seminars,
Quilt Show, and
Workshops

For More Information send a 52 cent stamp.

Princeton, WI. #16

Quilts & Quilting

Mon -Fri 8:30 - 5
Sat 9 - 3

607 W. Main St.   (414) 295-6506
P.O. Box 362   54968   Est: 1971
Owners: Sandy & Ron Mason
1800 sq.ft.

Custom Machine   Free Quilting Brochure
Quilting Since 1971
Complete
Quilt Shop
Fabric, Notions,
Books, Classes
Quilted Items
Gift Shop—Quilts
Baby to King

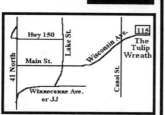

Neenah, WI #17

Holz's Pfaff Sewing Center

Mon - Fri 9 - 5:30
Thur til 8
Sat 9 - 5

132 W. Wisconsin Avenue   54956
(414) 722-8262   Est: 1945
Owner: Roy Holz   4000 sq.ft.

100% Cottons,
Notions, Fashion
Fabrics. Hard to
Find items.
Authorized Pfaff,
Babylock and
Singer Dealer for
Sales and Service.

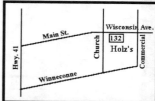

Neenah, WI #18

The Tulip Wreath

Mon - Fri 9:30 - 5:30
Thur til 8
Sat 9:30 - 5

115 W. Wisconsin Ave.   54956
(414) 725-9585
Owners: Debbie & Cindy Sypek
Est: 1990

100% Cotton
Fabrics —
Hoffman
Horton
Kings Road
Alexander Henry
Plus Lots More

Wisconsin Rapids, WI #19

The COTTON Thimble
FOR YOUR QUILTING NEEDS

Tues - Fri 10 - 5
Sat 9 - 3

240 W. Grand Ave.   54495
(715) 424-1122   Est: 1993
Owner: Carol Prahl

500 Bolts plus 100%
Cottons
Books, Patterns,
Stencils, & Quilting
Notions.

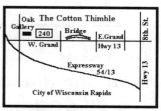

Chippewa Falls, WI #20

Nine Patch Quilts-N-Crafts

Mon - Fri 9 - 5:30
Sat 9 - 5

17 W. Central Street   54729
(715) 723-5931   Est: 1993
Owners: Lina LaRonge & Barb Dekan
1500 sq.ft.

Gifts, Amish
Quilts, Fabrics,
Fine Quality Yarns,
Quilting & Knitting
Supplies.
New Wool Batts,
Poly Batts,
Recarding Service.

Rice Lake, WI #21

Busy Bobbin

Mon - Fri 9:30 - 5
Sat 9:30 - 3

234 N. Wilson Ave.   54868
(715) 234-1217   Est: 1981
Owner: Diann Raymond   1000 sq.ft.

Large selection
100% Cotton
fabrics, patterns,
books, and
quilting notions.
Classes offered.

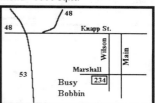

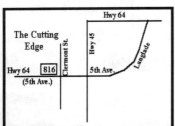

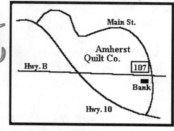

Singer —
A Quilter humming
along with her
sewing machine.

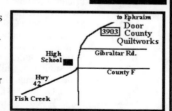

Wisconsin Guilds:
Tomorrow's Quilters, PO Box 248, Amherst, 54406
Baraboo Quilters, 901 Moore Street #15, Baraboo, 53913
Heart in Hands Quilt Guild, Box 12A, Boyceville, 54725
Lake Country Quilters, 1385 Countryside Lane, Brookfield, 53045
Piecemaker's, 1165 Parkmoor Drive, Brookfield, 53005
Fort Atkinson Piecemakers, 163 Hoopen Road, Cambridge, 53523
Cedar Creek Quilters, 1654 Summit Drive, Cedarsburg, 53012
Old World Quilters, 304 Larkin Street, Eagle, 53119
Cranberry Country Quilt Guild, 4483 Chain o' Lakes Rd., Eagle River, 54521
Village Quilters of Harvard, 212 Abbey Springs Drive, Fontana, 53125
Piecemakers Quilt Guild, 510 Grove Street, Fort Atkinson, 53538
Mixed Sampler Quilt Club, Box 133, Frederic, 54837
Menomonee Falls Quilters, W. 154 N. 11666 Daniels, Germantown, 53022
Heritage Quilters, 203 Beech, Grafton, 53024
Evergreen Quilters, PO Box 783, Green Bay, 54305
LaCrosse Area Quilters, W. 8154 Holland Drive, Holmen, 54636
Hudson Heritage Quilters, 874 Willow Ridge, Hudson, 54016
It's a Stitch Quilt Club, 3280 Highway P, Jackson, 53037
Rock Valley Quilters Guild, PO Box 904, Janesville, 53547
Southport Quilter's Guild, PO Box 1523, Kenosha, 53141
Mad City Quilters, 157 Nautilus Drive, Madison, 53705
Twilight Quilters Guild, 9 Leyton Circle, Madison, 53713
Darting Needles Quilt Guild, PO Box 603, Menasha, 54952
Covered Bridge Quilters, 13907 N. Port Washington Rd., Mequon, 53092
North Shore Quilters Guild, PO Box 17263, Milwaukee, 53217
Orchard Inn Quilters, 5510 W. Calumet Road, Milwaukee, 53223
Stitch it or Stuff it Quilters, 6551 N. 66th Street, Milwaukee, 53223
West Suburban Quilters Guild, 2621 N. 65th Street, Milwaukee, 53213
Wisconsin's Quilter's Inc., PO Box 83144, Milwaukee, 53223
Calico Capers Quilt Guild, RR 1 Gem Avenue, Montello, 53949
Evergreen Quilters, Box 426, Montello, 53949
Crazy Quilters, S. 70 W. 32864 W. Oak Place, Mukwonago, 53149
Patched Lives Quilt Guild, N. 53 W. 33511 Cumberland Drive, Nashotah
Pine Tree Needlers, Box 431-2, Wautoma, 54982
Wandering Foot Quilters, 8620 S. Howell Avenue, Oak Creek, 53154
Lake Side Quilters, 1350 Menominee Drive, Oshkosh, 54901
Patched Lives, Pewaukee
Hobby Quilters, PO box 362, Princeton, 54968
Lighthouse Quilters, PO Box 124, Racine, 53403
Around the Block Quilters, 940 E. Main, Reedsburg, 53959
Cornerstone Quilt Guild, 337 K Street, Reedsburg, 53959
Rhinelander Northwoods Quilters, 49 Lake Creek Road, Rhinelander, 54501
Friendship Quilter's Guild, 587 N. Park Street, Richland Center, 53581
Ladies of the Lake Quilters, 9200 Longs Road, Sayner, 54560
Shawano Area Quilters, 225 S. Main, Shawano, 54166
Sheboygan County Quilter's Guild, 2426 N. 25th Street, Sheboygan, 53083
Wild Rivers Quilting Guild, Box 1065, Spooner, 54801
Star Point Quilters Guild, PO Box 607, Stevens Point, 54481
The Stoughton Quilters, 404 W. Wilson, Stoughton, 53589
Prairie Heritage Quilters, PO Box 253, Sun Prairie, 53590
Casda Quilts, 2231 Catlin Avenue, Superior, 54880
North Woods Quilters, 709 W. Third Street, Washburn, 54891
Pine Tree Quilters Guild, PO Box 692, Wausau, 54402
Kettle Moraine Quilt Club, 4991 Hillside Drive, West Bend, 53095
Dells Country Quilters, #530 Highway 23 E., Wisconsin Dells, 53965
Rapid Fingers Quilt Guild, Wisconsin Rapids

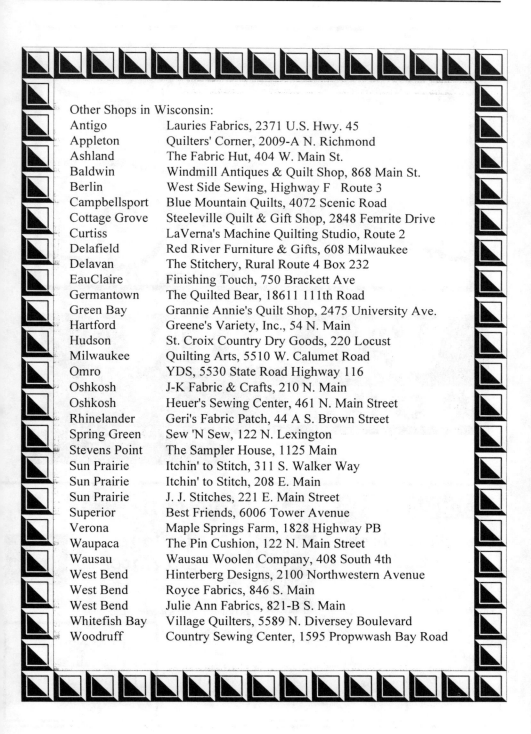

Other Shops in Wisconsin:

Antigo	Lauries Fabrics, 2371 U.S. Hwy. 45
Appleton	Quilters' Corner, 2009-A N. Richmond
Ashland	The Fabric Hut, 404 W. Main St.
Baldwin	Windmill Antiques & Quilt Shop, 868 Main St.
Berlin	West Side Sewing, Highway F Route 3
Campbellsport	Blue Mountain Quilts, 4072 Scenic Road
Cottage Grove	Steeleville Quilt & Gift Shop, 2848 Femrite Drive
Curtiss	LaVerna's Machine Quilting Studio, Route 2
Delafield	Red River Furniture & Gifts, 608 Milwaukee
Delavan	The Stitchery, Rural Route 4 Box 232
EauClaire	Finishing Touch, 750 Brackett Ave
Germantown	The Quilted Bear, 18611 111th Road
Green Bay	Grannie Annie's Quilt Shop, 2475 University Ave.
Hartford	Greene's Variety, Inc., 54 N. Main
Hudson	St. Croix Country Dry Goods, 220 Locust
Milwaukee	Quilting Arts, 5510 W. Calumet Road
Omro	YDS, 5530 State Road Highway 116
Oshkosh	J-K Fabric & Crafts, 210 N. Main
Oshkosh	Heuer's Sewing Center, 461 N. Main Street
Rhinelander	Geri's Fabric Patch, 44 A S. Brown Street
Spring Green	Sew 'N Sew, 122 N. Lexington
Stevens Point	The Sampler House, 1125 Main
Sun Prairie	Itchin' to Stitch, 311 S. Walker Way
Sun Prairie	Itchin' to Stitch, 208 E. Main
Sun Prairie	J. J. Stitches, 221 E. Main Street
Superior	Best Friends, 6006 Tower Avenue
Verona	Maple Springs Farm, 1828 Highway PB
Waupaca	The Pin Cushion, 122 N. Main Street
Wausau	Wausau Woolen Company, 408 South 4th
West Bend	Hinterberg Designs, 2100 Northwestern Avenue
West Bend	Royce Fabrics, 846 S. Main
West Bend	Julie Ann Fabrics, 821-B S. Main
Whitefish Bay	Village Quilters, 5589 N. Diversey Boulevard
Woodruff	Country Sewing Center, 1595 Propwwash Bay Road

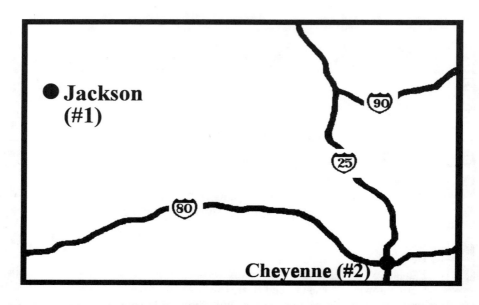

Jackson, WY #1

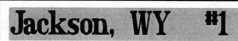

The Huckleberry Patch

Summer 9 - 7
Winter 10 - 6

180 West Center   83001
(307) 733-6824   Est: 1979
Owner: Jean Johnson   2000 sq.ft.

Custom order Quilts -- 800 bolts of Quilting Fabrics Top Brands at 10% below Retail.

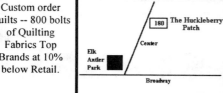

Cheyenne, WY #2

Heritage Quilt Shop

Daily 10 - 5:30

2622 Pioneer Avenue   82001
(307) 638-2002
Owner: Mary Genereux   Est: 1983

Fabrics, Books, 1000's of Patterns, Supplies and Classes. We carry Antiques and made ups.

I - 25 North to Randall Exit - Follow Randall to 27th street.

Notes

Wyoming Guilds:
Wyoming Heritage Quilters, P.O. Box 19081, Cheyenne, 82003
Paintbrush Piecers Quilt Guild, P.O. Box 258, Powell, 82435

Other Shops in Wyoming:
Casper	Prism Quilting, 143 N. Beverly
Cody	Crafty Quilter, 1262 Sheridan Ave.
Gillette	And Sew On, 2007 S. Douglas Hwy
Glenrock	The Kalico Korner, 103 W. Birch
Green River	Sew What Sewing, 351 Uinta Drive

INDEX

An Alphabetical listing of featured shops by name

Add stores you find here and
please send us a note about them.

Hope You Had A Nice Trip

**We will continue to update our guide on a regular basis.
If you own a shop or know of one we should be sure to include in
future editions of this guide, please drop us a note or
call (719) 685-5041.
Also if you have any suggestions for other information we could
include that would be helpful when you're traveling,
we'd appreciate hearing them.**

We welcome wholesale inquiries.